Understanding Counterplay in Video Games

This book offers insight into one of the most problematic and universal issues within multiplayer videogames: antisocial and oppositional play forms such as cheating, player harassment, the use of exploits, illicit game modifications, and system hacking, known collectively as counterplay. Using ethnographic research, Alan Meades not only gives voice to counterplayers but reframes counterplay as a complex practice with contradictory motivations that is anything but reducible to simply being hostile to play, players, or commercial video games. The book offers a grounded and pragmatic exploration of counterplay, framing it as an unavoidable by-product of the interaction of mass audiences with compelling and culturally important texts.

Alan F. Meades is Senior Lecturer in the Department of Media, Art and Design at Canterbury Christ Church University, UK.

Routledge Advances in Game Studies

Understanding Counterplay in Video Games

Alan F. Meades

Routledge
Taylor & Francis Group

LONDON AND NEW YORK

First published 2015 by Routledge

2 Park Square, Milton Park, Abingdon, Oxfordshire OX14 4RN
711 Third Avenue, New York, NY 10017

Routledge is an imprint of the Taylor & Francis Group, an informa business

First issued in paperback 2018

Library of Congress Cataloging-in-Publication Data

Meades, Alan F.
Understanding counterplay in video games / by Alan F. Meades.
   pages cm
Includes index.
   1. Video games—Social aspects. I. Title.
GV1469.34.S52R67 2015
794.8—dc23   2015004806

ISBN: 978-1-138-80492-0 (hbk)
ISBN: 978-1-138-54869-5 (pbk)

Typeset in Sabon
by codeMantra

Contents

List of Figures

List of Tables

Acknowledgements

This book is the product of over a decade of academic research exploring the ways that people play games, whilst playing multiplayer games very badly. The majority of this research was conducted between 2008 to 2013, when I was working on my PhD at Brunel University under the supervision of Professor Tanya Kryzwinska, and also whilst running the Digital Design Suite of degree programmes at Canterbury Christ Church University. I am incredibly grateful for the assured and confident supervision provided by Professor Tanya Krzywinska who managed the tricky task of giving me sufficient space to conduct my research while remaining a source of critical clarity. In addition to the financial support that I received I owe many thanks to my colleagues at Canterbury Christ Church University, who each contributed to a work and research culture that encouraged me to follow my curiosity. I would like to especially thank Professor David Bradshaw, Dr. Karen Shepherdson and Dr. Andy Birtwistle for continually seeing the potential in my work.

Some of the content published here appeared in much less unified form in a number of journal articles and book chapters, chapter two's exploration of incendiary user-generated-content builds upon an article published within *The Journal of Gaming and Virtual Worlds,* (Meades, 2010), while chapter four builds upon a number of articles and chapters for Vorhees, Call and Whitlock's *Guns, Grenades, and Grunts: First-Person Shooter Games* (2012a), *The Well Played Journal* (2012b), and *The Journal of Gaming and Virtual Worlds* (2013). I am enormously grateful for the robust feedback offered during the writing of these articles and chapters, and subsequently discussion with other game studies scholars as a result.

Despite all the gratitude that I owe my peers and fellow scholars, it would be impossible for me to do my research without the help of the hundreds of players that I played alongside, spoke with, and who had the patience to explain to me the ways that they play. There are many who it would be improper to name, but I want to especially Ryan350, Tmbnc, Nickncs, Davidor, Rezzzo, and iHcJames in particular - I'd take an arrow to the knee for any of you.

Lastly, Rachel, Elsie and Rose, who cared for me as I hunched over console and computer for many months. Elsie I hope that this in part answers your question about what a video game is, or at least what it can be. I want to thank my father, Ivan Meades, for always being willing to read and review my work, and to say that as you've always said, it's a dead fish that swims with the stream.

REFERENCES

Meades, A. (2010). Imaginary Monsters: Game 3.0 and the rise of the transgressive player. *The Journal of Gaming and Virtual Worlds,* 2 (2), pp.115–134.

Meades, A. (2012a). More Bang For Your Buck–Hardware Hacking, Real Money Trade and Transgressive Play within Console Based First Person Shooters. In Voorhees, Call, & Whitlock, *Guns, Grenades, and Grunts: First-Person Shooter Games,* London: Bloomsbury, pp.199–223.

Meades, A. (2012b). Why we Glitch: process, meaning and pleasure in the discovery, documentation, sharing and use of videogame exploits. *The Well Played Journal, 2 (2).*

Meades, A. (2013). Infectious pleasures: Ethnographic perspectives on the production and use of illicit videogame modifications on the Call of Duty franchise. *The Journal of Gaming and Virtual Worlds,* 5 (1), pp. 59–77.

Introduction

This book explores the concept of counterplay in contemporary video games, primarily from the context of action-orientated video games based on Microsoft's Xbox 360 games console and surrounding player cultures. The term "counterplay" is repurposed here to encapsulate play that is understood as oppositional, anti-social, and even criminal by its players and observers. Counterplay can therefore be regarded as being counter to the general expectation of compliant conventional play and instead contains a dynamic that works against rules, against other players, seeks alternate ways of playing and potentially different pleasures. As we shall see, there are a number of other terms that capture some of this dynamic – *cheating, trolling, grief-play, transgressive play, abject play, dark play etc.* – but instead, counterplay is used here in an attempt to simultaneously differentiate between these terms and to present a less pejoratively loaded term to better emphasize what I believe to be the universality of counterplay. This is an attempt to recognize that while this is a form of play defined by its working against a rule, against consensus, against etiquette, or against law, it is both frequent and widely adopted. This book will trace a cross section of counterplay practices – *incendiary user generated content, grief-play, collusion, the use of exploits, hardware hacking, and illicit software modification* – in an attempt to offer primarily a descriptive snapshot of practices, motivations, and, as a corollary, meaning. In so doing this book approaches counterplay in an ethnographic manner, entering counterplay communities, engaging with counterplayers, and simultaneously recognizing the various competing discourses that are used by counterplayers, victims, observers, and the establishment alike to (il)legitimize these acts. Ultimately it is hoped this book offers the reader some insight into what forms counterplay takes, how it is conducted, and to better understand the reasons we counterplay.

When I meet new people and explain my research, after I've clarified precisely what I do and what I mean, I'm frequently met with the same earnest, apologetically concerned questions revolving around *why? Why study counterplay* when it is so often something that undermines and erodes conventional, legitimate play, something that almost all of us hold dear? *Why spend time with and give voice* to the trolls, vandals, and idiots who seek to undermine and subvert the games and systems we care so deeply about? *Why not study something better* to do with play, something more wholesome?

My answer is always the same – because it's important, because it matters, and because when I play video games, counterplay is something I see, have to respond to, and occasionally conduct myself. It is something I recognize during play but this does not always tally with much that I read in game studies, and this interests me even more. One could argue the motivation for learning more about counterplay is to better protect against it, but as we shall hopefully see, counterplay is by definition evasive and protean and would inevitably find other opportunities to manifest itself. Instead my aim is to assist with the development of a body of work that records counterplay activities and engages with their protagonists in order to better understand counterplay as a social practice and to see it for what it is: a challenging, oppositional, but integral part of play, an indivisible facet of all play including that which is compliant and benign.

It should be stressed this book does not offer a descriptive taxonomy enabling the reader to identify player types or gamer groups, and while there are points at which groups of players will be referred to in the collective, this is intended for clarity as opposed to suggesting there are any essential group characteristics. Instead this book is about describing what players do rather than what they are. It isn't about gamers, or griefers, or hackers, although these terms are certainly used, but it is about ways players choose to play and the argument that many players engage in many forms of play. Instead of seeing a reductive identity based on the way of play with which an individual is seen to have engaged, thus isolating players into groups, this is about the universality of play and therefore counterplay.

It is important to note this book is not presented to ignore the implications or repercussions of counterplay. It does not disregard its damage on account of the universality of counterplay, nor is it apologetic about counterplay, but simply addresses the observation that detailed overviews of these practices are missing within the existing literature. It is also to state plainly that, as it is part of play, counterplay and other forms of hostile, antisocial, and illegal play necessitate further scrutiny and understanding, and should not be simply ignored.

Lastly, there is a moral imperative for studying counterplay that recognizes that despite the discourses that frame it as abject, counterplay is something many players conduct and experience. It is therefore for many a meaningful cultural practice, despite its damaging and even illegal status. Recognition of this does not diminish the impact or apologize for the counterplayer but it shifts the mental image of the counterplayer from a senseless, wanton transgressor who only opposes into someone who has chosen to play with rules for reasons, and with awareness of the stakes and penalties. This normalizes counterplay and challenges the reductive position that simply views counterplayers as vandals and criminals, as griefers, glitchers, hackers, and modders and, by definition, all other as both normal and benign.

1   What is Counterplay?

The concept of counterplay was first applied to video games by Nick Dyer-Witheford and Greig de Peuter, who saw video-game development and, by extension, the consumption and use of video games by players as an act of "Empire", an exploitative structure in which value was extracted from workers and players alike (2005). For Dyer-Witheford and de Peuter, "Digital games are produced by and productive of the multi-layered arrangement of military, economic, and subjective forces associated with the form of imperial power. ..." This, through concepts such as "work as play" and the commercial adoption of game mods, constituted an "apparatus of capture".

While this kind of system is not necessarily problematic in itself, there are times where unfairness, inequality, and exploitation may be sensed, such as the incompatibility of game development careers and family life, or when players realize the content they are producing is effectively subsidizing the development of the game for which they have already paid. In cases where individuals become aware of the exploitative context, they may push against and resist its power, something Dyer-Witheford and de Peuter call "counter-mobilization":

> Game designers and audiences creatively re-orienting their playful dispositions and intellectual capacities towards the subversion of the very logics of expropriation, commodification, and corporatisation that sustain the digital play industry in particular and global capital in general.
>
> (Dyer-Witheford and de Peuter 2005)

It is this application of playful dispositions and intellectual capacities within the context of video-game development and consumption that constitutes counterplay, a way of playing that works against the video-game production, video-game consumption, and therefore ways of playing that interrupt, fracture, or subvert the experience of play or the process of becoming a player. Dyer-Witheford and de Peuter talk of counterplay in the same way as other more recognizable forms of resistance and opposition, connecting a "wide occurrence of tactical media, activism, free and open source software, and distributed computing generating tumults through the circuits of Empire" (2005).

Looking back at Dyer-Witheford and de Peuter's counterplay ten years on we can see a number of changes within video-game development and distribution, such as the rise of indie gaming, the emergence of alternate platforms and delivery methods, and the widespread adoption of networked online game-play. Some of these changes may have made game development more equitable, but the shift to online play and increasingly mandatory Internet connections has profoundly altered the relationship between developer, publisher, platform-holder, and player. Video games are often purchased through online systems, require connections and updates to operate, are subject to security challenges that mitigate against unauthorized modifications or piracy, and player behaviour is subject to scrutiny and captured as metric data in order to encourage appropriate play and to inform future designs. This is a strong example of the apparatus of capture that Dyer-Witheford and de Peuter write about and the immaterial labour of playing games.

Simultaneously, players have increasingly become the very content of video games, such as in the case of competitive multiplayer games such as the *Call of Duty* franchise (2003-present), around which much of this book is focused. In these games, players become teammates and, more importantly, opponents, and it is their human intelligence and strategizing that become the compelling challenge of the game, not the game content. This shifts the meaning and role of games and players. The games become more like platforms or spaces that players populate, and as many would confirm, a *Call of Duty* game without other human players soon becomes a rather dull affair.

Yet despite this, there are times when the platform and use of players-as-content fail or become conspicuously exploitative, such as the bewildering cases where games fail to adequately act as platforms and to deliver their promises. We see this in *Battlefield 4*'s conspicuous launch issues, such as the in-game-lag, the rubber-banding as the server and player are repeatedly synchronized, or the outright server failures that boot players to the title screen at random, the result of apparently insufficiently tested code and an inadequate hardware infrastructure. A similar story is seen with Ubisoft's *Assassin's Creed Unity*'s (2014) hugely problematic launch and review embargo policy. The game, launched in November 2014, had an embargo that forbade games sites and media outlets from publishing reviews set to twelve hours after release, at which point many players would have purchased the game, not wishing to miss the launch window. Shortly after its release, and in the face of widespread consumer protest, Yannis Mallat, CEO of Ubisoft Montreal and Toronto, announced, "At launch, the overall quality of the game was diminished by bugs and technical issues" and after releasing three major patches responding to over three hundred reported flaws, Ubisoft announced its intention to discontinue the premium "season pass" for the release, offering those who had purchased it a free game as compensation (Jackson 2014). In a different way we see the same failure in *Halo Master Chief Collection*'s (2014) curious decision to ship with only one 65gb capacity blu-ray disc and require all players to download a 20gb core-data file, not an update, before they can play. These examples, alongside the cases of on-disk DLC or "bullshots", where the promotional imagery fails to correspond with the final game, draw the relationship of players and game institutions into sharp relief. The idea of a game-as-platform and the player as content feels inequitable, exploitative, and problematic.

Within the model of the contemporary video game that utilizes players as content, the security and reliability of the network, its platform, data, operation, and service become an intrinsic part of the game, and the attitude and behaviour of players become equally critical to the game experience. Players take on the role that would have been given to NPCs in previous pre-networked games. However, players are autonomous and unpredictable, and unlike NPCs may readily go off-script. This necessitates the careful management of players, both within the game and beyond, and thus video games now utilize player managers who engage with players and keep them excited and on-message. These managers actively interact with players through social networks, responding to queries, questions, and suggestions and doing whatever is necessary to establish and maintain meaningful interactions, sustain appropriate player populations, and the long-term success of the games.

Despite these significant changes since Dyer-Witheford and de Peuter's paper, it might be tempting to say very little differs structurally. Video games are still imperial, they still rely upon development cultures of work as play, are global, utilize immaterial labour, and thematically support military-industrial perspectives. But what has changed considerably is the individual player's relationship and visibility within the system. Each individual, whether in-game, on a social network, or a video-game forum, has become a constituent part of the system as customer, as an opponent within a multiplayer game, as a metric with which to compare progress, or another voice within a community. Each player inadvertently contributes to the success of a game through a multitude of channels: purchasing and reviewing a game online, commenting on forums, responding to community tweets, or simply playing the game.

This is a highly advantageous system for developers and publishers, offloading some of the conventional work of game algorithms, advertising, and community-building onto the players themselves, but this is also precarious due to the reach and connectivity of networked systems and communities. If players are content and complicit, their positive attitude will harmoniously reinforce the game product, but when there is dissent, the networks become channels for protest, targets for attack, and spaces for counterplay. It is the behaviours that run counter to the expectations of contemporary video-game play systems, not necessarily the creation and circulation of incendiary content, the grief-play, the harassment of commentators, the hacking and attacking of gaming networks, and the myriad ways of undermining and challenging expectations of play that constitute contemporary counterplay.

In 2010 Tom Apperley revisited the concept of counterplay, shifting it from Dyer-Witheford's and de Peuter's vision of counter-mobilization to a more generalized antagonism between the digital game ecosystem and players, and in particular its "encoded algorithms":

> Counterplay challenges the validity of models of play that suggest digital games compel the players to play according to encoded algorithms, which they must follow exactly in order to succeed. Instead, it opens the possibility of an antagonistic relationship between the digital game and player. An antagonism that is considerably more high stakes than the player overcoming the simulated enemies, goals and challenges that the game provides, rather it is directed towards the ludic rules that govern the digital games configurations, processes, rhythms, spaces, and structures.
>
> (Apperley 2010, 102–103)

And, as we have already identified, when other players constitute a significant part of the digital game by becoming competitors, allies, or content producers, as they do in almost all multiplayer games, the antagonism of counterplay may equally be channelled at or through players. Thus counterplay shifts in its meaning. Initially it consisted primarily of antagonism towards structures of development and consumption but later expanded to include a hostility towards the game, its systems, and, by extension, rules, other players, community networks, and as Apperley states, "configurations, processes, rhythms, spaces, and structures" (2010). Thus counterplay is in opposition to the experience of play, the units that enable the system to operate, and its commercial prerogatives.

Counterplay is in contrast to the norm and, through its opposition, the structures, contexts, and expectations related to the game: etiquette, rules, its spirit, and discourses of legitimacy, ideology, and/or law. To engage in counterplay is to embrace the implicit risk of being identified and punished. Thus counterplay shares aspects of, and overlaps with, a number of other similar concepts within game studies: games of order/disorder (Sutton-Smith 1977), dark play (Schehner 1988, 2013), pre-rational play (Spariosu 1989), agonistic play (Spariosu 1997), transgressive play (Aarseth 2007), countergaming (Galloway 2006), deludology (Kücklich 2007), and bad play (Myers 2005, 2010). While each has its own specific peculiarities and variations, they can generally be understood as ways of playing that prioritize anti-structure and the opposition of rule.

This denial of rules is especially problematic when placed within the context not of play but of gameplay – the playing of formal or organized games, as the existence and observation of rules are considered by many as an intrinsic factor. Let us remember video games are simulations constructed out of encoded rules and other logical statements that are carefully interwoven to create game-play that is enjoyable and meaningful. Many scholars have offered a definition of games that sketches their controlled, rule-based nature and therefore the edges of counterplay. Bernard Suits' attempt in *The*

Grasshopper, Games, Life and Utopia (1978, 41) is, for me, one of the most useful for approaching counterplay:

> To play a game is to attempt to achieve a specific state of affairs [prelusory goal], using only means permitted by rules [lusory means], where the rules prohibit use of more efficient in favour of less efficient means [constitutive rules], and where the rules are accepted just because they make possible such activity [lusory attitude].
>
> (Suits 1978, 41)

The important elements are that game-play necessitates behaviour informed by the restricted means enabled by the rules, and this in turn is part of the "lusory attitude" of the player – the appropriately playful way of approaching a game. The lusory attitude is then the willingness to be restricted rules in order to play a game. Without this attitude, play can still take place but not game-play, and therefore the experience is not fun or pleasurable in the ways originally set out by the designers of the game. Marc Prensky makes the link between a game and rules even more clear:

> Rules are what differentiate games from other kinds of play. Probably the most basic definition of a game is that it is organized play, that is to say rule-based. If you don't have rules you have free play, not a game.
>
> (Prensky 2001)

Counterplay is not a game, is not game-play, but may still consist of a different, divergent mode of play. Within a non-digital game the lusory attitude is precisely that. Despite the infinite possibility of behaviour and activity as defined by the rules of physics, the game player chooses to adopt the inefficient means. However, in a video game some of this decision-making is taken from the player and resides in the affordances offered by the game simulation.The game is coded to require certain behaviours, will only respond to certain stimuli, and rewards certain activities over others. Therefore the game system enforces some degree of alignment with lusory activity irrespective of the players' attitude. Instead of proactively choosing to adopt the rules, one could, as Espen Aarseth does, see the rigid code-based rules of a video game not as a platform and possibility but a reduction and imposition (2007):

> By accepting to play, the player subjects herself to the rules and structures of the game and this defines the player: a person subjected to a rule-based system; no longer a complete, free subject with the power to decide what to do next.
>
> (Aarseth 2007, 130)

This reminds us that playing games can therefore be regarded as only one, rather restrictive way of playing, and we can imagine a continuum of play, with regulated game-play on one end and chaotic, unbound free play on the other, archetypes Roger Caillois defined as "ludus" and "paidia" respectively (2001, 1961). For Caillois, paidia was a natural form of play, "common to diversion, turbulence, free improvisation, and carefree gaiety", a pleasurable, spontaneous, and often physical activity (2001, 1961, 14). In contrast, ludus represents paidia bound by "arbitrary, imperative, and purposely tedious conventions" (Caillois 2001, 1961, 13). The rules may be arbitrary and tedious, but what they create is a set of pleasurable activities with purpose and meaning that can be communicated and thus become shared and collective. The benefit of becoming subservient to arbitrary and tedious rules is the pleasure and communality of game-play. The activity transforms into something more meaningful than the sum of its parts, and as anyone who plays games will attest, this can be euphoric. Play shifts from being individual, carefree turbulence into something regulated and formal. We become players, teams, and in doing so we can work together and compete in a collectively meaningful social activity.

While the written or coded rules of the game are fundamental in constituting the game, player, and game-play, these rules are subject to constant challenge, renegotiation, and redefinition. As Jesper Juul explains, "Gameplay is not a mirror of the rules of the game, but a consequence of the game rules and the dispositions of the game players" (Juul 2005, 88). Game-play is therefore the product of contestation. Within non-digital games the originator decides the rules that are then validated or altered when other players inhabit the game and its spaces. Within video games the same process occurs, but as De Paoli and Kerr point out (2010), alteration or inscription is restricted by the extent to which the game is flexible and how much is allowed to be changed, and thus is a limited and contentious alteration. Players can only redefine the rules in ways the game has been coded to allow or must introduce change in aspects other than the coding of the game, such as by agreeing with others to play in certain ways, including boycotting elements or introducing additional concerns, something understood as "house rules".

In *Rules of Play* (2003) Katie Salen and Eric Zimmerman differentiate between three different kinds of rules: operational rules; constitutive rules; and implicit rules (129–30), the varying levels of malleability they offer, and the way they affect our understanding of player identities. Operational rules and constitutive rules can be understood as the restrictions dictated by the game code, the way a video-game space operates, such as the movement it enables, and then the rules of the game itself. Operational and constitutive rules are automatically enforced as the software is executed. By contrast, implicit rules are social in the sense they refer to the expectations of appropriate play and shift more flexibly in accordance with the attitude and preferences of the players. However, while the operational and constitutive rules are enforced by the structure of the game and are uniform, implicit rules can also vary between individual players and groups, who may each hold differing attitudes of what game-play should look and feel like. This raises the distinct possibility that the way an individual or group choose to play, their house rules may be considered odd, deviant, or plain wrong.

Table 1.1 Salen and Zimmerman's three kinds of rules.

Kind of Rule	Description
Operational rules	which are "… synonymous with written out "rules" that accompany boardgames and other non-digital games"
Constitutive rules	"… the underlying formal structures that exist "below the surface" of the rules presented to players. These formal structures are logical and mathematical"
Implicit rules	"… these rules concern etiquette, good sportsmanship, and other implied rules of proper game behaviour"

(Salen & Zimmerman, 2003, pp.129–30)

The malleability of implicit rules highlights that it is natural for different groups of players to adopt varied ways of playing the same game. It also illustrates that game-play is not simply defined by the rules encoded into a game but is determined by the behaviour and the perceptions of players. The realities of game-play are therefore unpredictable, and only take form once players fully inhabit the spaces. Additionally, game-play may differ between groups who may regard the play of others as inappropriate and abject. This betrays that players form different tastes for play and are very much conscious of the acceptability of other players' play.

This resonates with Michel Foucault's concept of "the normalizing gaze", which he describes as "a surveillance that makes it possible to qualify, to classify and to punish" (1977, 184). This is the process by which behaviour is observed, scrutinized, and judged, and its relationship to what is considered normal identified and communicated. It is this process that players engage in as they flexibly create implicit rules and create game-play, identifying what is normal and correct and all that sits beyond. This idea that players are constantly assessing and judging the play of others is something we will return to repeatedly through this book. It not only creates the sense of counterplay but seems a process of which all players appear conscious. The definition of appropriate play is therefore dependent on the observation of rules within a profoundly social, and therefore shifting, context. Games enable varying levels of rule flexibility, and the player finds themselves and their actions defined by the game structure but also the pervasive scrutiny of other players. This is in constant renegotiation and contestation.

While up until now counterplay has been seen as a player's active violation of rule, the normalizing gaze and implicit rules introduce the possibility that counterplay can be something identified by other players when they witness distasteful or offensive play. There could be situations in which counterplay has nothing to do with willful opposition but could be play that is called foul and defined as counter by others. Video games offer players a great deal of latitude for different ways of playing the game, leading to different approaches, strategies, and behaviour. When subject to the normalizing gaze, such as multiplayer environments or social contexts, some of these will be interpreted as allied or opposed to the spirit of the game.

OBSERVING ABNORMAL PLAY

The identification of other players' behaviour as abnormal or contrary to the rules or spirit of the game frequently occurs. One example is the case of "dominant or complete strategies" (Juul 2002, 327). These occur when the player becomes aware of the underlying processes in a game, particularly its constitutive rules, and identifies a predictable optimal way of playing: the strongest weapon, using an unblockable attack, or even a pattern of apparently random events such as enemy spawn locations and times. A growing awareness of these exploitable opportunities often develops as a player becomes increasingly familiar with a game they are playing, the product of hours of sustained inhabitation of a game space, but the dominant or complete strategy applies this in the extreme. Raph Koster repurposed Robert Heinlein's concept of "grokking", describing it in relation to games as when "you understand something so thoroughly that you have become one with it and even love it ... beyond intuition or empathy" (Koster 2004). At this point the game takes on a different meaning. It is perhaps as least challenging as possible, but while some might find this boring, other players enjoy the experience of flow, the movement and progress it allows, and the way this allows the game to be used for other purposes.

The player who groks a game to the extent they adopt complete or dominant strategies is seen in loaded terms. According to Thomas M. Malaby, this removes the contingency of the game, or "that which could have been otherwise" (Malaby 2007a). Dominant and complete strategies are seen by many as meaningless and abject, counter to the expectations of play, moving from leisure to something else, something Malaby presents as "a retreat from the demands of the new" that "signals a disposition that does not want to be performatively challenged" (Malaby 2007a).

Malaby's response betrays the extent to which play is subject to a normalizing gaze, and how emotive and entrenched assumptions are. For Malaby and many others, play is dependent on chance or, rather, games are to be played in relation to an inflexible conception of play. Play that is seen to deviate from the slowly evolving model of appropriate play is seen as problematic and even corrupting, and as a result our popular understanding of play has shunned these difficult, negatively perceived forms. These offensive, incompliant, dangerous, and illegal manifestations of play have been comprehensively isolated from our lexicon of play. In exchange, we read play as benign and games as regulated and predictably safe. Anything else, such as where our actions remove unpredictability from the outcome of a game, or where we alternately we remove the checks and balances that restrict how far a game goes and the risks its participants are exposed to, contradict what we understand as play.

Roger Caillois suggested corrupt play is a selfishly primitive urge that needs to be controlled and restrained to best "contribute usefully to the enrichment and the establishment of various patterns of culture" (2001, 55). This betrays that individualistic and potentially risky examples of play, such as counterplay, are regarded as abject and at odds with community and consensus. By contrast, acceptable play is thus configured as an activity almost entirely devoid of risk, ambiguity, and offense. Other theorists regard the boundaries between play and game-play with more flexibility. For instance, Ian Bogost argues that "understanding games as a medium of leisure or productivity alone is insufficient" (2011, 7) and offers a list of other uses of games that challenge our understanding of appropriate play.

From Bogost's perspective, game-play is just one form of play that games enable, alongside other practices including reverence, music, pranks, transit, branding, electioneering, promotion, snapshots, texture, kitsch, relaxation, throwaways, distillation, exercise, work, habituation, disinterest, and drill. Certainly some of these uses of a game space are regarded as incompatible with or oppositional to game-play, and thus can be viewed as counterplay.

Espen Aarseth argues video games create an expected model of play, an idealized player who understands and is willingly compliant with the rules and activities presented by the designer. He labelled this "the implied player" (2007, 133), which is what I mean by compliant or normative play. The problem Aarseth saw was that not all players are capable or inclined to comply with the expectations set by the implied player. They may be unable to meet the minimum levels of dexterity demanded by a game, unwilling to invest time to grind through early levels, or simply reject aspects of the game because they find them unenjoyable. This resonates with Apperley's version of counterplay and those players who work against and challenge the implied player model, engaging in "transgressive play" (Aarseth 2007). Aarseth challenges the reading of game-play as a utopian ideal, reframing it within the context of video games as domineering restriction, a "prison-house of regulated play" against which some players naturally rebel (2007, 133).

This progresses counterplay further. It can be instigated against mechanisms of game development and consumption; against the rhythms and structures of the game; it may be identified through the activity of the normalizing gaze; and now may be conducted in rejection of the expectations placed on the player through the "tyranny" of game-play and appropriate play. Aarseth presented transgressive play as:

> A symbolic gesture of rebellion against the tyranny of the game, a (perhaps illusory) way for the player subject to regain their sense of identity and uniqueness through the mechanisms of the game itself.
>
> (Aarseth, 2007, p. 133)

The power of the implied player, appropriate play, and the model of game-play already change what it means to be a player, and we see different kinds of players, ways of playing become increasing read not as activities but as identities. Katie Salen and Eric Zimmerman, for example, differentiate between the standard player (akin to Aarseth's implied player) and other abnormal forms: the dedicated player, the unsportsmanlike player, the cheat, and the spoilsport (2003, 268). These other kinds of players reject or counter aspects of the game and are defined by their lusory attitude, adherence to rules, and interest in the game itself.

Table 1.2 Salen and Zimmerman's player types.

	Degree of lusory attitude	Relationship to rules	Interest in winning
Standard Player	Possesses lusory attitude	Acknowledges authority of rules	Typical interest in winning
Dedicated Player	Extra-zealous lusory attitude	Special interest in mastering rules	Intense interest in winning
Unsportsmanlike Player	Sometimes resembles the Dedicated player, sometimes resembles the Cheat	Adherence to operational rules, but violates implicit rules	Intense interest in winning
Cheat	Pretends to possess lusory attitude	Violates operational rules in secret	Intense interest in winning
Spoil-Sport	No pretence about lack of lusory attitude	No interest in adhering to rules	No interest in winning

(Salen & Zimmerman, 2003, p.276)

The dedicated player possesses an over-zealous alignment with the game and play too hard, the unsportsmanlike player breaks etiquette in order to win, the cheat clandestinely violates rules to succeed, while the spoilsport is disinterred in the game and does something else in the game space instead. Needless to say, counterplay can be found in dedicated, unsportsmanlike, cheating, and spoilsport behaviour. While this way of thinking about and categorizing players is very useful if the aim is to highlight difference and deviance from the norm, this leads to a tendency to not see these as momentary ways of playing but as types of player identity. We see cheats, spoilsports, and the ranks of normal, compliant standard players. This highlights difference but says very little about the practices utilized, their motivations or pleasures. While Aarseth suggests a resistant approach, much like Dyer-Witheford and de Peuter's counter-mobilization, it fails to acknowledge that players might simply find this behaviour intrinsically enjoyable rather than feeling a sense of tyranny that needs to be opposed. Aarseth paints it as resistance to the specifics of the game, not as play.

In contrast, Richard Bartle's Hearts, Clubs, Diamonds, Spades (HCDS) player model (1996) recognizes these intrinsic pleasures, articulating four player types: achievers, explorers, socializers, and killers, which describe the various activities players tend to find enjoyable. If not carefully designed and managed, each of these player types can manifest itself in extremes and negatively impact a multiplayer game's dynamic, such as the socializer who turns a game into a chat room. Crucially in HCDS, and his later expanded model (2005), Bartle recognizes these are predilections and ways of playing rather than identities, even explicitly warning against the reading of activity as identity (2012), and argues that over time, players frequently change their play styles and what they enjoy. This only confirms what we know from experience – even those players who routinely break rules don't always do so, and different types of play suit different moods and points in our lives. Counterplay is part of a repertoire of play that, when conducted, may go too far or become mean-spirited, but this does not prevent the player from generally playing in an appropriate, standard fashion. A player can counterplay and do so with viciousness, when it feels like the right thing to do.

This raises an interesting connection between counterplay and rules. Games are defined by rules but they restrict play. Some respond to this restriction by counter action while others may see it as violating an idealized conception of how to play – in other words, the implied player. Finally, this strongly highlights the fact that players are constantly observing and assessing the play of others, and are subject to similar scrutiny that places individuals into categories and asserts identities: standard player, dedicated player, unsportsmanlike player, cheat, spoilsport, or many more.

CHEATING AND COUNTERPLAY

One of the most universally recognized counterplay activities is that of cheating. It is also one that has received some of the most attention within game-studies research. By looking at the way cheating has been theorized we are able to trace two differing approaches within game studies that offer further nuance to the ways games, players, and counterplay are handled. The first can be considered a formalist approach, originating primarily from the computing/software design school, which prioritizes the game and diminishes the complexity of the player. Work from this approach often offers definitions and taxonomies to enable the identification and subsequent protection of systems against counterplayers and does not care for the reason they have done something but generally only the outcome. The game takes priority. By contrast we can also trace a situationist approach, originating from sociological/humanities schools that prioritize the player over the game, presenting vignettes and testimonies of individual players and presenting all play as situated, contextual, and meaningful.

Each approach serves a different purpose. Formalist approaches tend to offer a systematic overview but could be accused of being a blunt and inaccurate instrument as a result of the overarching assumptions and generalizations needed to create persuasive and applicable models. By contrast, the situationist approach, with its intense detail and focus on contextual manifestations, offers interesting detail but might be seen to lack a wider applicability. One is too generalist, the other too granular. The formalist approach favours the game (and the mechanism of design, development, and operation) while the situationist stance prioritizes the player (and the consumption, use, and rejection of the structures explored by formalists).

Accordingly, these also tend to either see counterplay as a simplistic rejection of rules or a nuanced social activity. While each stance in isolation is potentially problematic, it is through the combination of these two approaches that game studies best progresses its understanding of play. It is worth mentioning this book most closely adopts a situationist approach, presenting counterplay as an important natural repercussion of games as culturally situated phenomena and challenging the extent to which counterplay is oppositional to the games and their structures.

Yan and Randell's article "A Systematic Classification of Cheating in Online Games" offers a representative overview of a formalistic approach, listing fifteen forms of cheating, ranging from "misplaced trust" to "denying service to peer players" and "compromising game servers" (2005, 2–4). What is interesting about this classification – which, it should be noted, presents similar categories as the work of Parker (2007), Yan and Choi (2002), and Webb and Soh (2007) – is the breadth of what is considered cheating, ranging from the use of distributed denial-of-service (DDoS) network attacks and social-engineering techniques such as "pretexting" (obtaining partial information in order to persuade and deceive) to "phishing", the classic false bank e-mail, for example (Yan and Randell 2005, 2–4). The formalistic approach does not attempt to situate the social or cultural contexts of cheating. It doesn't particularly concern itself with what cheating means, it simply describes its forms. Here. cheating is defined by the rules of the game as set out by the designers, or at the discretion of the game operators. Yan and Randell's definition of cheating makes this distinction clear. It is behaviour a player adopts:

> To gain an advantage over his peer players or achieve a target in an online game is cheating if, according to the game rules or at the discretion of the game operator … the advantage or the target is one that he is not supposed to have achieved.
>
> (Yan & Randell 2005, 1)

In contrast to formalist definitions, situationist approaches are typified by a tendency to view play as a temporal and situated response to a specific set of circumstances. Scholars such as T. L. Taylor (2003, 2007, 2009), Mia Consalvo (2007, 2009), Julian Kücklich (2005, 2007a, 2007b, 2008, 2009), Geoff King and Tanya Krzywinska (2006), Thomas Malaby (2007a, 2007b), and Sue Morris (2003), among others, have contributed towards a situationist understanding of games and, more specifically, counterplay activity such as cheating.

T. L. Taylor's work highlights the subjective and relative nature of the definition of cheating and, by extension, other forms of counterplay such as grief-play, pointing out the reliance on outside agents and contexts within its definition. "These categories – griefing and cheating – are both socially produced and only made meaningful via contextualisation. … The meaning within the game is based on something other than formal structures, which often leave significant spaces of ambiguity" (2009, 51–52). Counterplay is therefore a product of the gulf between what is intended by the designer and the social aspect of games, the implicit rules, and the ambiguity of interpretation and use – in other words, the range of ways that individuals play.

This is also recognizable in Mia Consalvo's research on cheating, in which she observes significant ambiguity over what players considered cheating, finding that many players were willing to adopt or even condone cheating under the right circumstances (2007, 93). Players described cheating as "anything other than getting through the game all on your own" and "breaking the rules of the game", but many argued cheating was only possible when another human player was disadvantaged (2007, 88–93). Consalvo's player/cheaters identified inequality caused by an activity as being the core definition of problematic cheating. According to the respondents, it was not simply the breaking of rules that constituted cheating but doing so in a way that disadvantages another player. This raises scepticism over whether cheating can even occur in a single-player game in which there is no disadvantaged other and the progress and activity of the player are not shared, and thus compared, with others. Disadvantage can surely only occur in situations in which an individual's play is influenced by the activity of others, such as on multiplayer games or those with an element of competition or reporting in its broadest sense: leader boards, gamer points, or progress announcements shared on social networks. Perspectives such as this present a play ecosystem in which players are constantly observing and contextualizing play for impact, inequality, and unfairness while simultaneously deciding when and under what circumstances the authority of rule can be appropriately suspended and ignored. This is not as clear cut as Yan and Randell's taxonomy of cheating, and questions what legitimate authority the game operator, designer, or publisher have to define what constitutes cheating – and, by extension, counterplay. Players appear to routinely make normative judgements about the behaviour they experience and engage in, balancing their observations in relation to the specific contexts of the game, and it is this that determines cheating the cheat and thus counterplay.

Players offered a range of reasons for contextual motivations for cheating, rationalizing them through being "stuck" in a game, for the implicit pleasures of the cheating experience, to enable "time compression", or simply as a way to "be an ass" (95–101). And, as indicated by these points at which cheating is adopted, cheating did not always receive universal prohibition from the player base but ambiguity. Consalvo observes the player base appeared to accommodate groups of players who had varying predispositions to kinds of cheating and even groups where cheating becomes an important mode of play: "In the world of multiplayer cheaters, a subculture of cheaters can subscribe to its own beliefs about skilled gameplay and the clever exploitation of game resources" (2007, 123). For these groups, cheating is part of the implicit rule set, a mark of appropriate play, and therefore the way to achieve status and reputation both within the cheating subculture(s) and those of the standard player.

Just through this rapid sketch of cheating we have exposed a complex set of overlapping and competing perspectives and concepts. Players cheat when they feel the need, as a product of the gulf between what games enable a player to do and what they are expected to do, and when there is an absence of clearly defined rules and expectations. Also, as Aarseth suggests, when rules are too restrictive or visible they may also motivate counterplay. Taking a similar stance to Aarseth but speaking in terms of tension instead of tyranny, Julian Kücklich argues games are "entities in which the impulse to play is inextricably linked to the desire to cheat" (2007a, 355). The constant restriction of game-play creates a desire for disorder, but cheating might additionally can be used as a means to better understand or grok the game as a way of playing with the materiality of the game. This brings us confusingly full circle to players who love the games so much, cheating is one of the ways of getting closer to them. Counterplay becomes a way of making even more meaningful bonds with the game. Cheating "can help us attain knowledge about a game more quickly than by playing by the rules, it is also possible to see cheats as tools that allow us to gain a more profound insight into games and how they are put together" (Kücklich 2007a, 359). Alisson Gazzard paints a similar picture with the "aberrant player" who deploys cheats as and when is necessary:

> The player may seek to find an easier/quicker way of completing certain sections. They may want to explore the "algorithm" further to re-instate the experience of "flow" ... or extend the other pleasures of the game in some way ... [and] seek out new ways of playing the game. ... (2008)

This implies cheating may serve purposes other than simply being a rejection of rules. It may act as a trapping of a gaming subculture but also implies cheats and cheating may have their own positive benefits, values, and meanings that are not always evident from a formalistic perspective. This is not to say cheating is compatible with game-play, nor to allude to it being entirely opposed to the game either. Cheating may not be about what it initially appears to be, as Consalvo puts it. "It may have nothing to do with advancing the game or gaining skill. The player is gaining more enjoyment from the game, in a variety of ways" (2007, 104).

There are other, more ambiguous forms of counterplay that still have the capacity to violate and damage, such as subversive manifestations of player-productivity, when players produce things in games or with games that violate rules and expectations. This is neither entirely breaking the formative rules of a game nor necessarily harassing a player but introducing elements or interacting with elements in ways that are deemed inappropriate or offensive, or that intrude on protected aspects of copyright and intellectual property. Player productivity in this manner can be understood as the result of unsanctioned "grassroots convergence" seen across the spectrum of media interactions and fandom, where players become focussed on the "archival, annotation, appropriation and recirculation" of the game, irrespective of sanction (Jenkins 2006, 18).

In these situations the game publisher is obligated to intervene and attempt to remove or invalidate the content lest they see their intellectual property eroded or, more problematically, the intellectual property of others. Unfortunately such intervention risks being perceived by the players as domination. Esther MacCallum-Stewart (2007) discusses the impact of the perception of inequality, specifically within the context of self-governance, within Linden Lab's *Second Life*, which resonates with imposition. In *Second Life*, players are encouraged to self-govern. However, developer intervention makes any sense of sovereignty meaningless. The authority of the developers can overrule the power given to the *Second Life* users, exposing its precarious nature, and thus some believe the only means of asserting power and agency is to protest and oppose. For MacCallum-Stewart, *Second Life* thus becomes "an anarchistic state where players are often profoundly unhappy with their lot, but have little ability to change it" (2007, 201). Cory Ondrejka acknowledges a similar dynamic within MMOs, suggesting "draconian approaches ... simply move the protest onto forums, blogs, and the web" (Ondrejka 2005, 16). Subversive manifestations of player-productivity such as incendiary user-generated content are pushed beyond the immediate jurisdiction of the game authorities. Thus counterplay permeates far beyond the initial reach of the game, finding root in pockets beyond, where it is documented, discussed, and no doubt future events are planned.

RULES, CONTRACTS, AND LAW: MANAGING COUNTERPLAY

There are other ways of counterplay that go far beyond cheating, such as those activities that, due to their nature, spill out of the jurisdiction of game rules and into contract law and criminality – for example, some cases of hardware hacking and illicit modding. Counterplay is necessarily defined and characterized by violation. Each example is seen to break an expectation of behaviour, a rule of a game, a contract, or law that defines the acceptable and the profane. Unlike conventional games, additional rules and laws hedge in video games. They are commercial entertainment products worth millions of dollars and as such, they are given legal protection and classified under copyright law as literary works to maintain profitability and to protect the investments of the corporations that produce them. This takes the form of giving legal protection to the technical methods used to secure the game systems and services under copyright law and the regulation of negative or problematic behaviour through the application of terms of service agreements and contract law. In the case of the Xbox 360, on which much of this study takes place, players are subject to multiple overlapping levels of restriction, and this is consistent with other console video-game systems

- The implicit rules that define how a game is to be played properly, according to the players;
- The operational and constitutive rules of the game that define how it is to function and be properly played according to the designers;
- The End User License Agreement (EULA) and Terms of Service that define how the player is able to interact with the game as a piece of software;
- The various laws that restrict behaviour within the public more generally, such as The Criminal Justice and Public Order Act 1994 and the Computer Misuse Act 1990 and those that protect copyrighted works such as the European Directive 2001/29/EC or the US Digital Millennium Copyright Act (DMCA).

In addition, when the player joins online and multiplayer environments they are subject to additional restrictions.

- The Xbox LIVE Terms of Use that determine the way in which the Xbox LIVE system can be interacted with;
- The Xbox LIVE Code of Conduct that determines how a player should behave when using Xbox LIVE;
- The specific game Code of Conduct that specifies what types of behaviour are sanctioned within its online element e.g. banning policies.

The expectations, rules, and laws violated during counterplay in turn take the form of a number of distinct practices with varying labels, levels of potential damage, and significance. This can be seen in the Code of Conduct for *Call of Duty: Modern Warfare 3* (2011), which explicitly defines the types of counterplay behaviour and the associated penalties. These align with some of the counterplay forms we will explore in this book. The Code of Conduct includes "boosting, glitching, hacking", "modifying the executable", "organizing cooperative or single game play for the purpose of gaining ... in-game unlocks", "Exploiting map holes ... glitch[es], and participating in modded lobbies", "demonstrating an offensive in-game gamer tag", and "verbal abuse, harassing, or other related behavior deemed as universally unacceptable to other players" (2011).

The *Modern Warfare 3* Code of Conduct is predominantly enforced through limiting access to the game by banning player accounts and referring credentials to Microsoft to enable the console(s) involved to be banned from the service directly. This Code of Conduct, while specific to *Modern Warfare 3*, is consistent with those found on the other *Call of Duty* releases but also other games on the Xbox 360. By contrast, the game End User License Agreement, in this case from *Call of Duty: Black Ops* (2010), is primarily concerned with regulating player interaction with the software and the protection of rights of ownership and copyright. The user is prohibited to do any of the following:

> Reverse engineer, derive source code, modify, decompile, disassemble, or create derivative works of this Program, in whole or in part.

> Hack or modify (or attempt to modify or hack) the Program, or create, develop, modify, distribute or use any software programs, in order to gain (or allow others to gain) advantage of this Program in an on-line multiplayer game settings including but not limited to local area network or any other network play or on the Internet. (2010)

Similar restriction is placed on the user from the platform-holder, Microsoft, which prohibits certain behaviour on its online gaming network, warning against offensive behaviour, activities that undermine the operation of the Xbox LIVE service, gaining unauthorized access to aspects of the service, and actions deemed to damage the experience of play. Some offenses warrant an immediate permanent suspension, including, without limitation, hacking, modding, fraud, severe racial remarks, nudity on the various camera peripherals that can be connected to the systems, repeated creation of inappropriate gamertags or profile content, or posting viruses or URLs to viruses

While much of the counterplay activity is penalized and addressed through the invalidation of player accounts and consoles, there is scope for some violations to be move into more powerful forms of regulation, particularly those relating to intellectual property. Since the development of the World Intellectual Property Organization copyright treaty (WIPO), in 1996, residents of the US and Europe have been subject to a more explicit set of laws related to copyright use. Established as the European Directive 2001/29/EC and the US Digital Millennium Copyright Act (DMCA), these laws define the offense of circumventing security measures designed to limit access to copyrighted works. While it was originally devised with the VHS Macrovision encryption technology in mind (it is explicitly mentioned in the DMCA statute), within the digital sphere it takes on a much more ambiguous and powerful application, effectively protecting any work that deploys an "effective technological measure" for protection. The ambiguity of this definition allows the DMCA to be applied liberally and to many different contexts, even potentially beyond its original scope and purpose.

Activity that violates the DMCA or equivalent, irrespective of whether play or not, shifts into a criminal act. The DMCA places a level of culpability on the owners of the technologies and services that allow it, such as the gaming platform manufacturer, in order to motivate a rapid response to the violation, as well as holding a penalty of up to five years in prison for the one conducting it. This presents a legally powerful control and makes anyone found to have violated this, such as hardware hackers and illicit modders, potentially subject to the full interpretations of the law. Despite the potential severity of DMCA violation, hardware hackers and illicit modders are generally reprimanded through invalidations and software/hardware countermeasures. However, there have been occasions when courts of law are used, such as when individuals or companies are seen as particularly damaging or when one assumes the platform-holder desires to send a message to the playerbase. These situations must be carefully managed by the corporate parties in particular since without care, they may also become configured in the same ways Ondrejka and MacCallum-Stewart warn against, becoming motivation for yet another cycle of counterplay, as will be explored in Chapter 5 in the discussion of the Graf_Chokolo, Geohot, and Opsony case. The point here is that within the context of counterplay, players frequently play in violation of rules and the law. Curiously, there seems to be something about play that makes some players willing to break rules and even the law. Perhaps it is that the outcomes of counterplay are pleasurable, seen "as direct, immediate, and engaging as those of good play" (Myers 2010, 16). But also, they are escalatory, may evolve into something much more significant without the players realizing, and irrespective of this counterplay, players can be at real risk of material loss and even incarceration.

Games law expert Greg Lastowka offers some perspective on why a player might feel so willing to break laws within the context of gaming, suggesting it may be "due to the fact that games constitute a rival regime of social ordering. The rules of games are inherently in tension with the rules of law" (2010, 106). This tension is what enables games to occur, such as the difference between boxing and affray, but games are not entirely controlled by law in the same manner as normal life. However, while this enables game-play, it also means players may be conscious of this tension and more inclined to regard the law as entirely extraneous to play. In the context of non-digital play and with caveats over the severity of the infraction, this is not necessarily an issue, but video games as commercial products are less resilient to this kind of activity. Within video games, the various Terms of Use, Code of Conduct, and End User License Agreements attempt to bridge and rationalize the difference between legal and illegal activity, reminding players of the legal frame to video-game play, yet this is often unsuccessful. Games are generally understood socially as being separate from ordinary life. In addition, the intense and utter absorption they demand and their non-productivity place them conceptually out of synch with the law. Instead they are controlled by rules, which can be bent or opposed.

Despite the social disconnection of play and legal restrictions, this is not something that is recognized in law. Instead, the law offers a level of protection to video-game designers, operators, and publishers that sits beyond the expectation of many players, who are preoccupied with their play. Lastowka presents a useful overview of the relationship between law and video game play:

> The law generally respects the exclusive right of virtual world owners to control the functioning of the key technology at play. ... In addition, the law generally enforces the contractual agreements drafted by virtual world owners. ... Property and contract are reinforced and

extended by anti-hacking laws that prohibit unauthorized access to the machines hosting virtual worlds. [And] ... copyright law allows virtual world owners to enjoy the additional benefit of copyright control over the code of their virtual worlds.

(Lastowka 2010, 180)

David Myers argues that game-studies literature largely fails to acknowledge the implicitly oppositional or transgressive nature of play, which he sees as "most frequently non-serious and therein bad, ignorant, destructive, and/or illegal" (2010, 20). Performance Studies researcher Richard Schechner introduced a similar concept, dark play, seen as a process of playing "in which even the rules of play are subverted or sabotaged ... when alternative, often mutually contradictory, realities are brought into contact with each other" (1988). For Schechner, this was not especially unusual or abject but one of the varied manifestations of play, which he saw as a "continuous creative-destructive process". In addition to its capacity for subversion and defiance, dark play contains the escalatory unpredictability we have touched on already, where "actions continue even though individual players may feel insecure, threatened, harassed and abused" (Schechner 1988, 4). Lastly, another of Schechner's core characteristics of dark play is its sheer ambiguity, even going beyond the limits and boundaries that delineate play.

> Dark play may be conscious playing, but it can also be playing in the dark when some or even all of the players don't know they are playing. Dark play occurs when contradictory realities coexist, each seemingly capable of cancelling each other out, as in the double cross.
>
> (Schechner 1988, 12)

I believe it is dark play that most effectively captures the range and breadth of counterplay, as used in this book. Dark play violates at least three principles that underpin contemporary Western play values.

- Non-observance of rules and expectations that form a game. Dark play rejects rules but does so in an unpredictable manner. Some rules may be forgone while others adhered to, or rules may be erratically or inconsistently adopted.
- The absence or unreliability of metacommunicational signals that conventionally signal play or non-play. In dark play there is uncertainty over what is being played, when, or by whom. The signals are incomplete, untrustworthy, or entirely omitted.
- The application of violent and destructive, unrestrained play. Dark play can embrace violence, causing damage to individuals, systems, or groups (physical, emotional, financial, symbolic etc.) and is therefore full of risk. As a result there is no way of reliably anticipating how far dark play might go or the stakes for those involved.

From these distinctions we see that dark play is nebulous, protean, and utterly unreliable. Players are not necessarily aware they are playing, nor the risks involved. We cannot identify its boundaries – we do not know when, where, and what form it will take, and we have no certainty over if, when, or how it will stop. Dark players each hold differing levels of awareness and influence of the game at hand, but even those with greatest insight still have no guarantee of controlling what is in play. Dark play is perhaps then best regarded as a semi-autonomous performance or dance, one that can be guided and nudged but never truly controlled. It depends on protagonists and victims, both of whom are subject to similar risks and uncertainties, and it is only understandable when one is certain it has ended. When the sequence of actions is placed in a temporal and social context and subject to "reperformance as narrative" (Schechner 1988, 14), dark play is stripped back and rationalized, seen in the cold light of day as antagonism, theft, vandalism, or much worse.

When occurring, dark-play performances are conducted with disregard for the potential risks and without the expected metacommunicational triggers that would normally signal a change of affairs and enable protective defensive strategies such as the definition of safe words or boundaries. These signals might include the absence of a knowing wink, the wry grin, or the spontaneous ripple of nervous laughter that betrays something is afoot. As a result, the lack of signals creates players (perhaps best understood within a theatrical context) who are oblivious yet central to the performance. These "nonplayers – innocents, dupes, butts, anxious loved ones – are essential for the playing to continue; the reaction of the nonplayers is a big part of what gives dark play its kick" (Schechner 1988, 14). There is no warning signal that something is afoot, new boundaries or limits are never established, and all involved are therefore subject to risk.

At its core, Schechner's dark play signals a perceived inconsistency in Western configurations of play as a concept that has been entirely divorced from its manifestations, which are oppositional, vindictive, nebulous, or dangerous. Instead, play is framed as beneficial and benign, and once play is decided to have crossed a line of taste, protocol, or law, it is no longer play but simply violation or deviance. Of course, Schechner is not the first to have offered a critique of Western play values or challenged assumptions about its benign nature. We see it in Brian Sutton-Smith's recognition of "the hidden character" of children's play (1997), full of "secret clubhouses and forbidden activities such as stealing, vandalism, gambling, drinking, and watching prostitutes" (1997, 121). We see a similar dynamic in Mihai Spariosu's exploration of a classical Hellenic "pre-rational play" (1989) or "agonistic play" (1997) that revels in the mastery of the victor over consideration for the defeated. In relation to video games, we also see connections with David Myers' "bad play", "extreme risk-taking (and risk-enjoying) … which is harmful to the self or others; and play that is against the rules" (2010, 17). It is important to stress that the player/protagonist enjoys this play. Frequently it only becomes apparent how extreme or dangerous it has become, and the extent that rules and laws have been violated, after the play has ended.

These arguments present dark play as common and intrinsically linked to conventional play. The difference is that it is duplicitous, embraces outcomes or methods that violate opinion, and contains risk that frequently causes harm. This is not to suggest dark play must result in harm to victims or players, or that others need necessarily recognize it: Instead dark play may simply pass without recognition or retribution, like a "kick me" sticker slapped onto the back of a classroom victim, that falls to the ground without instigating violence, or the lone driver who floors their accelerator in the middle of the night without the blink of speed camera or the wail of police siren. Dark play contains these pleasures of risk, of violation, and of personal agency that resonate through such acts, even extending to the vicarious pleasure of knowing of, but not performing, dark play – the thrilling anticipation of awaiting a practical joke's performance.

Dark play can be regarded as another game layered onto the existing context, which may or may not be one of game-play. It may offer advantage to playing, such as a poker cheat who slides a winning card out of their sleeve, or be entirely unrelated, such as stealthily tying a teammate's laces together while waiting on the substitute bench. This game is individual and pleasurable. It is part of play.

Before exploring specific examples of counterplay it is useful to retrace the qualities we have explored.

- Counterplay is a dynamic and free form of play closely linked to paidia and in contrast to restrictive game-play;
- It may oppose any element of the system that constitutes a video game and may do all of this intentionally or unintentionally. Its identification occurs within the social realm;
- The counterplayer is often attributed a special status. They are differentiated and their actions are frequently associated with identities e.g. griefer, cheat, hacker;
- Counterplay acts may be conflictingly viewed as legitimate uses of game spaces by different player groups or stakeholders;
- Participatory and fan production cultures have extended the scope and frequency of potential counterplay engagements due to players interacting with video games on a productive and closer emotional level;
- Counterplay makes use of ambiguity and the absence of enforced rules, but it also emerges within contexts where rules are applied too stringently and visibly;
- Counterplay has an escalatory danger;
- Counterplay is pleasurable;
- Counterplay is only really understood when it has finished or, to be more precise, once counterplay is finished it is translated into a narrative that explains its motivations, purpose, and meaning.

This allows us to define broad modes of counterplay, listed in a subjective order of escalating risk, in terms of the danger they pose the video-game system and, by penalty, the protagonist:

- Incendiary, offensive, or oppositional player productivity e.g. obscene user-generated content;
- Offensive or asocial player interactions e.g. grief-play;
- Non-adherence to rules e.g. breaking etiquette or promises;
- The exploitation of game system vulnerabilities e.g. cheating and the use of exploits;
- Unsanctioned peripheral modification e.g. the creation and use of auto-fire controllers;
- Unsanctioned hardware hacking e.g. consoles that have had security countermeasures removed;
- Homebrew and illicit software development and use e.g. modification programs;
- Game and system piracy and copyright abuses e.g. the use of game ISO images;
- Illicit game modification e.g. modified *Call of Duty* matches;
- Unauthorized access to video-game systems and access/distribution of content.

This chapter has explained how counterplay is defined and how it is understood within game studies – what it is, how it is regulated, and what relationships it has with game rules and game-play. While this has given insight into how it can be defined, it has not particularly helped us to grasp how it might be understood. The normalizing gaze and the notion of reperformance as narrative have indicated the understanding of counterplay occurs after the act has been decided to have finished, whereby meaning and significance are attributed through reference to a normative external frame. But what are these frames and where do they come from? These frames are the discourses that offer tightly packed bundles of meaning that can be applied to counterplay or any other form of transgressive violation for that matter. It is therefore important to explore these in detail.

While this sketches out the complexity of counterplay from a game-studies perspective, there is the additional problem that it is an activity that does not occur in cultural isolation. Despite discussion of the magic circle of game-play, the reality is that video games are now culturally, economically, and socially significant artefacts. What happens within games affects people, businesses, and our understanding of the world. In addition to this, game-play and, in this case, oppositional game-play, is regarded as a problematic transgressive activity not simply within the boundaries of the specific match, game, or platform but within society generally. As a result they are not subject to the order of power and meaning within games, nor subject to being called foul by an umpire but subject to the monolithic discourses by which we make sense of deviance, oppositional behaviour, and crime. This presents further challenges for the video-game researcher and is something we will explore in more detail in the next chapter.

GAMEOGRAPHY

Assassin's Creed Unity. 2014. Ubisoft.
Call of Duty: Advanced Warfare. 2014. Activision. Sledgehammer Games.
Call of Duty: Black Ops. 2010. Activision. Treyarch.
Call of Duty: Black Ops 2. 2012. Activision. Treyarch.
Call of Duty: Black Ops Rezurrection. 2011. Activision. Treyarch.
Call of Duty: Ghosts. 2013. Activision. Sledgehammer Games.
Call of Duty: Modern Warfare. 2007. Activision. Infinity Ward.
Call of Duty: Modern Warfare 2. 2009. Activision. Infinity Ward.
Call of Duty: Modern Warfare 3. 2011. Activision. Infinity Ward / Sledgehammer Games.
Call of Duty: World at War. 2008. Activision. Treyarch.
Halo: Master Chief Collection. 2014. Microsoft Studios. 343 Industries.

REFERENCES

Aarseth, E. 2007. "I Fought the Law: Transgressive Play and The Implied Player." *Situated Play, Proceedings of DiGRA 2007 Conference*, 130–133.
Apperley, T. 2010. "Gaming Rhythms: Play and Counterplay from the Situated to the Global." *Amsterdam Institute of Network Cultures* [online]. http://www.networkcultures.org/_uploads/TOD%236%20total%20def.pdf. Accessed June 22, 2012.
Bartle, R. 1996. "Hearts, Clubs, Diamonds, Spades: Players Who Suit MUDs." http://www.mud.co.uk/richard/hcds.htm. Accessed January 8, 2012.
Bartle, R. 2005. "Virtual Worlds: Why People Play". http://www.mud.co.uk: www.mud.co.uk/richard/VWWPP.pdf. Accessed December 10, 2010.
Bartle, R. 2012. "Player Type Theory: Uses and Abuses." http://casualconnect.org/lectures/design/player-type-theory-uses-and-abuses-richard-bartle/. Accessed July 10, 2012.
Bogost, I. 2011. *How to Do Things with Videogames*. Minneapolis, MN: University of Minnesota Press.
Caillois, R. 2001 [1961. *Man, Play and Games*. Urbana: University of Illinois Press.
Consalvo, M. 2007. *Cheating: Gaining Advantage in Videogames*. Cambridge, MA: MIT Press.
Consalvo, M. 2009. "There is No Magic Circle." *Games and Culture* 4 (4), 408–417.
De Paoli, S. and Kerr, A. 2010. "The Assemblage of Cheating: How to Study Cheating as Imbroglio in MMORPGs." *The Fibreculture Journal*, 16.
Dyer-Witheford, N. and de Peuter, G. 2005. "A Playful Multitude? Mobilising and Counter-Mobilising Immaterial Game Labour." *The Fibreculture Journal* [online]. http://journal.fibreculture.org/issue5/depeuter_dyerwitheford.html. Accessed July 2, 2011.
Foucault, M. 1977. *Discipline and Punish: The Birth of the Prison*. New York: Vintage Books.

Galloway, A. R. 2006. *Gaming: Essays On Algorithmic Culture.* Minneapolis, MN: University of Minnesota Press.

Gazzard, A. 2008. "Grand Theft Algorithm: Purposeful Play, Appropriated Play and Aberrant Players." MindTrek'08, October 6–9, 2008. Tampere, Finland: ACM.

Jackson, M. 2014. "Assassin's Creed Unity Season Pass 'discontinued', free game offered." http://www.computerandvideogames.com/481815/assassins-creed-unity-season-pass-discontinued-free-game-offered/. Accessed December 2, 2014.

Jenkins, H. 2006. *Convergence Culture.* New York: New York University Press.

Juul, J. 2002. "The Open and the Closed: Games of Emergence and Games of Progression." *Computer Games and Digital Cultures Conference,* Tampere University Press, 323–329.

Juul, J. 2005. *Half-Real: Video Games between Real Rules and Fictional Worlds.* London, England: The MIT Press.

King, G. and Krzywinska, T. 2006. *Tomb Raiders & Space Invaders.* London: I.B. Tauris & Co. Ltd.

Koster, R. 2004. *A Theory of Fun.* Phoenix: Paraglyph Press.

Kücklich, J. 2005 "Precarious Playbour: Modders and the Digital Games Industry," The Fibreculture Journal, Issue 5 2005, http://five.fibreculturejournal.org/fcj-025-precarious-playbour-modders-and-the-digital-games-industry/. Accessed December 2, 2014.

Kücklich, J. 2007. "Homo Deludens." *Convergence,* 359.

Kücklich, J. 2007b. "Wallhacks and Aimbots: How Cheating Changes the Perception of Gamespace." In Borries, F. v., Walz, S. and Bottger, M., eds., 118–124. *Space Time Play: Computer Games, Architecture and Urbanism.* Berlin: Birkhauser Verlag AG.

Kücklich, J. 2008. "Forbidden Pleasures – Cheating in Computer Games." *The Pleasures of Computer Gaming,* 52–71: Jefferson, N.C.: McFarland & Co.

Kücklich, J. 2009a. "Virtual Worlds and their Discontents." *Games and Culture,* 4 (4), 340–352.

Kücklich, J. 2009b. "A Techno-Semiotic Approach to Cheating in Computer Games: Or How I Learned How to Stop Worrying and Love the Machine." *Games and Culture,* 4 (2), 158–169.

Lastowka, G. (2010). *Virtual Justice: The New Laws of Online Worlds.* New Haven, Connecticut: Yale University Press.

MacCallum-Stewart, E. 2007. "The warfare of the imagined – building identities in Second Life." *International Journal of Performance Arts and Digital Media,* 3 (2). Intellect, 197–208.

Malaby, T. M. 2007a. "Ganking the Meaning out of Games." http://terranova.blogs.com/terra_nova/2007/02/ganking_the_mea.html. Accessed June 27, 2012.

Malaby, T. M. 2007b. "Beyond Play: A New Approach to Games." *Games and Culture,* 2 (2), 95–113.

Morris, S. 2003. "WADs, bots and mods: Multiplayer FPS games as co-creative media." *Level up: Digital Games Research Conference:* Utrecht, Holland: Utrecht University. November 4–6, 2003.

Myers, D. 2005. "What's good about bad play?" IE 2005 Proceedings of the second Australasian Conference on Interactive Entertainment: Sydney, Australia. p133–140. November 23–25, 2005. Creativity & Cognition Studios Press.

Myers, D. 2010. *Play Redux: The form of computer games.* Ann Arbor: The University of Michigan Press.

Ondrejka, C. 2005. "Changing Realities: User Creation, Communication, and Innovation in Digital Worlds." http://ssrn.com/abstract=799468. or http://dx.doi.org/10.2139/ssrn.799468. Accessed December 2, 2014.

Parker, J. 2007. "Cheating by Video Game Participants." Proceedings of CGSA 2006 Symposium, Canadian Games Study Association CGSA.

Prensky, M. 2001. "Fun, play and games: What makes games engaging?" http://www.marcprensky.com/writing/. Accessed October 17, 2012

Salen, K. and Zimmerman, E. 2003. *Rules of Play: Game Design Fundamentals*. Cambridge, MA: MIT Press.

Schechner, R. 1988. "Playing." Chick, G. and Sutton-Smith, B., eds. *Play & Culture*, 3–19.

Schechner, R. 2013. *Performance Studies: an introduction*. New York: Routledge.

Spariosu, M. 1989. *Dionysus Reborn: Play and the Aesthetic Dimension in Modern Philosophical and Scientific Discourse*. Ithaca, New York: Cornell University Press.

Spariosu, M. 1997. *The Wreath of Wild Olive: Play, Liminality, and the Study of Literature*. Ithaca, New York: Cornell University Press.

Suits, B. 1978. *The Grasshopper: Games, Life and Utopia*. Edinburgh: Scottish Academic Press.

Sutton-Smith, B. 1977. "Games of Order and Disorder." *Newsletter of the Association for the Anthropological Study of Play*, 4, 19–26.

Sutton-Smith, B. 1997. *The Ambiguity of Play*. London, England: Harvard University Press.

Taylor, T. L. 2003. "Power Gamers Just Want To Have Fun?" In Raessens, M.C., ed. Utrecht: Utrecht: Universiteit, 300–312.

Taylor, T. L. 2007. "Pushing the Borders: Player Participation and Game Culture." In Karaganis, J. ed. *Structures of Participation in Digital Culture*, 112–132. New York, NY: Social Science Research Council.

Taylor, T. L. 2009. *Play Between Worlds: Exploring Online Game Culture*. Cambridge, MA: The MIT Press.

Webb, S. D. and Soh, S. 2007. "Cheating in networked computer games: a review." *Proceedings of the 2nd International Conference on Digital Interactive Media in Entertainment and Arts,* 105–122.

Yan, J. and Choi, H. J. 2002. "Security Issues in Online Games." *The Electronic Library*, 20.

Yan, J. and Randell, B. 2005. "A Systematic Classification of Cheating in Online Games." *NetGames '05 4th ACM SIGCOMM Workshop on Network and System Support for Games,* New York: ACM, 1–9.

2 The Challenges of Studying Counterplay

While the previous chapter led to a functional definition of counterplay from within game studies and video-game culture, it is necessary to remember that acts of opposition, countering, aggression, and violation – transgressions – are universal and not particular to a video-game context. Wherever rule and order exist, by definition so too do their mirror images of misrule and counter-acts. We see cheats, bullies, and law-breakers throughout society, and these have been subject to extensive study and theorization. As a result there is a significant body of literature that attempts to rationalize, explain, and respond to counter-acts, but more widely within society there are a number of popular discourses of legitimization that serve the same purpose. These are culturally specific in terms of being based on a wide range of social, political, cultural, religious, and economic influences, and equally, these discourses are subject to change over time. For the researcher attempting to make sense of transgressive activity such as counterplay, discourses are problematically monolithic, presenting an often dominant context, meaning, and justification in either the absence of or simply drowning out the voice of the protagonist. Discourses often make up the entire scope of meaning applied to a counterplay act, dominating the available motivations, dynamics, and interpretations. Transgression and the discourses that surround it are therefore crucial to this study.

Transgression can be understood as violation of rule or moral principle. These principles often demarcate important boundaries within society, such as between the sacred and profane, the normal and the abject, the compliant and the criminal. We largely see these boundaries through interrelated social and legal frameworks such as rules and laws, which are informed by collective opinion and solidarity. They come to feel like common sense or the opinion of the majority. In this respect, the law, or similar boundary, can be considered a "visible symbol" that represents this consensual solidarity regarding behaviour and protects the central cultural and economic interests of society (Durkheim 1982, 64).

The idea of a body of individuals, a collective or a mass, is something we will return to time and again through the discussion of transgression and counterplay. These are the people, the members of society, the public, who decide how something is understood or comes to be. As we shall see, transgression is heavily reliant on the general public as it is the way they respond to an act of violation and the discourse they finally accept that controls meaning. There are a number of terms we could use – the proletariat, the multitude, the demotic – much like the terms used to explain counterplay touched on in the previous chapter, but each comes with its own biases and associated baggage. We shall therefore use the neutral term "public". By this I do not simply mean compliant average players, although it contains these, but the public at large with their varied voices and opinions, including ardent gamers, counterplayers, designers, intellectual-property lawyers, cybercrime investigators, non-gamers, and so on. The public does not exclude particular individuals and counterplayers also contribute to the way such acts are understood, but there are certainly individuals and groups that have greater influence: experts, policy-makers, and spokespeople. This resonates with the core argument of this book: counterplay is one way of playing within a broader repertoire and there are many people within the public who occasionally counterplay. For the sake of argument, the public, as I use it here, means all the people who contribute to the understanding of a transgressive act.

There are other points in this book where we will need to differentiate between other parts of the public. The terms used include "the establishment" to speak of those with disproportionate influence or a dominant position, such as, in this case, game developers, publishers, platform-holders, and IP lawyers; "the playerbase" to restrict the selection to only the players of a specific game less robust but somewhat useful; and "counterplayers" and "compliant players". Remember this is temporal and situational, since players flip-flop between modes as and when they need to signify an oppositional or supportive stance. While the transgressive act may be individual, the response it calls for is collective.

Those who transgress break expectation, rules, and laws, and in so doing step into dangerous territory that places them at risk of penalty and questions the authority of the rule and, as a corollary, the autonomous power of the transgressor. A tension is formed around what happens next. Will the rule be reaffirmed and the transgressor reprimanded, or will they evade penalty and therefore have shown a new space of opportunity and behaviour? Transgression is therefore dependent on rule. It not only works against them but needs them in order to have any power. As Chris Jenks suggests, transgression such as counterplay is not about getting rid of rules but "is a deeply reflective act of denial and affirmation" (Jenks 2003, 2). There are other interesting aspects to the way transgression works. Transgression doesn't end when the activity breaking the rule does but instead works on a "hail and response model" – the transgression invites, not demands, that something happen as a result. The thing has happened is often momentary but its power, its damage, and menace come from what occurs next.

Transgression is seen as a curious, simultaneous denial and affirmation, a playing against and with rules that simultaneously objectify and break, in so doing calling for a response. The transgressive act lacks the potential to change directly but instead issues a call to the public and establishment for a response that either reaffirms the rule or exposes its irrelevance and causes change. This is a crucially important distinction as it moves transgression away from mere rejection or circumvention. Instead it becomes dialectical, a forcing-open of dialogue, a challenge for response, and a retracing of boundaries. Michel Foucault further expands on this concept, describing transgression's relationship with the limit of rules:

> A limit would not exist if it were absolutely uncrossable and, reciprocally, transgression would be pointless if it merely crossed a limit composed of illusions and shadows. ... Rather, their relationship takes the form of a spiral which no simple infraction can exhaust.
>
> (Foucault 1977, 33–35)

While transgression is defined by a hail-response dynamic, transgression does not, cannot, fully take place in visibility. It cannot hail too soon or too loudly for the simple fact that it is likely to be challenged and stopped before it reaches its full potential. Instead transgressions emerge from the shadows and half-light of partial obscurity. As Schechner points out, much of the power of dark play comes from this hidden and duplicitous nature, developing in the shadowy ambiguity until it is ready to be performed, unveiled, and completed (1988).

Thus counterplay acts are often only identifiable and visible after they have taken place, after they have concluded and been called foul, explained, and rationalized – again, Schechner's reperformance as narrative and the normalizing gaze. The normalizing gaze enables the public to understand what has taken place and why, and to eventually reach agreement on what kind of response it necessitates. This process is open to some contestation as consensus is formed, and it is here the discourses that explain transgression compete for dominance. It is the prevailing discourses that suggest and inform common-sense ways of understanding the transgressive, and thus counterplay acts, as they are tested and applied dynamically by the public. It is therefore essential to explore the prevailing discourses that legitimize and illegitimize transgression, as these influence the ways counterplayers, compliant players, the playerbase, and the establishment come to approach and understand counterplay as an activity.

TRANSGRESSION AS PATHOGEN

It is possible to trace the origins of the discourse of pathogenic transgression, at least in terms of its language and general structure, to Emile Durkheim's *The Rules of the Sociological Method* (1982). In this text Durkheim articulates the importance of the average, the commonplace, or normal in society and, by contrast, non-normative (non-normal) behaviour. Durkheim presented "social facts" that were considered normal behaviour for "a given social type ... at a given phase of its development, when it occurs in the average society of that species" (Durkheim 1982, 97), the point being that social facts are the measure of appropriate behaviour, are important, and indeed aspirational. Durkheim prioritizes normality over difference, articulating three non-normative stances: the different, the deviant, and the criminal, each increasingly opposed to social fact. Behaviour that fails to adhere to the expectation of social fact is abnormal, different, deviant, and criminal. Durkheim's model places emphasis on the value and importance of conformity, seeing agreement and consensus as not just the building blocks of society but as core to the long-term health of society as an ecosystem. Seeing society in biological terms, social facts and normality are healthy, while difference, deviance, and criminality are unhealthy. Normal, healthy behaviour promotes solidarity, continuity, and union, while unhealthy or pathological abnormality promotes individualization, fragmentation, and interruption (Jenks 2003, 25). Abnormality threatens the equilibrium of a system, and if allowed to expand and be replicated, jeopardizes the security and survivability of the whole, much like a cancerous mutation transgression is regarded as problematic and pathogenic.

This captures some of the pathogenic capability of the transgressive act, largely dependent on its potential to radically bring about unpredictable change. Once a rule has been violated, once its authority has been challenged and a response demanded, unless it is dealt with rapidly, visibly, and with conviction it opens up the potential for further transgression, replication of the transgressive act by others, and the violation of other rules. Unless the infection is quickly sterilized it may spread until it cannot be regulated and thus becomes pathogenic, the previous social system dies and is replaced by another.

The biological element of this discourse has diminished since the late 1800s when Durkheim was writing, but its core principles of dangerous infectious deviance – distrust of ambiguity, an emphasis on the normal, and hostility towards the different – still resonate today. This discourse now manifests itself in the ways that abnormal, deviant, or criminal elements are presented as escalatory threats, as the thin end of the wedge that jeopardizes the ultimate security of the system and risks instigating a descent into chaos. It is a discourse frequently employed by the establishment, who often have the most to lose if a system or boundary changes, and conversely, it is something underplayed by subordinate groups seeking change or whose tastes differ from the norm.

The discourse of pathogen has become the dominant way of understanding and (il)legitimizing deviance and criminality, although we now live in a time where difference (but not too much difference) is celebrated or at least tolerated. However, pathogen is just one of the discourses that compete for meaning. There are other subordinate discourses that jockey to make sense of transgressive acts. We will explore four subordinate discourses of transgression that originate from a range of practices and have been recognized by a number of scholars:

1   Transgression as resistance: a direct opposition to rule, boundary, or law, which recognizes but contests the power it holds. It attempts to bring about change through undermining the logic of rule, introducing chaos, and opposing authority in the hope that boundaries are redrawn through public consensus;
2   Transgression as mastery: recognizes but disregards the power and authority of the rule. It is an act that asserts mastery of the protagonist, placing them in a dominant position. Unlike resistance, mastery does not seek to bring about change since for the transgressor, the rules, boundaries, and laws have been circumvented;
3   Transgression as identity: this is based on violation of rule as a means of creating and/or maintaining the identity of the transgressor. Transgression as identity does not tend to challenge authority directly but instead works in contrast to and within these dynamics in order to create individual and group identity;
4   Transgression as carnival: carnivalesque transgression is focused largely on the pleasures of transgression and misrule. It does not seek long-term change, nor explicitly rejects the authority or power, nor does it carve out any meaningful durable identity. Instead the carnival is based on the socially meaningful pleasures of fluid group membership and anonymity, of attacking and laughing at others, and thumbing noses at the establishment.

We will now take time to look at these discourses in more detail, tracing their complexities and the key literature from which they originate.

TRANSGRESSION AS RESISTANCE

Resistance can be understood in its most abstract sense as when an act is instigated in direct opposition to a stimulus such as a rule, mandate, or prohibition. It is the natural oppositional force of a subordinate entity against the will of the dominant.

Resistance is largely determinant on the perception of inequality, a sense that a rule or law is unfair. This is subjective in the extreme and naturally follows from the discourse of pathogen and being labelled as abnormal, deviant, or criminal. The inequality is perceived by the subordinate or the disempowered, who can choose to complain through mechanisms of hegemonic resistance such as courts of law. Alternatively they may engage in transgressive resistance, including civil disobedience or direct action. Transgressive resistance becomes a potentially explosive, temporary means of challenging or reversing the force of the edict, ignoring rules, law, or convention due to a greater injustice. The hope is that the transgression will spur change by shocking the system or at least force the issue into debate and lead others to question the authority of rule. For those who do not share the perception of inequality, it is deemed unnecessary, senseless, and merely pathogenic. The disenfranchised can fleetingly assert power and control even though they have no authority to do so. They resist the power relations projected onto them, which has the capacity to stretch out over time or space, undermining the authority of rule, its logic, and power. If we think of many of the social movements of the twentieth century such as the African-American Civil Rights or Indian independence movements, these used civil disobedience and transgressive resistance as a mechanism of bringing about change and employed the discourse as a way of legitimizing the transgressive acts.

Traditionally, resistance has come to be seen as an act that actively seeks recognition and recruitment, not just to highlight the illegitimacy of a rule but to convince others of this stance. Therefore there has been a tendency to judge the legitimacy of resistance according to the number of individuals who share its stance. The more people who see inequality, the greater the likelihood of its escape being framed by the discourse of pathogen. This occurs when resistant movements reach a tipping point and what formerly seemed deviant becomes common sense. Under the right circumstances, isolated acts of individual resistance may tessellate into a more cohesive communal form. Each act of resistance, even those that are neutralized, may contribute to the momentum of the cause. This is transgression as pathogen inverted.

This view of resistance has become somewhat outmoded, however. In *What is Resistance?* (2005), Rebecca Raby challenges the prevalence of the communal and recruiting aspect of contemporary resistance, arguing instead it is now often individual, fractured, and personal. This changes the dynamic of resistance, as it enormously reduces the likelihood of it coalescing into a movement with sufficient support to become legitimized and elicit meaningful change. Instead resistance retains the oppositional stance but no longer maintains the need to organize or to find recognition. It no longer hails with the same intensity, nor cares for the response.

As a result, postmodern resistance does different things, while those who engage in it "may be less able to celebrate collective, organized, oppositional resistance, [though] they do address complex flows of power relations, fragmented, constructed subjectivities and local and individualized activities" (Raby 2005, 161). Resistance can then be subjective and instanced, manifesting itself in the way the protagonist chooses. This creates a situation in which a matrix of individual transgressions are motivated as resistance but one that seeks neither momentum nor connection.

The issue here is that postmodern resistance describes a huge range of acts and behaviours. J. Patrick Williams (2011, 93), faced with such range, offers some way of articulating the similarities and interconnections between postmodern resistant acts. This is done by describing the formal character-istics of resistance such as its mode, its scale, and its visibility (94–106). Williams argues resistance works along a passive/active axis according to how direct the challenge is to the rule. If it is direct opposition, it is active resistance, while if it seeks to evade the rule, it is passive resistance. Secondly, resistance exists on a micro/macro scale that can be used to think about the target of the act, the type of response it elicits, and/or the extent to which it originates from individual or group activity. Micro resistance works on the individual scale, meso scale being the scale of groups and institutions, while macro scale focuses on wide-scale issues such as economic systems or political ideologies. Thirdly, an overt/covert axis exists that describes the extent to which resistance is visible and recognized by targets and observ-ers alike. Overt resistance is a vocal and public proclamation of opposition and refusal, while covert resistance occurs secretly. Covert resistance may take the form of an act with double meaning and double inscription that is correctly deciphered only by those who are complicit or in the know. As we shall see, this resonates with the discourse of identity. The example of double inscription highlights the challenges of exploring postmodern resis-tance, in which the recognition of resistance may only be possible to certain members of society and the curious situation where resistance may not even be recognized in plain sight.

At its core, resistance builds on dialecticism, which sees conventional power structures being opposed, destroyed, and rebuilt, leading to a new reality, a synthesis. Resistance is defined through the possibility of bringing about change through the challenge and opposition of rule. Within the con-text of counterplay, resistance would be play seeking to bring about change.

TRANSGRESSION AS MASTERY

The discourse of transgression as mastery has its basis in the concepts of the slave/master relationship, the master morality, and the Übermensch as seen in the writing of Frederick Nietzsche and later developed by Georges Bataille. In *Thus Spoke Zarathustra* (1969, 1883) and, more explicitly, in *Beyond Good and Evil* (2003, 1886), Nietzsche contemplated the origins of moral concepts such as justice, law, conscience, and social responsibility. Unlike Durkheim, who saw solidarity and community in average, common-sense social facts, Neitzsche's thesis was that normative Judaeo-Christian morality was a limiting constraint that dominated and subordinated human potential. Instead of solidarity and continuity emanating from the normal, Neitzsche saw a system that prevented members of society from being free, turning them into slaves. When expressed as the slave/master model, the anger felt from being subject to constant social domination is inverted and channelled back onto the individual as guilt and cynicism. The individual becomes slave to the master of socialization, surrendering their desires and potential in exchange for consensus and normality. For Nietzsche, the slave morality, typified by negativity, pessimism, and cynicism, is contrasted to an ancient Greek master morality, now subjugated, which prioritized values of strength, wealth, and health. Nietzsche's argument was that a return to the emancipatory master-morality was preferable to the continuation of the repressive slave morality, even though this would require refusing to be bound by social restrictions and therefore be transgressive.

Nietzsche's master-morality is best captured in his figure of the Übermensch, an individualistic manifestation of aristocratic values that rejects the slave-morality and the fear of social rejection and censure. The Übermensch asserts a will to power that does not recognize the legitimacy of the restrictions and pursues its aims with self-control, self-affirmation, and self-determination, irrespective of the social and moral implications. Nietzsche's work, in particular the Übermensch, has historically been utilized and distorted to support the agenda of extremist and peripheral groups as a way of introducing sweeping radical change, such as the Nazi party and anarchist movement, who utilized its image as a model of radical and amoral change.

Georges Bataille's writing developed some of the themes implicit in Nietzsche's work, particularly those related to the limitations of morality and the desire for freedom. Strongly critical of capitalist economics and their impact on human relations, Bataille developed a "general-economy" that sought emancipation and sovereignty through conspicuous waste and the creation of "no-use-value". The logic is that waste and "no-use" free the protagonist from the limitations of economics in their broadest sense: the need to stockpile surplus necessitated by the constant repressive fear of failed harvests, hard times, and scarcity. Through consumption in excess, creating waste and loss, and an economy of unproductivity, the individual defies the restriction of economics and becomes something like Nietzsche's infinitely free Übermensch. Through rejecting the need to generate profit, Bataille's transgressive rejects the fear of the future and becomes steadfastly focussed on the bodily now. The acts refute the authority of restriction and represent absolute individual freedom and a profoundly spiritual recognition of the individual will, even though this likely leads to oblivion.

This is what is meant by transgression as mastery: becoming free not just from a rule but from all rules, from the restrictions and expectations of the system, to go beyond its limit and become lost within it, freed by the taking, the assertion of a master morality. However, this talk of freedom fails to recognize the implications of continuing to ignore the authority of and thus the violation of rules. Eventually the transgressive will be penalized. Mastery is an unsustainable strategy. From such a perspective the transgressive element takes on another valence as a noble, self-exhausting step towards sovereignty and human liberation. This is the transgressor who continues despite the inevitability of prosecution; it is the willful transgression that anticipates destruction. It creates spectacle that symbolizes freedom, although its concern is not with the emancipation of others or the improvement of a situation, just the individual rising above it.

Returning from the lofty heights of emancipation to the reality of the manifestation of mastery, it is transgression that continually defies the rules. It has a longstanding thematic resonance within computer culture and video-game culture and is perhaps most clearly understood when it takes the form of the hack. While hacking is often regarded as anti-social, illegal, or degenerate, its development as a practice revolves around ideas of total access to information and the rejection of any barriers to access. According to Steven Levy, the early hacker communities embraced a "hands-on-imperative" that argued "all information should be free", irrespective of notions of ownership (2001, 40–45). This masterful approach to information manifested itself through the necessity of the circumvention of security systems, reverse engineering, and social engineering, all techniques to erode the barriers that prevent access, justified on the basis that "access to computers – and anything which might teach you something about the way the world works – should be unlimited and total" (Levy 2001, 40).

Transgression as mastery can be considered an individualistic mode of transgression. The protagonist rejects the authority of restriction that surround them and becomes symbolically free, going down in a blaze of glory. Mastery thus differs from resistance by rejecting the authority of the rule and systems instead of opposing it and also rejecting the authority of the public. Unlike resistance, mastery does not seek recognition or agreement; it simply does what it wishes. The reasoning, the justification, and the purpose are all defined by the individual. Within counterplay this would be playing with no care for the rules or laws, the impact on others, or the eventual repercussions on the protagonist.

TRANSGRESSION AS IDENTITY

In contrast to resistance's attempt to change power relations and mastery's freedom through circumvention, the discourse of identity frames transgression as a way of expressing individual or communal identity. Transgression that focuses on identity doesn't seek to contest the power of rule like resistance, or to completely reject authority as seen in mastery, but instead aims to create spaces and practices outside the immediate gaze of power or, contrastingly, where alternate realities, power structures, and identities can be created and maintained. Transgression as identity is therefore closely linked to the concept of subculture, in which divergent identities are expressed through the deployment of unusual, deviant, or transgressive practices and rituals, at all times in contrast to a sense of the conventional. The point here is that identity is created through violation of rule but in a way that ideally neither triggers widespread penalty nor seeks to engage with or change the power structures and is therefore sustainable indefinitely.

Dick Hebdige, considered one of the pivotal scholars in subcultural identity, saw it as being communicated through stylistic acts including argot, demeanour, and image – the ways subcultural members talk, act, and look, respectively (1979). This may take the form of the adoption of intentionally distinctive slang or impenetrable speech, by behaving in ways that violate normative etiquette and rules, and by engaging in overtly transgressive acts – for example, from Hebdige's punk context, vandalism, affray, and the use of illicit drugs. From this perspective, opposing the establishment and orthodoxy – and, for this opposition to be periodically recognized by other outsiders as well as the public – is to signal subcultural membership. Once within a subculture the individual is able to gain status that may be missing or unattainable within conventional social groups.

Pierre Bourdieu's (1990) notion of distinction is critical to this discourse. He argued that in addition to economic capital, other forms existed, including cultural capital (individual cultural knowledge signalled by certain predilections or tastes) and social capital (the advantages of having a durable network of social ties and recognitions), and these were instrumental in maintaining class structures, creation of consensus, and ultimately policing the way discourses are applied. Bourdieu saw distinction or taste and the rejection of the tastes of others as one of the core ways groups created and sustained exclusive spheres, differentiated between identities, and ultimately enforced hierarchical mechanisms of power and control.

This application of distinction works as effectively for a subordinate individual as it does for someone within the establishment. Through behaving in certain ways and demonstrating "manifested preferences", the individual is able to signal membership, identity, communality, and hierarchy. Status can be established and capital generated, and in subcultural groups this may take place through rule-breaking. Transgressive identity offers a framework for the subordinate to carve out their own spaces and legitimacies, irrespective of the normative interpretation of their activity. Thus apparently deviant or transgressive activities may be the expression of, or creation of, subcultural identities that serve to legitimize the behaviour within the context of group identity and create spaces in which alternate power can be established.

Similar to Raby's observations about resistance, subcultural identity has also been affected by a postmodern turn, as seen in the post-subcultures work of Sarah Thornton's exploration of rave culture, identity, and behaviour (1995). Whereas modernist perspectives of identity emphasized the communal, spatial, and behaviourally coherent, postmodern identity is in permanent flux and renegotiation, and therefore does not have clearly defined boundaries, argot, demeanour, image, and thus identity.

Thornton's post-subcultures work rejects the notion that identity is necessarily collective, instead arguing subcultural identity can take place through modes of consumption and individualization, echoing the passive-active continuum of resistance. Buying the right kind of products, using them in the right way, wearing the right clothes, or consuming the right kind of illicit substances for Thornton become the markers of distinction and definitions of subcultural identity. However, these signals are also diffuse and prone to misinterpretation. In addition, the nature of contemporary society accentuates this diffusion. Behaviour and consumption may align the protagonist with a subculture with which they have no immediate contact and instead rely on the Internet to develop and maintain these bonds. Within this context the protagonist deploys the subcultural style, adopting the argot, demeanour, and image of the group with which they identify, but to the observer, that lacks an awareness of the subcultural context, the cues may be missed, and the act may simply appear idiosyncratic or deviant.

Applying subcultural identity explicitly to games, Jon Dovey and Helen Kennedy present the notion of technicity, "identity based on certain types of attitude, practices, preferences and so on and the importance of technology as a critical aspect of the construction of that identity" (2006, 17). Thus the digitally facilitated and located subcultural style could be playing the right games in the right ways, as contrasted with the playerbase, perhaps having a predilection towards certain illicit ways of playing, highly dexterous ways of playing, or simply expectations of duration and commitment to multiplayer gaming. From this perspective, the argument is that engaging in counterplay may be seen as the right way to play by a specific subculture, and identity that aligns with subculture is formed through counterplay practices. Playing against the rules may be a way of taking on an identity.

TRANSGRESSION AS CARNIVAL

The final prevailing discourse we will trace is that of transgression as carnival, or the carnivalesque. The carnival is notable in its negation. It doesn't seek to change anything; it recognizes the power of rule; and it has a contradictory and shifting attitude towards group and individual identity. Carnival is nebulous and tricksy. It is ultimately about the sheer joy of transgression, of the risks involved, and the pleasures of opposing and berating mechanisms of control, rule, power, and other pitiful wretches who stray into its sights.

The discourse of transgression as carnival historically revolves around the idea of a descent into a temporary period of collective antagonism and hostility, owing much of its documentation to the work of literary theorist Mikhail Bakhtin. Bakhtin's book *Rabelais and His World* (1984) explores the carnival as depicted in the work of Renaissance writer François Rabelais, notably his *The Life of Gargantua and of Pantagruel* novels (2006, 1562–1564). The carnival took place throughout Northern Europe during the Middle Ages and Renaissance, as a period of festivity where laypeople were permitted to behave in ways far beyond the boundaries of conventional societal norm. The carnival was orientated around "ritual laughter" that took form through physical "ritual spectacles" such as the crowning of a fool-king, "comic verbal compositions" that ridiculed those in power, and use of bawdy and offensive language known as "Billingsgate" (Bakhtin

1984). It represented a wide-scale but temporary period of frivolity, subversion, parody, and ridicule, where individuals and the feudal structures of power (ecclesiastical, monarchical, legal, economic) were openly challenged and humiliated. For Bakhtin, the carnival represented a time-constrained descent into transgression:

> ... temporary liberation from the prevailing truth and from the established order; it marked the suspension of all hierarchical rank, privileges, norms, and prohibitions. ... It was hostile to all that was immortalised and completed.
>
> (Bakhtin 1984, p.10)

Ritual laughter was universal. It challenged, ridiculed, and humiliated the feudal structures of power (ecclesiastical, monarchical, legal, economic), something that was potentially a capital offense outside the carnival. Yet despite or perhaps because of the inherent danger attributed to such acts, the carnival was not the conspicuous activity of an individual or minority group. Instead it was all-encompassing, collective, and anonymous, making use of masks and disguises and involving all who ventured near. Despite its communality it is wrong to assume the carnival necessarily championed the weak. Instead it was indiscriminately hostile towards its targets. The carnival "violently abuses and demonizes weaker, not stronger, social groups – women, ethnic and religious minorities, those who 'don't belong' – in a process of displaced abjection" (Stallybrass and White 1986, 19). The carnival was a period of misrule and hostility that played with motifs of excess, death, decay, and mortality, and in so doing became a symbolic leveller. Carnival spoke very much of the seductive power of the crowd and Victor Turner's concept of "communitas" (1974). Communitas is the social bond that forms between individuals within a crowd, such as the carnival, and may be seen in the right circumstances as the fuel that drives subversion, transgression, and even revolution. Communitas prioritizes solidarity, equality, and a sense of joy that is unanimously hostile.

> Communitas is, essentially speaking and in its origins, purely spontaneous and self-generating. ... It is essentially opposed to structure ... closely hedged about by rules and interdictions – which act like the lead container of a dangerous radioactive isotope.
>
> (Turner 1974, 243)

Carnival has become an important theme in relation to the study of transgression, not necessarily because of what it constituted but rather what it represented to the people. The carnival was not dialectic. It did not serve to change political or social relations, it did not create a persistent identity, it did not assume authority, nor escape the grasp of the dominant, but instead represented an antagonism towards the structures of society itself. It reminded all of their vulnerability and corporeality, and is now regarded as a cathartic acknowledgement and defiance of the brutally repressive nature of life in the Middle Ages.

From our modern perspective it is difficult to fully grasp the nature of the carnival that Rabelais documents. Unsurprisingly, as a cultural practice it was subject to sustained restriction and legislation by the establishment until it either ceased or abandoned ritual laughter and hostility as core dynamics. Thus the contemporary carnival is spectacular, celebratory, and communal but neither critical nor malign. There is instead a tendency for us to view the historic carnival "as the vulgar practices of a superstitious and vulgar population" and a "purely negative phenomenon" (Stallybrass and White 1986, 9). Yet this approach makes us likely to miss that, for its participants, ritual laughter had a "special philosophical and utopian character" (Stallybrass and White 1986, 12), "when it triumphed over the fear inspired by the mystery of the world and by power, boldly unveiled the truth about both. It resisted praise, flattery, hypocrisy. This laughing truth, expressed in curses and abusive words, degraded power" (Bakhtin 1984, 92). The symbolic laughing truth is perhaps the true transgressive danger of the carnival, as John Jervis points out: "Humour exposes the pomposity, the pretensions, the arbitrary nature of the given order; it involves unexpected juxtapositions and category transgressions; innate adaptability and creativity possible; it is parodic and reflexive" (Jervis 1999, 17). In so doing, the carnival and the ritual laughter that it invokes hold dangerously subversive connotations, flattening hierarchy. It "contains something revolutionary ... [as] only equals may laugh" (Herzen in Jervis 1999, 18). Despite the discontinuation of the carnival as a distinct cultural form, there is a sense we still hold a human need for its symbolic laughter and criticality, and as a result we now seek out other ways to satisfy these desires.

> People have the real need ... to doff the masks, cloaks, apparel, and insignia of status from time to time even if only to don the liberating masks of liminal masquerade.
>
> (Turner 1974, 243)

As a result, carnival has entered the "cultural world of the imagination" (Jervis 1999, 24), where it becomes an attitude as opposed to a behaviour tied to time and space. We enter a position where the carnival may be individually invoked whenever and wherever we see fit, leaving us in a "strange carnivalesque diaspora" (Stallybrass and White 1986, 190). This is similar to postmodern resistance or identity but applied to the simple pleasures of misrule. Leisure, conspicuous consumption, binge-drinking, extended adolescence, hen-parties, spectatorship, raves etc. all contain distasteful aspects that ridicule the normative, emphasize the bodily corporeal, and embrace ritual laughter. These pleasures represent a reconnection with the carnival.

Cultural criminologist Mike Presdee argues contemporary carnival lacks the explicit collective nature of the historic carnival and its clear demarcation in space and time. Carnival becomes asynchronous and individual. However, this lack of synchronicity fundamentally alters carnival's ability to generate communitas and flexibly support coalitions, alliances, opponents, and the rites of reintegration that mark its end and the reinstatement of conventional authority. As a result the participants become socially suspended and isolated, the carnival never quite ends, and we are "left with disappointment, dissatisfaction, discontent and the expectation that the carnival of crime will be performed, must be performed, again and again" (Presdee 2000, 48). This discourse views transgressive acts as an expression of the human need to invoke and descend into misrule, and the social function of ritual laughter and universal hostility. It is transgression to laugh at others and to seek a ripple of laughter through fellow carnival-goers. Carnival is transgression conducted to elicit a laugh, to take a cheap, mean shot, to ridicule and to attack, to feel alive and to remind the establishment of the precariousness of their authority. Carnivalesque counterplay would be transgression to cause a laugh, to ridicule the powerful or systematic, to enjoy attacking another, and to temporarily undermine authority.

Each of these discourses of transgression ultimately resonates around power or, to be more precise, present a justification for a different interaction with power. In pathogen, we sense the establishment's fear of power loss; in resistance, we seek a change to power balance by any means necessary; in mastery, power is assumed by the rejection of the authority of others; within identity, we seek the power to articulate new identities and foster new hierarchies; and in the carnivalesque, power and the principle of power – all power – is to be ridiculed, debased, and undermined.

APPLYING DISCOURSES OF ILLEGITIMACY

There are inevitably other discourses applied within society, and certainly other cultures and communities may observe other dynamics, but the five introduced here can be considered the dominant ones within a European perspective that compete to inform how transgression is to be understood, rationalized, and justified. The problem is these discourses compete organically and all around us, and thus it is impossible to fully escape their influence and be objective. This means the task of the researcher intending to explore counterplay is a difficult one, as counterplayers, those identifying counterplay, and the researchers themselves are inevitably influenced by the discourses – and in turn, these become the natural grooves to slip into when understanding transgression. This makes it hugely problematic to confidently ascribe motivation to a counterplay act, especially where the protagonist is unable to comment. This highlights the importance, wherever possible, of going directly to the counterplayers and seeking to document their actions, motivations, and contexts, but also being aware of the influence and reach of these discourses. In cases where we are unable to do this, as illustrated in the following example of incendiary user-generated content (UGC), the prevailing discourses offer potential reasons and justifications and this may skew the interpretation of the act.

INCENDIARY USER-GENERATED CONTENT: A CASE STUDY

Using incendiary user-generated content as a case study is intended to highlight the challenges and issues associated with attempting to ascribe motivation and meaning to counterplay acts without access to the testimonies of counterplayers or victims involved. We will do this by identifying a number of incendiary examples of user-generated content that violate expectations, terms of service, or etiquette, and thus appear primarily produced as violation and counterplay.

To clarify, user-generated content is the name given to the outputs created within games that enable players to create and often share things: objects, levels, constructions, images, videos etc. For example, in Maxis' *Spore* (2008), players design creatures that inhabit their games and then subsequently dynamically spread into other players' games as they connect to the central game-servers. Other examples include car livery and paint jobs in many racing games, and even fully playable game levels in the *LittleBigPlanet* series (2008-present). While the expectation is that players will create what is relevant to and compliant with the theme and tone of the game, within these situations there is naturally plenty of latitude for subversion and counterplay.

Common examples of incendiary user-generated content include the representation of genitalia and coitus, such as the comical and artistic creatures from *Spore* (known as Sporn) captured mid-thrust; a profusion of *Call of Duty: Black Ops* (2010) player emblems in which a gun is emblazoned with a crude phallus stencil; or a fair few *LittleBigPlanet 2* (2011) levels that focus on the manipulation and often bringing together of many mechanical genetalia. Other common themes are the inclusion of profanities and swear words, spelled out through the placement of items such as the smutty animé pornography produced by players using *Halo 3* (2007) custom levels.

Figure 2.1 Incendiary user-generated-content, suggestive level design in Halo 3.

Whereas the performed counterplay is generally fleeting and temporary, incendiary user-generated content persists after its initial creation. It is there to be encountered, shared, and distributed until steps are taken to remove it from the game ecosystem, although this may not be possible where the user-generated content is then remediated, duplicated, and dumped onto other platforms such as YouTube or web pages. Thus while performed counterplay is fleeting, incendiary user-generated content can be scrutinized by the player community over a period of time, can be judged, consensus reached, and reprimand sought. Unlike the performances that are fleeting and can only be described by their immediate witnesses, incendiary user-generated content is more robust, can be reviewed and scrutinized, and thus likely to elicit strong consensual responses from the public and establishment.

We will touch upon six examples of incendiary user-generatedcontent originating from four different games in order to highlight the scope of this activity but also the challenges associated with its scrutiny:

- *Rudette*: a creation in *Spore* that takes the form of two yellow anthropoid creatures in coitus. While the creature-creator game function was designed to create an individual creature, with careful modelling and arrangement this resembles two creatures copulating;
- *Fuck-slug*: also produced in *Spore*, this green caterpillar-like animal has a ridge of protrusions on its back that clearly spells out "FUCK";
- *Nazi-car*: a user-generated car decal for Turn 10's *Forza 2* (2007) racing game, applied to a 1957 Mercedes 300SL, that includes a swastika, "Heil Hitler", and "White Power", in addition to other offensive fascist iconography;
- *9/11 Level*: a *LittleBigPlanet* level where the player becomes a passenger on an aeroplane that smashes into the World Trade Center towers, which burn and eventually collapse;
- *Homer Sporeson*: a creation of a *Spore* creature that unmistakably resembles Homer Simpson;
- *LBPdius*: a playable mechanical recreation of the first level of Konami's *Gradius 2* (1988) within *LittleBigPlanet 2* (2011).

It should be stressed that these user-generated content examples are not especially representative of the content created and shared where games allow it, but simply make up part of the repertoire of content experienced. The frequency, largely determined by the attitude of the playerbase and the way such transgressions are dealt with, results in a player encountering this kind of content quite innocently during everyday play. Spore creatures spontaneously inhabit the game worlds of other players to create the sense of an unpredictable and organically dynamic galactic ecosystem. The Nazi-car was visible within the conventional *Forza 2* car marketplace before being reported and removed, although it subsequently reappeared a number of times, and players of *LittleBigPlanet* could potentially access *9/11*, *Gradius*, (1985),

Figure 2.2 Incendiary user-generated-content, Homer Sporeson in Spore.

and other levels simply by browsing the available user creations from the core game interface. This easy or spontaneous spreading of user-generated content is likely the reason why these examples found a sufficient number of observers with a sufficient a range of dispositions that the user-generated content became known, was banned, and then documented and shared on YouTube or similar sites due to its reputation as celebration or in disgust.

As we have already noted, counterplay exists on a scale of perceived volatility, threat, and objection. In its least potent forms, victim and witnesses alike may ignore it. It may titillate and amuse, it is different and perhaps deviant, but not yet abject. However, more potent examples have the potential to elicit moral outrage. This is naturally a difficult distinction to make as tastes and perceptions of offense differ. Some may find something amusing while others see offense.

These examples do not appear to explicitly target or victimize an individual or group and thus are diffuse as opposed to focused transgressions. The depictions of coitus, genetalia, or obscenities are without context or intent, resulting in low-level censure that either brings a chuckle or tiresome yawn as opposed to indignation. Of course, this depends on where and how this content is encountered and the sense of harm it may cause the audience. For example, in a game that already deals with explicit or graphic themes, where the player shoots opponents and stabs them with combat knives, the intrusion of the occasional crudely modelled phallus or swear word, while potentially jarring, is of little impact. This audience is already exposed to challenging and complex issues. However, the same is not true if the intrusion occurs on a family-friendly side-scrolling platformer such as *Little-BigPlanet*. Where transgression occurs within spaces utilized by vulnerable groups or in ways that target already discriminated groups and individuals, the act takes on further meaning and harm. It becomes a slur or an attack and is therefore much more likely to cause widespread condemnation.

There are examples of incendiary user-generated content that do target vulnerable groups or that flippantly handle complex and socially or legally sensitive subject matter, such as the Nazi-car and 9/11 examples. These trespass on much more troubling content than the previous puerile examples: global terrorism, the Holocaust, and race-hate. One might assume the motivation for each of these examples is the same, to cause as much offense as possible, but this is difficult to ascertain. The examples of coitus and profanities are relatively mundane by comparison, part of the lexicon of everyday transgression, the graffiti we might encounter on the way to work, expression of a transgressive sort. It perhaps goes without saying that the use of racial slurs and other aggressive forms of vitriol are also prevalent online, exacerbated by the relative anonymity of online environments. While not using this to apologize or to excuse the counterplayers of their actions by virtue of being the least severe examples, we then reach a situation where we begin to think about levels of transgression, and the notion of how far is too far. Is a crude depiction of coitus less problematic than one that has greater fidelity? If so, was the intention of the creator of the latter to offend and the former to amuse? Was this created to cause offense or is it a by-product of the illicit thrill of engaging with an incendiary subject matter? Was this produced to undermine the game or is it a mischievous playing with the game? These are the kinds of questions that incendiary user-generated content raise but that we cannot reliably answer.

This raises issues is a problematic dilemma. To what extent can we be assured a (counter)player produced the user-generated content in a "counter" frame of mind? And alternatively, to what extent were they simply playing? Which of the prevailing discourses do we apply and how might these alter the meaning of the act? What might the motivations be? What can we actually ascertain from these examples? And, finally, does this matter?

This also highlights a peculiarity of transgression related to its hail and response interaction with the public and establishment. While for many, counterplay is experienced as a performance – something done or said in a game context that opposes or subverts expectations, a refusal or a circumvention of rules – there are some instances where this act takes form or is documented and therefore continues to conduct the transgression each time it is encountered or replayed. In this situation the hail that demands response comes time and time again, and the likelihood of response increases as the transgression is seen, heard, or felt by a wider and more diverse audience. An example of this is the creation of user-generated content such as in games where players are invited to generate and design items, to customize the way things look, or in some cases create entirely new interactive experiences within a game, especially when the content created is deemed transgressive or incendiary. When shared, when viewed, or when used, the incendiary nature of the user-generated content becomes apparent. It violates the rules and expectations, such as through the dissemination of obscenity, copyright infringement, or intentionally offensive material.

This is made even more challenging when we explore other forms of user-generated content that are deemed transgressive for their infringement of copyright and intellectual property. Examples include the careful modelling of an unmistakable Homer Simpson creature in *Spore* or the recreation of Konami's 1988 arcade classic *Gradius 2* within *LittleBigPlanet 2*. It is unlikely these were intended to shock or to offend, and both are evidently the product of careful reference, awareness, and engagement with both the game as platform and the thing emulated. Therefore one would assume this user-generated content is an expression of fondness for the original referent, something Henry Jenkins calls "lovemarks" (2006, 68) and, by association, a positive attitude towards the game as platform.

These items and practices are often documented and archived outside the games they concern, such as on YouTube, websites, and social networks. Faced with such a range of examples existing in forms beyond their original contexts, how does the researcher go about making sense of these motives, meanings, and processes? How might we understand these acts or artefacts? Are we simply forced to adopt inductive reasoning, allowing us to say this user-generated content was probably produced to offend but saying nothing of the reasons for wishing the offense, whom it was aimed at, and what potential pleasures this might have caused? In the absence of input from the counterplayer and an understanding of the processes conducted we are hostage to the discourses of legitimacy.

We could argue each of these examples of incendiary user-generated content are pathogenic and their existence is likely to offend other players to the extent they will leave the game and tell others to do the same. We might speculate that people may be offended to such an extent that lobby groups are formed and the media contacted, resulting in a public-relations disaster and a decrease in stock price. Likewise, in cases where games are used as platforms for the distribution of hate-speech, incite racial tensions, or other illegal activities, there is the risk the platform-holder may be regarded as complicit and culpable for these actions. Lastly, copyright law, enshrined in the DMCA, places significant responsibility on the platform being used to distribute and access the infringing material. Unless dealt with swiftly, the platform-holders may find themselves legally responsible for the activities and copyright violations of their users. All of this frames incendiary user-generated content as something that threatens the health of game development and the system of consumption, damaging the experience of play, the future development of games, extending and escalating beyond the original transgression.

Inversely we might wonder whether these were the intentions of the (counter)player, to what extent they hoped their user-generated content would cause such offense that the game development would be challenged. We might wonder whether there were specific issues, a design decision, an economic process, or something that had been done that warranted this resistant activity, and whether they hoped this would lead to change. In the case of Homer Sporeson or LBPdius or any of the examples for that matter, it is potentially the case that if the user-generated content was produced in a resistant mode, its inevitable removal from the game could be the kind of action that motivates this very behaviour. Even if the administrators are only responding to law and the discourses of pathogen, this can still cause dissatisfaction as it may be regarded as injustice by the counterplayer. Cory Ondrejka acknowledges this dynamic within MMOs, suggesting "draconian approaches … simply move the protest onto forums, blogs, and the web" (Ondrejka 2005, 16). This could be the motivation that shifts incendiary user-generated content onto YouTube, the web more generally, and to be replicated and distributed further.

There is certainly a resonance with mastery within the incendiary user-generated content explored here, but again we are left simply to guess. Was the content produced in a spirit that knew of the violation but simply didn't care about the context or the risk of penalty? Did the counterplayers decide to produce fuck-slug, the 9/11 level, and the Nazi decals for themselves, irrespective of the rules and expectations and without the need to distribute and share? In the case of the LBPdius level, on account of the technical proficiency and time required one would assume it was an implicitly enjoyable act, conducted either in denial of the authority of intellectual property law or, adversely, ignorance of the violation.

We might wonder if the counterplayer is attempting to develop a reputation by producing incendiary user-generated content, perhaps by producing examples that are highly impressive but illicit (certainly a potential dynamic in LBPduis), or simply by being repeatedly offensive or part of a group who are known for their abrasiveness. The Nazi-car most clearly resonates with this, raising the notion that the counterplayer is a neo-Nazi sympathizer to their worldview. The incendiary user-generated-content becomes a proclamation of their identity. Yet once again we can only assume this.

Lastly the carnival, the hostile ritual laughter that attacks and ridicules the establishment, can be seen throughout the incendiary user-generated content. We can trace it in the sexualized and scatological Spore creatures that resonate with billingsgate and bodily excess, daring us to laugh with or be offended by the content. We sense displaced abjection in the insensitive handling of 9/11, and a willful violation of boundaries that delineate what must be spoken about sombrely and with restrain. Lastly, we see it in the creation, distribution, and use of the incendiary user-generated content, which invites us to fleetingly take part of a now technologically distributed carnivalesque crowd, temporarily donning digital anonymity and doing things we know we shouldn't or wouldn't. Thus a player goes through the motions of playing with Rudette, tells others about it, takes a screen-grab, shares it with a friend, and lets out a guilty chuckle. But once again we can only guess. Each of these could resonate or not at all, and instead we simply see the influence of the discourse.

The challenge here, and the point of swiftly sketching out these practises and prevailing discourses, is making sense of and understanding counterplay as an activity. It is very much possible for an observer to ascribe any of the prevailing discourses to any example, and to form a logical and reasonable justification. This is possible as the discourses are established and, in their own ways, coherent. We see a matrix of pathogen, resistance, mastery, identity, and carnival, and thus can hypothesize and project motivation and judgement onto the counterplayer through the normative gaze. This highlights that it is essential when attempting to understand counterplay that we step beyond these discourses or recognize their existence and influence, and instead focus on four things: documenting the process of conducting counterplay; considering its form and nature; engaging with counterplayers and, where possible, the played directly; and attempting to capture the immediate contexts of its manifestation. While this does not prevent leaving the judgement of motivations and meaning to the competing of the discourses by doing so, at least it enables us to observe from a more informed perspective. This highlights the need to directly engage with the counterplayer and counterplay forms, rather than rely on its documented form, which has already been subject to the normative gaze of the discourses of legitimacy.

We will now approach a number of counterplay themes and practices while engaging with this process. Over the following chapters we will explore grief-play, boosting, glitching, hardware-hacking, and illicit software-modding. Hopefully, by doing so we will better be able to explore what it is that counterplayers do and how, and enable us to better understand counterplay in video games.

GAMEOGRAPHY

Call of Duty: Black Ops. 2010. Activision. Treyarch.
Forza 2. 2007. Microsoft Studios. Turn 10 Studios.
Gradius. 1985. Konami.
Gradius 2. 1988. Konami.
Halo 3. 2007. Microsoft Studios. Bungie.
LittleBigPlanet. 2008. Sony Computer Entertainment. Media Molecule.
LittleBigPlanet 2. 2011. Sony Computer Entertainment. Media Molecule.
Spore. 2008. Electronic Arts. Maxis.

REFERENCES

Bakhtin, M. 1984. *Rabelais and His World*. Bloomington: Indiana University Press.
Bataille, G. 1987 [1957]. *Eroticism*. London: Marion Boyars Publishers Ltd.

Bourdieu, P. 1990. *The Logic of Practice*. Cambridge, UK: Polity Press.

Dovey, J. and Kennedy, H. W. 2006. *Game Cultures: Computer Games as New Media*. Berkshire: Open University Press.

Durkheim, E. 1982. *The Rules of Sociological Method*. Trans. W. D. Halls. London: The Free Press.

Foucault, M. 1977. *Discipline and Punish: The Birth of the Prison*. New York: Vintage Books.

Hebdige, D. 1979. *Subculture: The Meaning of Style*. London: Routledge.

Jenkins, H. 2006. *Convergence Culture*. New York: New York University Press.

Jenks, C. 2003. *Transgression*. London: Routledge.

Jervis, J. 1999. *Transgressing the Modern: Explorations in the Western Experience of Otherness*. Chichester: Wiley-Blackwell.

Levy, S. 2001. *Hackers: Heroes of the Computer Revolution*. London: Penguin.

Nietzsche, F. 1969 [1883]. *Thus Spoke Zarathustra*. London: Penguin.

Nietzsche, F. 2003 [1886]. *Beyond Good and Evil*. London: Penguin.

Ondrejka, C. 2005. "Changing Realities: User Creation, Communication, and Innovation in Digital Worlds." SSRN: http://ssrn.com/abstract=799468. or http://dx.doi.org/10.2139/ssrn.799468. Accessed December 2, 2014.

Presdee, M. 2000. *Cultural Criminology and the Carnival of Crime*. London: Routledge.

Rabelais, F. 2006 [1532]. *Gargantua and Pantagruel*. London: Penguin.

Raby, R. 2005. "What is Resistance?" *Journal of Youth Studies*, 8 (2), 151–171.

Schechner, R. 1988. "Playing." Chick, G. and Sutton-Smith, B., eds. *Play & Culture*, 3–19.

Schechner, R. 2013. *Performance Studies: An Introduction*. New York: Routledge.

Stallybrass, P. and White, A. 1986. *The Politics and Poetics of Transgression*. London: Routledge.

Thornton, S. 1995. *Club Cultures: Music, Media and Subcultural Capital*. Cambridge, UK: Polity Press.

Turner, V. 1974. *Drama, Fields, Metaphors*. Ithaca: Cornell University Press.

Williams, J. P. 2011. *Subcultural Theory: Traditions and Concepts*. Cambridge, UK: Polity Press.

3   Approaching Grief Play

The last chapter illustrated the complexity and challenges associated with making sense of counterplay without access to the protagonist or process, largely because of its ambiguity of meaning. In response this chapter will explore grief-play by looking at objectified counterplay (like the incendiary user-generated content) but also by talking with grief-players, those who have been victimized, and exploring the processes and wider contexts that frame it. It should be stressed that this process of research stops at the direct performance and participation of grief-play on ethical grounds. For more on the implications of not doing so, it is worth looking at the scholarly outcry at David Myers' adoption of the vindictive and annoying *City of Heroes* (2004) character Twixt (Plunkett 2009). Grief-play is therefore approached by interview and analysis but not direct participant observation, on the grounds that grief-play causes distress.

Let us begin to approach grief-play with an example of objectified grief-play, a YouTube video produced by a group called *I Can Has Grief?* who predominantly produce videos of griefing *Minecraft* (2009) players. The video documents a griefing session on *Minecraft*, complete with the lead griefer's perspective voice-over, alongside text-logs and occasional speech from the other protagonists and victims. It can be treated as documentation of a griefing act, yet we should still recognize it has been edited and published, focusing on the most destructive points and dramatic interactions with the victims, and is therefore more than an objective documentary. Let us be clear, this is entertainment.

The video finds us on the victim's *Minecraft* server. It is lush, colourful, and blocky. We see buildings and bridges the player has created around the topology, and a gargantuan staircase that stretches upwards, straddling the crest of a mountainside. There are four other members of the griefing group visible on screen, all of whom are furiously swinging their pick-axes to smash the structures to bits. The lead griefer recording the video begins to speak:

> OK, so we are calling out for everyone to come to spawn to collect their free gift of free diamonds while we wreck it because it's all unprotected. I'm starting to take apart these stairs by the way. ... This is *so* dumb the whole place is unprotected ... we're unbuilding! ... this guy's trying so

hard to get me to stop, he's like, jumping around me. … I'm gonna put one block of lava here and then run … in the side of this building so it just burns. … I'm gonna watch. … Isn't it pretty? It's burning. … Woo, there's a bridge. Let's get rid of that!

(*I Can Has Grief?* 2012)

While the specifics of *Minecraft* may be unfamiliar to the reader, it is likely you recognize the nature and tone of the griefer's monologue as he and his fellow co-conspirators go about their business unabated. This is much the same as a playground bully, dominating the victim while offering a monologue to both the immediate griefers and the wider audience and, in this case, distributed: "Why do you keep punching yourself Meades? Why do you keep punching yourself Meades?" It is a statement not only about immediate domination but is one that stretches out into time and space, making the point that others are aware of the situation but are not intervening. The domination by the griefer is absolute for the duration of the situation until the griefer decides they have finished or an external authority intervenes. Within the context of the YouTube video the audience is further expanded beyond the traditional schoolyard bullying context, being replayed and watched by individuals around the globe who may add their comments, thoughts, and likes, and in so doing extend the duration and insult of the griefing act and, one would assume, some of the transgressive pleasure of dark play for the griefers.

For those unfamiliar with Mojang's (now Microsoft's) *Minecraft* (2009), it is a game primarily about the mining, collection, and then construction, with many thousands of cubic blocks within a colossal low-fidelity 3D world. While *Minecraft* was initially envisaged as a survival construction game in which the player was pitted against zombies, skeletons, and explosive creepers, it has become famous for being a platform for freeform creativity and construction, with many players spending huge amounts of time building complex and detailed environments. The monologue comes from a video titled *Minecraft Griefing – Protect Yo Sheeit* (2012), which presents thirteen minutes of a longer griefing raid in which an unprotected game server, presumably the product of scores of hours of planning and careful clicking, is systematically unbuilt.

I should make it clear the griefers doing the unbuilding get very little from the experience. While smashing things with pick-axes gives the player resources, these can only be used on the server they originate from, the server the griefers will shortly be banned from once an administrator responds to the support requests. The grief-play therefore leads to no progression within the context of the game. Instead, this appears to be solely about inconveniencing others, the pleasures of transgression, the foolishness of the server-owners for not adequately protecting the space, and the desperate and ineffectual attempts of the victim to get the griefers to relent. This is about upsetting another player. This is grief-play.

This video has been watched some 930,000 times, and the *I Can Has Grief?* channel's nineteen videos have chalked up nearly fourteen million views. This video is well received by its viewers, with over five thousand "Likes" and around one thousand "Dislikes". It is regarded as an entertaining video and has generated modestly successful viewing figures. The channel contains a number of other videos that focus on grief-play, the most popular being *HOW TO become Admin on almost ANY Minecraft server WITHOUT Hacks!* (*I Can Has Grief?* 2011), with almost three million views. This details a process of impersonation and the gullibility of *Minecraft* players, suggesting that by simply saying, "I'm from PlanetMinecraft [a well-regarded *Minecraft* review website] and I'm reviewing servers to be featured on our site" and then later asking to be made a "server operator" to test the specifications of the server, the griefer is often given full control of the game (*I Can Has Grief?* 2011). After this, the video shows a number of servers where this has worked and the chaos and distress caused as the griefer uses server commands to swap the status of blocks, crash hardware, sever network connections, and infuriate players as they gradually realize they have been duped. The most spectacular examples are where sky blocks are turned into lava or sand, raining fire on the entire world, burning everything down, or covering the world with a deep layer of blocks that must be picked away at individually, thus effectively destroying the server on account of the magnitude of the task at hand.

This is a rather consistent example of grief-play, resonating with unilateral domination, performance of the act to immediate and distributed audiences, the entertaining pleading squeals, threats, and protestation of the victim, and the eventual conclusion of the grief – in this case when the griefers are kicked from the server and are finally barred by an administrator. While it shares aspects of conventional playground bullying, online grief-play also overlaps with the notion of trolling, common on the Internet and other online environments. The difference between griefing and trolling is difficult to determine and many people I interviewed used the terms interchangeably. The general consensus is that trolls tend to work individually by getting under the skin of other players, as opposed to necessarily causing damage or preventing play. A troll works in the realm of psychology and mind games while the grief-player takes a more physical and immediate stance. Yet for both of these forms of grief-play, the aim is to gain pleasure from the distress of others, whether through carefully antagonizing them within the game or by wasting their time and destroying what they have accumulated through their efforts.

As grief-play is about dominating others and altering the power relations within a game-space through this domination, it is not restricted to the deployment of any specific technologies or methods. Somebody could engage in grief-play by exploiting or misapplying game rules, by using cheats or software exploits, by using hardware hacks that alter the flow of the game, or using modified instances of the game. Grief-play is simply a way of playing in which the primary aim is to play with other players and your relationship with them, imposing power, preventing them doing what they wish, and generally undermining their efforts. As a result there is significant potential for ambiguity within the interpretation of grief-play as it is about causing another player discomfort and harm. While in some games such as the *Minecraft* example above, it is evident when play becomes grief. However in others, such as those that include competitive multiplayer, it is not always possible for observers to determine whether it is grief or simply the natural domination of a defeated player. This ambiguity is partly what the grief-players exploit, often utilizing the gulf between what is expected, what is occurring, and what is perceived, as with the process where the *Minecraft* players realized their newly promoted server operators were not from PlanetMinecraft but were grief-players.

GRIEF-PLAY THEORIES

Grief-play, like cheating, is another concept that has received relatively serious scholarly attention. Grief-play can be distinguished from cheating by ascertaining how much benefit the activity causes. Generally, cheating confers some kind of goal-orientated advantage whereas grief-play is primarily about the response from other players. It is not done primarily to progress in the game but to cause distress. In grief-play, advantage becomes transformed into power-imposition. It becomes not so much about getting better at or progressing in a game but about playing by dominating other players. Chek Yang Foo and Elina Koivisto define grief-play as "intentionally engaging in actions that disrupt the gaming experience of other players" (2004), and see it working across a range of behaviours: harassment, power-imposition, scamming, and where grief-play occurs inadvertently, greed play.

Put simply grief-play can be typified in the following manner:

> The griefer's act is intentional,
> It causes other players to enjoy the game less,
> The griefer enjoys the act. (2004, 246)

Yet while this definition certainly captures some of the perception of grief-play as an intentional and enjoyable act of harassment, it also betrays its weakness as a concept, in that it is dependent on ascertaining the intent and pleasures that surround it. More problematically, compliant game-play, as opposed to grief-play, is also intentional and pleasurable.Tthe only difference is that grief-play causes another player to enjoy the game less. Put simply, grief-play is playing in a manner that causes someone to enjoy a game less. The other constituent parts, the intent and pleasure, are no different from game-play. This dependency on judging the intent of a grief-play act is open to wide misreporting and observers may regard some compliant play as grief-play. Therefore, for me, grief-play is largely a social construct and comes once again from the normalizing gaze and reperformance as narrative. In a later book that touches on grief-play from a formalistic perspective, Chek Yan Foo offers a taxonomy that details the range of forms it takes, including greed-play that acknowledges the ambiguous edges where grief-play can occur.

Table 3.1 Foo's taxonomy of grief-play types.

Categories	Subtypes
Harassment	Slurs
	Intentional spamming
	Spatial intrusion
	Event disruption
	Stalking
	Eavesdropping
	Threatening
Power imposition	Use of loopholes
	Rez-killing
	Newbie killing
	Training
	Player blocking
Scamming	Trade scamming
	Promise breaking
	Identity deception
Greed play	Ninja-looting
	Kill-stealing
	Area monopolizing
	Item farming

(Foo, 2008, p.79)

Foo's taxonomy of grief-play contains a huge range of activities, from slurs and interruption to targeting inexperienced players, breaking promises, area monopolization, and item farming. If we accept Foo's taxonomy, being verbally abused is grief-play, as are glitching, identity deception, masterfully dominating a game space, and repeatedly, mechanically accruing items. Providing it is intentional negatively impacts on the play of others. Foo's taxonomy, through the definition of greed-play, removes the need for the distress caused to the victim to be pleasurable to the protagonist and instead suggests any activity that is intentional and causes distress is therefore grief-play. This places the onus entirely on the victim – quite rightly so, perhaps – who feels their play has been damaged. Thus we enter a situation where, in addition to acts that fit into the intent-distress-pleasure model, we also entertain an intent-distress-obliviousness model.

To make things even more complex, some of the acts in Foo's taxonomy are not necessarily malicious according to the social context of play and the implicit ruleset. A group of friends may embrace trash-talk or banter in a game as they might down the pub; glitchers may use game exploits to explore the game space or to create new games in consensus; or it may become common practice to farm certain items in certain locations or be known that a certain clan resides in one area or has a predilection for a certain set of activities. The point here is that in each of these situations, there could reasonably be a player who is unaware of or opposed to these implicit rules (which also differ from those initially set out by the designers) and thus offense, distress, and grief-play may be seen where it was not intended.

This line of discussion is not to excuse griefers, to suggest it is phantasmagorical, or to condone a permissive approach but to highlight that the most important thing about grief-play is not necessarily what is done but how it is interpreted by the players involved, taking into account the implicit rules that have developed and the extent to which a player is disadvantaged. Once again it becomes about making judgements about the intent of the protagonist, ascertaining whether it is legitimately an act conducted to disadvantage other players. Another worthwhile consideration is the intentionality, and thus replication/extension and risk, of the grief-play act, the domination of players in a manner sufficiently disruptive and therefore costly in terms of player time and effort for it to have a meaningful negative impact on play. Examples might include preventing or restricting play, destroying items or statistics that have taken considerable time to accrue, or making the play environment so hostile or distracting that play is diminished or compromised. If these processes can then be repeated so the cost is magnified, then even better. For me, this is the mark of grief-play: to waste another person's time, their efforts, and to repurpose the precious minutes, hours, and days they have dedicated to their play for your own ends. This is to say your time is more important than theirs.

STUDYING GRIEF-PLAY

Due to its sensitive nature and negative connotations, it is relatively difficult to find players who acknowledge they engage in grief-play and who are willing to discuss their behaviour. While there are many who are prepared to broadcast their activity in a form similar to *I Can Has Grief?*'s videos, this is still part of the bravura performance of grief-play, a boastful monologue instead of dialogue, and when contacted, few were willing to talk. Fortunately, through engagement with a number of gaming websites and through extensive play, discussion, and research, I was able to talk to a number of grief-players. Many were willing to talk but not on the record, while others would do so providing they remained anonymous. Evidently grief-play holds significant social censure, with the majority who grief-played keen not to be directly identifiable. Despite this censure, my own play experiences and many people I spoke with suggested grief-play, or the perception of having play intentionally and thus maliciously diminished others, appeared relatively commonplace. As an illustration, in undergraduate theory classes

I teach, I routinely discuss my research and ask students whether they recognize activities and processes. For the last four years I've used rough-and-ready surveys to ascertain whether students have experienced grief-play and other counterplay forms in both protagonist and/or victim roles. Perhaps surprisingly, out of the students who played games online (the majority), more than half agreed that at times, they had engaged in grief-play – an admission that normally came with a ripple of embarrassed laughter. Similar proportions of students also suggested they had experienced grief-play but in subsequent discussions appeared rather ambivalent about it, suggesting an escalated or distressing case was an unfortunate but relatively rare occurrence. Perhaps this betrays there is a generalized, low-level performance of grief-play within many online communities, an opportunistic hostility that embraces play that distresses others, and as a result, this is generally accepted and ignored. It becomes simply the noise that surrounds videogame play but that is somehow distinct from the more extreme, premeditated instances.

What follows is based on interviews with a number of grief-players and those who regarded themselves as the victims of grief-play. It paints a picture of the practice of grief-play that is missing in Foo's formalistic work. While there is no suggestion this is statistically representative, since it is based upon few perspectives, it still contributes to our growing understanding of counterplay and crucially, unlike the challenges seen with user-generated content, it allows us to begin to explore motivations and meanings from a counterplayer's perspective.

TEAM KILLING IN *METAL GEAR ONLINE*

Ocelot introduced himself, saying he'd become a "renowned griefer" on the PlayStation 3 European *Metal Gear Online* servers (2008) and was viewed as an associate or accomplice of another player we'll call Psycho Mantis, who had a reputation across many *Metal Gear Online*-related forums as an "arch-griefer". Ocelot described himself as "an arrogant, annoying, person … often referred to as Psycho Mantis' right-hand man or his dog" and "renowned as a Team Killer". Team killing is the process, only possible in certain combinations of constitutive and operational rules, where the grief-player doesn't attack the opponents as expected but instead turns against their fellow teammates. Team killing is unexpected, and can negatively impact on the dynamics and flow of competitive play, undermining team progress as players await the conditions of being respawned into the game, preventing them from accessing or progressing towards goals and objectives, and damaging play statistics.

Shortly before I began interviewing Ocelot, Konami, the developer of the game, had announced its intention to turn off the *Metal Gear Online* servers, effectively euthanizing the game on its fourth anniversary in June 2012.

According to Ocelot, this announcement had resulted in an explosion of grief-play on the game, which in turn had reminded him of my project and made him think of contacting me. For Ocelot, who admitted to already having a taste for grief-play, whatever previous sense of risk attributed to being caught that once existed had now evaporated, replaced with a suspicion that Konami's announcement coincided with the dereliction of duty of the game administrators who policed behaviour. Instead, the responsibility of policing of *Metal Gear Online* now fell on algorithms that used metrics, such as the number of teammates killed, to automatically detect and respond to infractions by ejecting players from the game. There was a perception that the authority of rule was contested, and detection and enforcement of transgression had become brittle and hollow. The upsurge of grief-play Ocelot witnessed and contributed to was not borne out of a sense of resistance, nor of protest against the impending cancellation of the game, but instead took advantage of the ambiguity, futility, and opportunity the game now offered. It was Ocelot's opinion that *Metal Gear Online* now offered an unobserved and unrestrained play-space he was more than happy to utilize for his own ends, including grief-play.

It should be stressed that the awareness that the game was facing impending closure was not the thing that motivated Ocelot to begin grief-play, but that instead it was read as an invitation to resume it as mode of play, within a greatly reduced sense of personal risk. He admitted he had engaged in grief-play when the game was new but at that point, he was still very much interested in playing the game as intended. Over time, as he became accustomed to the game and it became increasingly boring, he sought new thrills alongside its conventional pleasures, including grief-play. This dual-play, where the player adopts grief-play as a simultaneous but discreet play practice, is dependent on careful separation and management of identity – the use of different aliases to play compliantly and others to grief-play. This was something Ocelot was well versed at through the creation of multiple "alts", separate, disassociated play profiles in order to grief.

> I play normally too, although I do have alts and I use one alt specifically to do well on, I use other characters to troll and grief. … If the opportunity arises I'd troll. … There's something about Metal Gear Online that works for me for trolling. It was just really fun. And I was really gutted when I heard that it was closing, because you can pick it up and go in there and everyone knows your name because you're universally hated.

This recognition and response from other players appeared key to the pleasures of grief-play for Ocelot, resonating with power imbalance and dark play. Ocelot and other griefers such as Psycho Mantis utilized this environment as a space for team killing, attacking their allies in addition to their opponents, which, due to the specific design of *Metal Gear Online*, was a catalyst for grief-play power-imposition and harassment. *Metal Gear*

Online is a game in which it is possible to attack and damage teammates as well as opponents. Of course it is generally unexpected and accidental rather than premeditated, as it makes the game more difficult for the whole team. Yet, perhaps in an attempt to normalize his actions, Ocelot was keen to differentiate between his behaviours from those of "real trolls", those who imported external prejudices and issues into the game, arguing it was the specifics of *Metal Gear Online*, and *Metal Gear Online* alone, that were right for him to grief.

> I'm not a troll by nature I don't sit on 4chan or go on YouTube and spam, it's just that this was so fun, some of the reactions you got were so intense, the big threats that you got were just funny.

The age of the game and the decreasing player numbers created a small and close-knit community, with so few players on the multiplayer servers the matchmaking system was forced to group players together to create viable matches and often led to large differentials in expertise and competence. The same issue of scarcity of players also effectively invalidated the algorithmic anti-grief countermeasures that would normally disconnect a player from a game when a set number of team kills had been registered. While Ocelot and Psycho Mantis were occasionally ejected on account of these counter-measures, the lack of players on the game's servers meant that on reconnection, they were invariably reunited with the very people they had just been harassing. "You'd end up straight back in the same game up against the same opponents, and we'd be like – we're back!".

Thus the griefing was repeatable, the victims hunted and imposed on until they abandoned the game and acquiesced to the griefing, or Ocelot and Psycho Mantis moved on to something else. This structure enabled grief-play to be manifested as harassment (slurs, intentional spamming, spatial intrusion, and event disruption) and power-imposition (newbie killing), where the aim was to kill team players, abuse them in their incapacitated state, and then go on to win the match. Ocelot was keen to suggest his team killing method soon became replicated among the small body of *Metal Gear Online* players, and for some was adopted as a new way to play the game – a new marker of an expert player.

> We'd just ruin the game. … It actually became more fun to kill the limit of people that you're allowed to on your team and THEN go on to win the game. Meaning more points and a higher level. … Once this starts it becomes a way to play, and a way that is best when you manage to get someone who's uninitiated into the game.

Ocelot highlights the organic nature of player culture and of implicit rule-sets. If certain actions are left unchecked for periods of time, they lead to replication and acceptance in some groups. Those uninitiated with the game, finding themselves at the brunt of Ocelot and other team killers, experienced long periods of inactivity as a result of griefing:

> You stun people, they're stuck on the floor and have to wait maybe two minutes before they wake up. During which time you can run around them just writing stuff on the text channel and they can't reply, so you can tell that they're just getting really annoyed.

The act of grief play became a process of power-imposition and harassment, preventing the other player from doing what they wished, wasting their time, and emphasizing this with vitriol. After two minutes of inactivity and domination, it is quite possible players would be immediately stunned on recovery, partly as a result of the differential between the skill, equipment, and mastery of the griefer and player, and they would once more find themselves trapped in limbo while being tea-bagged (where a victor repeatedly crouches on a fallen foe, acting out the humiliating placing of testicles on their body) and ridiculed via text chat.

> When *Metal Gear Online* got less popular it took 6–7 minutes for the matchmaking to put you in a game [and] ... in the mode I played you only get one life. If you were killed you'd have to watch the other players for five minutes.

Ocelot's team killing forced the victim to sit prostrate for five minutes or attempt to join another game, resulting in a delay of six or seven minutes, at which point there was strong probability they would still be reunited with Ocelot and Psycho Mantis. Ocelot's grief-play was dependent on a comprehensive understanding of the constitutive and operational rules to enable him to exploit the functionality of the game to his ends, and similarly, an awareness of the implicit rules his behaviour violated, offending and initially surprising his quarry. As this behaviour became well known, Ocelot relied more on his skill as a player, as opponents either attempted to evade his advances or team kill him. In this sense Ocelot's grief-play had forced the agenda for the players wishing to remain in the game. The game changed and shifted onto his terms, he played a central role in its proceedings, and thus play revolved temporarily around this altered context. While it is probable many would have breathed a sigh of relief when Ocelot finally departed the match with a plume of invective, there are likely to have been other players who noted what was done and how, and who conducted the same team killing at a later date. In contrast, those who were distressed or found the activity deeply disruptive would have already been compelled to leave the game.

As already touched on by Foo, grief-play can take many forms, providing it causes and is primarily about the offense of others, including the use of loopholes, what I refer to as glitching, and by extension any other techniques that allow play to be undermined and power wielded. For example, one modder who used illicitly altered versions of *Call of Duty: Modern Warfare 2* (2009) multiplayer code, known as "lobbies", specially designed a variant that stripped players of any accumulated experience points and unlocks, partly for retribution and partly for the sheer pleasure of grief-play.

Whereas modded lobbies often unlocked experience points and items for the player, this modder, known as Zakhaev, used reverse unlock lobbies known as "derank lobbies". Derank lobbies were used to damage and undermine the statistical profiles and removing the associated unlocks of players lured into playing them, initially those deemed to have played inappropriately by illegitimately improving their profiles by modding. While this may have been an act of retribution, Zakhaev got most of his enjoyment from the anguished responses of those he had deranked, and the deranking lobby became a barbed example of counterplay – a vindictive prank to humiliate, annoy, and cost victims time. Those who entered the matches discovered that at their conclusion, instead of being given the maximum number of experience points or a slew of new unlocks, the number of experience points awarded was prefixed by a minus sign, stripping the player of every unlock and accumulation they had earned, whether legitimately or illegitimately.

Figure 3.1 Grief-play, a Call of Duty "derank lobby" removing all accrued experience points and unlocks.

Zakhaev told me he had run five blocks of derank lobbies over a two-week period. To do this he used alternate player accounts and an elaborate process of identity deception and promise-breaking in which highly decorated and reputable accounts were used as props to deceive potential victims about the legitimacy and benefits conferred by what was really the derank lobby. He estimated he had "punished" around sixty players in this way. The accounts used to run the derank lobbies (aside from the diversionary, highly decorated account) were abandoned soon after on the assumption they would be banned as a result of player complaints, although Zakhaev and his friends logged into them to check for any messages the punished had sent. This often-vitriolic interaction appeared to be the primary pleasure of the grief-play session. However, Zakhaev was keen to frame it not only as entertainment but also as a moral imperative that aimed to reaffirm the importance of playing correctly, with or without mods.

> We did the right thing, but it was a lot of fun too, the messages were just so full on. ... People were just screaming, you couldn't make out what they were saying because they were so angry. ... We wouldn't say anything back most of the time, but sometimes we said we were Microsoft employees that had had enough, saying "this is payback, you've brought this on yourself". While other times we'd just say "you didn't get it properly and you can just start again and do it properly".

Zakhaev didn't only run derank lobbies but also played with his friends online in other illicitly modded versions of *Call of Duty*. While the intention appeared to be playing primarily with his friends, it was necessary to involve other players in order to have a fully populated game, with sufficient players on each team to make it viable. This meant other players were inadvertently subjected to the modified game environment and its new rules, and while some found it novel and enjoyable, others wanted simply to return to the conventional game. This was something that wasn't always possible, due to the design of the specific lobby modifications, and players found themselves either carrying the modified settings with them onto other games or being forced back into Zakhaev's game. Instead of being problematic, this became another source of amusement, Zakhaev stated.

> It keeps annoying them. ... Sometimes they end up back in the same game anyway and then that's when all the funny messages start – and they're like What are you doing, Leave me alone! ... They send you hate mail and rubbish. And I like that. I think it's very enjoyable.

What became apparent through talking with grief-players, including Ocelot and Zakhaev, was the extent to which they justified their grief-play as a reaction either against the behaviour of individual players or, alternatively, an abstract, generalized concept of the player. In Ocelot's case, he articulated that his grief-play was partly motivated by a reaction against what he saw as the "false kinship" projected by players in the game.

> What I find more annoying than people being rude or abusive to me is that kind of kinship everyone feels. If you're all playing a game

together there's a given that you're all enjoying it otherwise you'd do something else. But cheesy people on there write line after line of shite like good luck, good shot and it fills up the screen. It's false and unnecessary and works against the message of the game. I mean we're taking turns to kill each other wearing stupid Santa hats – it's competitive and impersonal by design.

For him, the grief-play was an arresting shock to a system partially used to reacquaint players with the job in hand – trying to kill each other in a counter-espionage stealth game. For him, the importation of positive gaming etiquette, such as complimenting players on a good game, was in violation of the core dynamic of play and outside what he saw as appropriate. Both Ocelot and Zakhaev appeared to protest and wish some degree of change, or simply wished to punish those deemed inappropriate and inauthentic players. This is similar to Zakhaev's distaste for other players' distorted profiles that he summarized as follows:

> You spend a lot of time nurturing your account and then it's your pride … and then on the leader board you're just wiped out by someone who's gone onto a lobby and they've got some stupid Kill/Death ratio with a minus on it and it's obviously not real. … You look at their stats and it's clear that they've hacked.

This was the motivation for some of Zakhaev's modding, the derank lobbies at least. Similarly *I Can Has Grief*'s video at the opening of this chapter can partially be seen as being in reaction to and entirely facilitated by the player's inappropriate play and not adequately protecting the server. However, in each case the response seems disproportionate and the justification weak: I think you've cheated, I'll strip you of all unlocks; you've not protected your server, I'll destroy it; people are being too friendly, I'll stop them from playing at all. What this alludes to is a hostile/virtuous cycle in which grief-play can at least be partially justified or motivated through a distaste for and rejection of the play of others, but this may be entirely asynchronous, the annoyance and dissatisfaction caused by individuals and the punishment meted out to others entirely unrelated to the original event.

Other grief-players were more prosaic about their activities. Jilk, for example, stated his relationship with grief-play and trolling "varied dependent on social, environmental or emotional factors" and while at the moment he didn't grief particularly often, there had been other times when antagonizing and trolling other players had served an important purpose, including "as stress relief" – a relaxing activity. A long-time multiplayer gamer, he saw this against a context of the increasing prevalence of this kind of behaviour: "Trolling behaviour has been constantly increasing, and now it is becoming part of the norm of gaming, almost acceptable within the community". So much so that, for him at least, the barriers between grief-play and legitimate competitive strategy were now eroding.

In competitive gameplay, trolling turns more to griefing, as you are trying to get any advantage possible, and griefing is a great way to try and make people focus on more than one thing.

Jilk then recounted a convoluted grief-play escapade in which a group of griefers placed a mole in the opposing team who was able to talk to both the opponents and the griefers independently. This was used to better co-ordinate grief-play.

> The person in the party chat would find out information of the people on the other team ... e.g. age. This would be our starting point, we'd troll the person who is either the youngest or the worst at the game, as the other people on the team are quick to defend that player. ... If people didn't leave, then they would quite quickly become either upset or defensive. Fortunately, when we were trolling, this was the exact behaviour that we were looking for.

Jilk's use of a mole allowed not only immediate trolling/grief-play but served as an information-gathering exercise for later, more important competitive games such as the Major League Gaming events his team were involved in. Once again, alternate and unknown player accounts were central to this process. As Jilk's team made use of the information to offend and infuriate, their opponents became destabilized, less co-ordinated, and at a competitive disadvantage. Despite the immediate competitive benefit, the process still resonated with the pleasures that other grief-players identified and aligning with aspects of Schechner's dark play.

> Trolling and griefing was always quite fun to do, more times than not we would be successful so to start you would have a feeling of accomplishment. Also because we would mostly do it during competitive gameplay there would be a feeling of risk to it, as it'd be dependant on how the other team would behave.

Jilk saw the response of the victims as being critical to the enjoyment of the grief-play act, but this too was subject to a normative gaze that defined what Jilk saw as an appropriate response to the stimuli. Sometimes players who were being trolled or griefed responded in ways that were unexpected and escalatory, and these were troubling not only to Jilk but other griefers I interviewed. Jilk recalled an example of an escalatory grief response:

> I remember when we were playing friendly games, we really upset a player, it was not purposeful, but that one time always stays with me. It doesn't stop me trolling/griefing, it just stops me going too far with it. The thing is that people I know still get messages now, from people trying to troll them because of what happened a long time ago. This is the way people instigate their feuds.

Let us make it clear what happened here. Jilk griefed a player who had responded in a way that was unexpected, becoming deeply distressed. In turn, more than a year after the event, Jilk and people associated with him receive hostile messages and are targeted for subsequent trolling and grief themselves, not necessarily by the person victimized in the original grief-play but by other interested parties. What Jilk paints is a tit-for-tat, escalatory digital gang war taking place in video games as grief-play is conducted and then replicated as retaliation by others and the development of long-standing grudges within some groups of players. Ocelot also encountered a similar escalation.

> I was winding one guy up online, I said something along the lines of "you're terrible, worship me" over and over and over again on the text chat, and he's written something along the lines of "you think you're better than me watch this". And then my PlayStation 3 turned off and made a weird noise like a dial-up modem.

Instead of quitting the game in fear, Ocelot, no doubt due to his familiarity with the roles and performances of grief-play through his own activity, took this further, inverting his previously dominant role and adopting the language and stance of a suitably sycophantic subordinate victim. This was not done to congratulate the griefer or to recognize the new power relations that had emerged but as a technique to learn more about the process used by the new dominant actor in the hope it might become a technique Ocelot could adopt later.

> I got back on and messaged him in the game and was like WOW, what did you just do? Because I was quite scared and I thought everything that comes with it, he must have used an IP address and I knew I was at threat, so I sucked up to him and pretended to be in awe because I wanted to find out what he'd done.

It transpired the player had utilized a Distributed-Denial-of-Service application known as Kane and Abel to identify and then flood Ocelot's IP address, a crime in the UK punishable with up to six months' imprisonment under the 1990 Computer Misuse Act. Whether or not this would have resulted in the PlayStation 3 behaving in the manner described, as opposed to simply losing its connection, is unclear and may well be embellishment, but even so, this serves to illustrate the breadth of the techniques deployed in grief-play and, perhaps most importantly, a pattern in which grief-play may become increasingly escalatory.

On this matter Ocelot admitted to having previously used other technology to assist with his grief-play, including lag switches, small devices that temporarily interrupt network traffic at the press of a button. If used correctly, the game can be tricked into misreporting the location of the player, making their whereabouts impossible to determine and generally making them invulnerable and invisible. However, Ocelot had found these devices unwieldy and was ultimately fearful of the implications of misuse, both in terms of damage to his equipment and violation of the law.

> To be honest with you I'm more interested in the hacking and lag switching, but because I'm not very good at it I go more for the trolling and grief-play. ... I'd love to be able to, you need to be really versed – once you start messing around you don't know what you're doing you could get in trouble.

Thus in the case of Ocelot, he was happy to continue to team kill and harass up until *Metal Gear Online* closed, but it highlights the pleasures of grief-play and that he was always looking for another technique to add to his arsenal. While he was fearful of hardware failure and the long arm of the law, there will always be other players who do not share this concern. These examples illustrate that grief-play is conducted for a host of reasons (enjoyment, distaste, retribution) and then replayed and repeated in response (retaliation). Add to this the notion that grief-play may be identified with a slight that was unintended (as in Foo's greed-play) and you have a potent and rather toxic cycle of escalatory grief-play or, less dramatically put, a play culture where grief-play is simply part of the lexicon of play – not unusual, not conducted by peripheral and disenfranchised members of the player base but something done to and done by everyday players and part of regular play.

LADDISH CULTURE

A number of players I spoke with talked about the idea of a "laddish culture", a primarily masculine, adolescent dynamic within multiplayer gaming that embraced hostility not entirely dissimilar to the idea of the adolescent gang. Within laddish culture, communication and interactions, both individually and within diffuse groups (anything from a randomized pre-match lobby to a more formalised gaming clan), had a character that was prickly and full of one-upmanship, manifested in endemic trash-talking, ridicule, claims of supremacy and dominance, and the ritual laughter of crowds. While the suggestion was not that this necessarily resulted in grief-play, it created a fertile environment from which it might emerge, with frequent boundaries of allegiance, jockeying for position, competition, the perception of offense, and the escalatory nature of counterplay. In these contexts things may be said and done that the individual would be highly unlikely to do outside the game.

The adolescent masculinity of video-game culture is likely to be no surprise to the reader, but it should be recognized this research was primarily conducted against the backdrop of mainstream console-video games, and largely combat- and warfare-orientated releases. This is not to suggest these games, being the equivalent of blockbuster movies, don't attract female players, but simply that the dynamics of the games and the way they are expressed tend to be rooted firmly in masculinity. Ocelot did not identify whether he meant laddish in terms of masculinity or as a reference to a laddish behavioural archetype that embraces overt competition, instead of feminized stereotypes that prioritize creativity and collaboration. Ocelot's choice of words may also fall into the hardcore gamer stereotype that paints gamers, rather than players, as socially inept and vicious man-babies, but this is not something I recognize in my engagements with players in multiplayer games, whether counter or compliant. Instead what I have noticed is a dynamic that reso- nates with the carnivalesque, full of ridicule and ritual laughter, twinned with the occasional situation when this escalates, causing offense and damage. For me this is no different to the kind of play that occurred in an adolescent playground or, for that matter, on the football terrace, down the local pub, or in the rugby changing room. According to Ocelot:

> It's like a typical laddish culture where just being rude to each other can just bring you really funny, funny things – but I guess that it wasn't interpreted as that especially by a lot of the foreign people who don't understand the flow of English.

Ocelot suggested he saw laddish culture across many digitally mediated and partially anonymous platforms, social media in particular:

> The second you go on anything that isn't standard Facebook or You- Tube, people just love for some reason bringing in racist comments or whatever and I've used plenty but not in a 4chan way where I'm saying really bad words. ... I'd never do it in real life but it does feel different on there. I can understand the way that it starts, they enjoy it so much that they lose perspective. But the moment you get in there it's everywhere, and the proper rules and policies are in complete ques- tion. Nobody is playing by the rules.

Henry Jenkins has discussed some of the gender affiliations of game-space, touching on the adolescent masculine mode of video-game culture (and, one would assume, other digital spaces such as those on the web), which appear to resonate with some of what Ocelot calls laddish culture (1995). Jenkins channels E. Anthony Rotundo's notion of "boy culture", which is seen as a "semi-autonomous" play-space that defines itself in distinction to the motherly values of the homely, feminine play-space. The home, accord- ing to Rotundo, was the women's sphere that "offered kindness, moral- ity, nurture, and a gentle spirit. ... [In contrast] the boys' world countered with energy, self-assertion, noise, and a frequent resort to violence, [and] ... willingness to inflict pain" (Rotundo in Jenkins 1995). Jenkins argues

Rotundo's core claims about nineteenth-century boy culture hold true for the "video game culture of contemporary boyhood" (Jenkins 1995). The vicious fun that Ocelot and Zakhaev articulate may be a manifestation of boy culture, an intrinsic aspect of masculine play that can occur in spaces of relative autonomy, such as those where there is rule-based ambiguity or some sense that identity and culpability are obscured by the use of alts or the simple distance of technology. The suggestion is not that women don't play these games and inhabit this laddish culture but that the dynamics that have developed in multiplayer games articulate through a masculine manner and lean towards what are understood as masculine ideals. Despite that association, they are perfectly enjoyable to women who play these games. The short version is that one would assume many women enjoy playing in this laddish play culture and engage in grief-play, and while it seems somewhat unnecessary to point out, one of the griefers on the *Minecraft* video that opened this chapter was female. However, having said this, the counterplayers I encountered during my research were almost entirely male.

In addition, laddish culture appears to embrace the universal hostility of the carnival ritual laughter, abusing any who enter the space. Laddish culture seems largely independent of the formal rules of the game and the terms of service and law. It defines its own limits and contexts and at times, this was manifested by some players in ways that were found offensive, problematic, or abject. In Ocelot's grief-play example it wasn't that the formal rules were entirely ignored but that their authority and reach were something that was under contestation, subject to the same hostility and challenge as other aspects of game-play.

> I don't think anyone had the rationale to read the TOS and say – lets go against that – so there's no – I'm confident that there's no evidence of rebellion against them. It was just fun … it came naturally.

The suggestion is that grief-play erupted naturally from the play, rather than a conscious rejection of rule, but it is inevitable that those who were griefing were aware of the extent their actions deviated. This was certainly the case with Ocelot's anxiety over using hardware methods. The impression that griefing and trolling had simply become part of the territory of online play, twinned with ambivalence towards it, was something shared by almost all players I spoke with. Jilk says:

> I don't think you can say this behaviour is justifiable in any way shape or form, but nowadays it is becoming more of the norm, and more socially acceptable within the gaming community. The only reason we implemented this behaviour was to win or to relieve stress. Was the behaviour acceptable? I'd have to say yes, because that's nowadays what gaming is. It is accepted. Times have changed and the audience of gaming has changed.

We might imagine laddish culture growing as one of the natural responses to an environment in which play is highly visible, individuals are constantly scrutinizing and subject to the scrutiny of others, and their play is assessed for suitability and captured as metrics – as a scoreboard, as a ranking, as a number of unlocks, number of likes or similar. While I'm describing how I regard much of video-game play, it would also equally cover other organized sports such as a football or baseball league. Much as these non-digital game contexts demonstrate, multiplayer games are social constructs that are capable of emphasizing hierarchy to varying degrees. In situations where play is captured as a metric, a hierarchy is possible to be applied – best defender, best goal-scorer, etc. – and for some, this will emphasize competition and rivalry, and this may be expressed in varying levels of hostility and appropriateness. I believe this creates a culture in which hierarchy is especially important, and thus activities that express hierarchical dominance, even through illegitimate means, become natural. This is the wider context Ocelot articulates as laddish culture and that expresses itself as grief-play. It enables individuals to say something about dominance and hierarchy as an act similar to Bahktin's carnivalesque, displaced abjection and ritual laughter – levelling and creating new, often inverted, power structures. Ocelot articulated this in a different way, saying that for him, grief-play, even hidden under the anonymizing layers of alternate player accounts, additionally enabled the development of identity.

> It was a game at first but then it became a space. You can only differentiate by uniform, the things that you buy for your character, but then to get notoriety and individuality you have to behave differently – it's like a missing feature from the game.

Ocelot argued the ability to be an individual, as opposed to a subject or player function, was poorly accommodated within *Metal Gear Online*. Therefore he adopted a role as a griefer as an alternate way of creating an identity. This could be seen as another way in which the griefer subverts the provided hierarchies, inventing their own way of getting recognition and feeling power.

> We managed to get a name for ourselves and as a clan, where people would know if any of us turned up the game it was going to go that way: we were going to fuck it up.

I quizzed many grief-players about those they had harassed or victimized. Often they simply viewed their activities as something exciting and amusing, as either bad luck for the victim or justified through the identification of distaste at the play of others – some point of etiquette or longstanding feud that justified the mistreatment of other players or at least turning them into a source of amusement.

Despite acknowledging the frustrating impact of grief-play, Ocelot was ambivalent about his victims. They were simply unlucky to be placed arbitrarily against or alongside him. Ocelot said he couldn't logically justify his actions entirely, they were motivated by fun, and egged on by the observation that as some of his victims replicated his actions, this ".took away any element of guilt", signalling the victims were in fact both compliant and open to becoming grief-players. Similarly, Zakhev removed any complication by seeing his actions as either retribution or, where he griefed other players, "spreading fun" and "60% of them enjoyed it". Finally Jilk rationalized grief-play through competitive advantage, apart from the one example that went too far. Through my discussions it became apparent that while grief-play was often ignored by victims and occasionally felt as a personal attack (and in some cases it was), for the most part grief-players were ambivalent about their quarry. It was as if they had been dehumanized and become like NPCs, just NPCs who had a tendency to get really upset. The point I am trying to make is that for the grief-player, it is the response, any response, which is important, not necessarily that it is the response of a specific individual. Nothing personal. This naturally leads us to consider the victim's perspective. How do they rationalize grief-play?

Davidor, a committed player and one of the administrators for a large *Minecraft* server, had extensive experience of having dealt with grief-play and, as appears natural, occasionally conducted it himself.

> Although I rarely grief and troll I have found myself at the rough side of it many times. It occurs on average twice a week but is focused around newer content and new releases. Seeing it also differs upon the person in question, for instance a newer player keeping to themselves will hardly see it. But for someone who is a higher player, of any influence within the gaming community, or simply rather good at the game, it can be a common occurrence.

Davidor argued the anonymity and visibility offered by multiplayer video games meant grief-play was often conducted as retribution, and the more extreme examples were often targeted against prominent individuals. One would assume this was to maximize the impact of an attack, but also the message about power relations and hierarchy this expresses. Attacking the prominent smacks of the levelling dynamic seen in the carnivalesque. It vocally states the important are not untouchable, and, for a short time at least, the griefer assumes a dominant stance. Davidor saw this as a logical decision, borne out of frustration and both the demands and opportunities of video games, where the player is one of many and has little opportunity to stand out from the crowd.

> Why follow the masses of people doing quests daily when I can kill the quest giver and watch them freak out? Why spend days building a virtual house when I can knock down these walls and see it collapse?

> Why spend three hours attacking a lonely noob when you can DDoS
> a streamer causing him and thousands of viewers to sit in darkness?

Davidor was well aware of the impact of this kind of counterplay through his
work as a server administrator and the way grief-play can willingly squander
months of accumulated work. He described a major *Minecraft* group-build,
in which eight players were constructing a scale model of the Colosseum,
using architectural drawings and photographs for reference. After more than
two weeks of work, the project was nearing completion, but Davidor and his
colleagues were to discover they had been targets of grief-play.

> We discovered that about five griefers had attacked at 4am one morn-
> ing with clients that let them remove the protection, allowing anybody
> to go to town on it. They had also deleted the Big Brother file meaning
> the backup was corrupted and we could not retrace their steps after
> the deletion. Overnight our Colosseum had been flattened and built
> into an array of what can simply be stated as male bits.

Weeks of work had been destroyed, or at least heavily vandalized, overnight,
but unlike the *I Can Has Grief?* Example, the server was unpopulated at
the time. Nobody was there to beg the griefers to stop or to respond in the
moment. Nor were the griefers necessarily party to the strife and anguish
they had caused, although as the griefers were never identified, they could
well have been other members of Davidor's group. At least, they were certainly unable to engage in interaction with Davidor and his colleagues to
maximize the enjoyment. Instead one must assume this was largely an escalatory and pleasurable act of destruction, a communal dance of laughter and
chaos as the griefers focused on unbuilding the Colosseum and rebuilding
penises, all the while imagining the response of the players. This suggests
that while grief-play is very much about the response of the victim, this
response can be imagined. Simply thinking of the impact of the grief-play
act, and therefore having to empathize on some level with the victim in order
to understand the meaning of the damage, seems pleasurable enough to
motivate grief-play. Despite all this, Davidor was prosaic about the incident.

> People destroying your own works and interrupting your gameplay can
> be annoying and stressful, but at the end of the day it is just a game. ...
> There are always angry and jealous people on the Internet, with an easy
> way to attack you with no real consequences for their actions. Letting
> them get under your skin is the worst you can do. ... Doing this can
> bring them back day after day, every time they are bored they know
> they can get a kick from your reactions so it's best to ignore. ...

For Davidor, established anti-griefing systems, such as filing reports to
administrators or GMs, was an important aspect of dealing with grief-play

but one that was procedural rather than likely to have any impact on the grief-play as it took place.

> Reporting isn't as useful as it could be, if it's one person being attacked they have no chance as the requests can take days to process. By this time they have been attacked and had their items destroyed, and frankly their gaming experience ruined. … In World of Warcraft, at the release of a surprise NPC offering a limited time quest, hundreds rushed to the area. Three players decided they would sit in over-sized mounts to block the NPC from anyone's view. After about half an hour people agreed to report these players and within two minutes a GM arrived to remove them … but in my experience single players can take up to a week if not more as group reports are the priority.

He saw group representation and co-ordinated reporting as the only effectual means of engaging with the reporting services, as the number of complaints being lodged was one of the ways administrators prioritized what situation to respond to next. Put simply, Davidor thought grief-play was endemic and there were too few GMs and administrators to deal with the constant stream of reports. Like Jilk, Ocelot, and Zakhaev, Davidor recognized an abrasive, competitive, and laddish culture exists within video games and for the individual, there was very little to do but acquiesce or ignore in the hope the griefers would move on. Interestingly, Davidor also spoke of "report-griefing", where the reporting system itself was reappropriated as a mechanism to conduct grief-play.

> A griefer approaches and offers a donation of some gold. He takes it with a merry thank you. This griefer then submits a report saying that this streamer tricked him and "stole" his money, the griefer's friends also report and a set of about 50 complaints are submitted, meaning instant GM, account blocked until further investigation and so forth …

Yet with reporting largely ineffectual in the short term, Davidor was also keen to emphasize that responding to the grief-play visibly in any way whatsoever was highly problematic. Even attempting to use techniques against a perceived attack was likely to prolong and escalate the activity, something Oceolot recognized when he griefed others. Faced with little recognition and response, grief-players tended to escalate the offensiveness of their activities in the hope of a response before eventually seeking other targets.

> They head on to verbal attacks, racial slurs and such in an attempt to get a response, and after this will often just leave to find a new more vulnerable target if they do not receive attention. … Aa lack of reaction means they have failed.

Lastly, Davidor spoke at length about the reasons he saw behind grief-play. Like Jilk, Zakhaev, and Ocelot, he saw retaliation as a prime motivation but regarded retaliation as an exceptionally broad concept. Davidor's retaliation could be motivated by frustration with progress in a game, frustration that another player is doing better, and the more commonplace notion of responding to an attack. But especially telling is that the retaliation need not be against the individual, group, or structure that is the source of the issue but against a symbolic target and act of misplaced abjection.

> Retaliation can also be on previous trolls, singling out people in the distant past that come to mind. Someone kill you when you were busy doing something? Then kill them back a future day and ruin their evening, even the score.

Add to this the boredom associated with video games and the jealousy that comes from constantly observing, judging, and comparing the play of others and Davidor encapsulates much of what underpinned the motivations of other grief-players with whom I spoke.

> Some succeed but many others fail and feel that they have been short changed. In that situation they pick something or someone out as a target and "they deserve to be punished". … With so many things to do in games people find the challenge bewildering and boring. They end up spending time doing the same old thing, grinding this raid, watching these people build etc. then they decide to change their routine. One way to fill this boredom is to interrupt other people's routines.

Davidor offers a different perspective to grief-play. He comments that the player has no real choice but to silently endure grief-play in the hope the griefer will depart. Of course this inaction is likely to mask the true damage or impact of grief-play on play experience, and the griefer is likely to assume their actions aren't quite as troublesome as they might seem. Within multiplayer games this silence becomes even more pertinent. If an individual within a multiplayer environment is being victimized and other players witnessing it remain silent in order to avoid becoming targets themselves, they are likely to be regarded as an amused and approving audience by the griefer, and as being aligned with the griefing act by the victim. The silence becomes tacit approval, a potentially misplaced signal that this behaviour is normal or acceptable. Therefore in such an environment, it is logical that a laddish abrasive culture develops. Individuals are unwilling to correct the behaviour and the institutional structures are often too slow to act.

From the perception of the establishment, the griefing practices discussed certainly resonate with the discourse of pathogen. They are acts that hold the potential to damage the played experience to the extent that victims and observers may abandon the game altogether. Griefing therefore does hold the potential to damage the commercial viability of the game. This notion of the cost of the griefing act in terms of time and effort appears of significance to the protagonist. Whatever the griefing prevents the victim from doing or accessing, the time that it costs them and ultimately the net cost of the griefing are important. In the case of the *Metal Gear Online* griefing discussed here, it is largely dependent on the awareness that the player is given little choice if they wish to continue to play. It is the sense of being dominated and reducing the latitude for alternate behaviour. They are forced to sit and read the abuse for five minutes, or alternatively they must reset and wait seven minutes to reconnect. The cost to the victim is at least five minutes of play, in the derank lobby the cost may be months of legitimate or minutes of illegitimate play, while in Davidor's Colosseum example, the cost was eight people's toil for a fortnight. It is this that has effectively been taken from them and it is this that creates the imbalance of power relations that the griefer appreciates. When the frustrations that are bound up in this erupt, then the griefer finds this even more enjoyable.

While it is tempting to immediately link grief-play with the carnivalesque on account of the chaos it brings into the game-space, this cannot be fully substantiated, following reflection on the basis that grief-play is neither unilaterally hostile, nor does it invite others to do the same. While the observation of grief-play might motivate some to copy it themselves, Ocelot was opposed to this practice, seeing it as another mark of player hypocrisy. While some might be able to grief alongside Ocelot and his master, it appeared preferable if the players remained as frustrated and ideally vocal victims – the bullied. The image captured here is of an act that appears primarily concerned with the generation of identity through the appropriation of game-space that demonstrates mastery, dominating opponents and other players and forcing them to play under the grief-player's terms. In the absence of overseers, grief-play becomes a highly efficient and even less easily countered way of expressing mastery and dominance over other players and asserting ownership of the space. While the act holds some pleasure, it is the response of the victim and the perception of other players that appear more significant.

GAMEOGRAPHY

Call of Duty: Modern Warfare 2. 2009. Activision. Infinity Ward.
City of Heroes. 2004. NCSOFT. Cryptic Studios.
Metal Gear Online. 2008. Konami. Kojima Productions.
Minecraft. 2009. Mojang.
World of Warcraft. 2004. Bizzard Entertainment.

REFERENCES

Foo, C. and Koivisto, E. 2004. "Defining Grief Play in MMORPGs: player and developer perceptions." *Proceedings of the 2004 ACM SIGCHI International Conference on Advances in Computer Entertainment Technology,* 245–250. New York: ACM.

Foo, C. Y. 2008. *Grief Play Management: A Qualitative study of Grief Play Management in MMORPGs*. Saarbrucken: VDM.

I Can Has Grief? 2011. HOW TO become Admin on almost ANY Minecraft server WITHOUT Hacks! https://www.youtube.com/watch?v=8faFqfPBpiE&list=UUQ MxWj0YVlPyEcSGW0sBmbw. Accessed December 1, 2014.

I Can Has Grief? 2012. *Minecraft Griefing – Protect Yo Sheeit*. https://www.you-tube.com/watch?v=N-ratUZxmeM&list=UUQMxWj0YVlPyEcSGW0sBmbw&i ndex=1. Accessed December 1, 2014.

Jenkins, H. 1995. "Complete Freedom of Movement: Video Games as Gendered Play Spaces." http://web.mit.edu/21fms/People/henry3/complete.html. Accessed June 23, 2012.

Plunkett, L. 2009. "College Professor Trolls For Science, Finds People Hate Him." http://kotaku.com/5308780/college-professor-trolls-for-science-finds-people-hate-him. Accessed November 12, 2014.

4 Boosting and Glitching

Whereas the previous chapter explored a wide range of counterplay forms – grief-play and anything from abusive language to the use of Distributed-Denial-of-Service attacks – this chapter focuses on one way of playing: exploiting video-game software. This will be done in two ways: one where the exploitation occurs as collusion between players, but without altering the expected function of the game; and another where the game is forced to deform and behave in unpredictable ways. These two forms are boosting and glitching respectively. In order to do so I will briefly touch on boosting, and then spend much more time focusing on glitching.

Boosting can be understood as the process of thoroughly understanding the underlying principles of the game, its constitutive rules, but rejecting the way it is intended to be played, its operational rules. While boosting, opposing teams might choose to co-operate in order to more efficiently accumulate the rewards that would normally contextualize competitive play. For example in a normal competitive match of *Call of Duty* a typical player kills ten opponents and gains one hundred experience points for doing so on account of the size of the map, the accuracy of the weapons, and the evasion of other players. If it is the experience points players desire, more than the experience of having killed an opponent, then it is entirely logical and much more efficient to agree all players should sprint to a position and take it in turns to kill one another. Thus each player might kill twenty opponents and get two hundred experience points at the same time. This is the core principle of boosting: understanding how the game works and the processes by which goals are reached, and finding ways of reaching the desired ends more efficiently through co-operation and collusion.

Glitching, by contrast, also makes use of an understanding of a game's constitutive rules and a partial rejection of its operational rules but does so through interrogating the fabric of the game to find exploitable points of inconsistency. The glitcher seeks out situations in which the game code contains undiscovered or unexpected functions that enable new ways of play, from a way of making a weapon more powerful, a quicker way of navigating the game environment, or occasionally game-breaking exploits that entirely undermine and subvert the game's function. Glitching is about understanding the game enough to identify when something is inconsistent or amiss and finding ways of exploiting it, whereas boosting is about understanding the game enough to see how its functionality can be subverted through organization and agreement. Placed in a real-world context, boosting would be like race drivers agreeing not to jockey for position in order to get the very best lap times, while glitching would be the discovery that a certain corner could be skipped without repercussion. As we shall see, this is an overly simplistic analogy but useful enough to use here.

There are even situations where a practice blurs the boundaries between boosting and glitching, as is the case of the *Destiny* "treasure cave" (2014). *Destiny* is a console-based, hybrid first-person shooter/MMO game created by Bungie, where players travel around (relatively few) locations in the solar system, completing missions, killing foes, and grinding to accumulate items dropped by foes on very limited frequencies. Occasionally, when a foe is killed they will drop an "engram", a spherical collectable that can be converted into an unknown item, such as a weapon, a piece of armour, or a consumable. These engrams are colour-coded by rarity, with rare blue engrams and legendary purple engrams being the most desired. Players rapidly determined through observation and experimentation that engrams were reliably dropped from adversaries within *Destiny*, irrespective of their strength, and therefore in order to most efficiently accrue engrams one would simply need to kill as many foes as possible. As a result players sought out locations that offered the most reliable source of numerous, but not too powerful, foes, as killing a horde of weak foes is preferable to killing a handful of powerful ones.

On *Destiny*'s release on September 9, 2014, players began to notice that one stretch of map, specifically a cave from which the insect-like Hive enemy type emerged, could be tricked into spawning groups of enemies every six seconds (the average for other places was more like forty seconds). Not only this, but the magic spot seemed to have higher engram dropping rates. In order to trick the cave to work properly, players had to stand a certain distance from its entrance and then kill any Hive in the area. If any players strayed too close to the cave, the spawning stopped. As the Hive were dispatched, the cave would fill with shining collectable items, ammo and engrams, which could be picked up when players decided. (This wasn't essential as *Destiny* allocates engrams on a per-player basis, meaning other players cannot pick up the engrams and any a player forgets to collect are automatically forwarded to a hub area postmaster.) Players would spend hours at the mouth of the cave, shooting into its depths, accruing highly desirable legendary engrams, weapons, and armour.

News of the treasure cave's existence spread rapidly and players began to change their play accordingly, venturing straight to it in preference to other environments in order to "farm engrams". As this required players not to violate the area immediately in front of the cave, players developed systems of warning and marshalling, jumping in front of and tossing grenades at players who stopped the spawn, getting into a linear formation by the boundary, and charging en masse towards the cave when someone lost patience in finding out what glowing engrams sat waiting in the cave for them. Beyond this, an additional practice developed, "AFK farming" (away from keyboard), whereby it was discovered a player could still earn engrams from being close to others who were killing foes instead of killing them themselves. In AFK farming a player would simply stand close to a fellow player shooting into the cave – and then go make a cup of tea. Bungie soon became aware of the treasure cave and its lore, and on September 25, sixteen short days after its discovery, it announced:

> The social experience of a cave farming run is amazing: the herding to get a team of Guardians all behind the line and firing in the right direction, the rush to grab the loot. ... But shooting at a black hole for hours on end isn't our dream for how Destiny is played.
>
> (Destiny Dev Team 2014a)

And then, in the patch notes that followed shortly after players were informed, at least with sense of humour, that:

> The Hive of the holy "Treasure Cave" have realized the futility of their endless assault on Skywatch and have retired to lick their wounds and plan their next attack.
>
> Respawn timers for monster caves in Skywatch have been normalized to 40 seconds (increased from 6).
>
> (Destiny Dev Team 2014b)

This offers an example that bridges both boosting and glitching. It is dependent on a critical understanding of the game and the ability not only to identify points of abnormality and inconsistency (the spawn rates and engram drops of the cave) but also to determine how it can be triggered (the location and non-trespass of areas), how it can be exploited (to rapidly amass engrams), and its collaborative or communal aspect (the development of treasure-cave protocol). Perhaps unsurprisingly, and in a nod to the previous chapter, it should be noted that on more than one occasion, I witnessed players who trespassed on the area immediately outside the cave, preventing spawning, who then proceeded to dance on the spot or point at glitchers until the thwarted engram farmers either logged out or found something else to do.

Figure 4.1 Glitching, twenty minutes worth of "Engram farming" on Venus in Destiny.

While the treasure cave was patched, players relocated to other anomalous places in the game, such as a certain spot on Venus I'm rather partial to, where the game can be fooled into thinking the player has left the area and enemies immediately respawned. The spoils of twenty minutes of engram farming in this way can be seen above. It should be stated that Bungie's light-hearted approach to the *Destiny* treasure cave isn't consistent with that of other developers and in many instances, both boosting and glitching are express violations of a game's terms of service and labelled as abject play, such as Activision's notion of "game abuse". The *Call of Duty: Ghosts* (2013) code of conduct defining boosting and glitching game abuse is described in the following way:

> **Boosting:** Any user who colludes with another user to exploit the game for the purpose of gaining XP, prestige, game score, weapon level, or in-game unlock.
>
> *Glitching*: Any user who abuses an exploit in game code or other established rule of play is subject to penalty. An example includes but is not limited to using a hole in the map geo to intentionally go outside of the map boundary.
>
> (Candyslexia 2014)

Players deemed to have resorted to boosting or glitching are subject to a range of penalties and public censure. For the first identified case, the player has elements of their game restricted. The multiplayer component is temporarily invalidated and all accrued experience points, unlocks, and progression metrics are reset. Repeat offenders have multiplayer elements of the game permanently invalidated, including options for offline split-screen multiplayer, and the player's account is omitted from all in-game leader boards.

Despite this risk, players have created websites to assist with and co-ordinate boosting and glitching. The Boosters Hotline was formed in 2008, presenting itself as a "worldwide cooperative videogame community", boasting in excess of 100,000 members. While it is ostensibly a generic gaming fan-community website, its major attraction is that it enables players to boost. Within the context of *Call of Duty* (The Boosters Hotline supports most popular contemporary multiplayer games), boosting consists of creating a multiplayer match solely populated by other Boosters Hotline members (a beachhead), who take it in turns to shoot each other in the head, or repeatedly win and lose objectives in order to accumulate experience points. The expectation here is that once the booster has fulfilled their obligation to boost and to boost others, they are free to utilize the spoils in games against conventional players. The booster therefore may boast an advantageous weapon or display a particularly desirable medal or award as a result of their actions.

As already implied, The Boosters Hotline is reliant on a structure of trust, obligation, and reputation. On joining the site, individuals must submit applications and are subject to scrutiny and verification before being integrated into the community. They are expected to provide their Xbox LIVE or PlayStation Network credentials for review, and respond appropriately to the messages and invites that now flow to these accounts from other Boosters Hotline members. Assuming they have been accepted, the player is free to apply to join a boosting game via a "shout box" on The Boosters Hotline website. The shout box lists available boosting games and the expectations of membership and obligation, such as an agreement to play for a certain period of time or until all players have reached a specific unlock objective. Players who fail to meet expectations are subject to probation, are likely to be declined invitation from further boosting matches, and may have site access removed. Likewise, those deemed trustworthy and reliable, especially those who perform admin functions or donate towards upkeep costs, are given preferential access to forum pages and boosting matches. For trusted members, joining a boosting game is as simple as "find a banner for the desired game, log into xbox.com, ask for an invite, push send and wait for an invite" (Boosters Hotline 2010).

As already alluded to, glitches differ from boosting in their application and relationship to the game. Glitches are generally discovered by an individual or small team, and are documented then shared with the general public, enabling subsequent replication. Glitching communities therefore function differently to The Boosters Hotline, serving primarily as distribution/publication channels. While there is still a definite need for glitchers to co-ordinate and share expertise while identifying and developing prototypical glitches, this can be done through a loose matrix of interpersonal communication channels such as instant messages, texts, and emails.

As a result, glitching communities share much more with other participatory culture forms, particularly that of the YouTuber, where videos are periodically released to the public alongside a certain amount of audience interaction via comments fields. As a result of the visibility of YouTube, ease of subscription, and sharing, it is relatively straightforward for particularly well-regarded glitching groups to become pivotal in the development and communication of glitches on a platform, as is the case with chaoticPERFECTION (2006–2014) and mapMonkeys (2006–2012). chaoticPERFECTION and mapMonkeys were both founded in 2006, and have subsequently become known as the two primary glitching entities on the Xbox 360 console. By October 2012, the mapMonkeys YouTube channel hosted ninety-three glitch videos that had been viewed over nineteen million times, with 45,000 channel subscribers. At the same point, chaoticPERFECTION's YouTube channel – its third, due to copyright claim-related account suspensions – hosted two hundred videos with 900,000 views and 2,500 subscribers.

Within such a context, being first to discover and publicize a glitch becomes critical for the status and standing of glitching groups, and glitching becomes a race to identify exploits or anomalies before others. Despite the inherent competition within glitching communities, it is a collaborative activity, best conducted in flexible and close-knit teams, and competition between glitchers is often suspended if it is likely to facilitate the development of new glitches. This means glitchers of varying ability and experience frequently work together and become known to each other. This acts as a way of inducting new glitchers into the practices but also serves as a way of rapidly assessing skills and reliability similar to The Boosters Hotline's vetting process. Additionally, this formation is also a pragmatic way of responding to the time required to effectively identify, develop, and document a glitch. The more glitchers willing to work on the same task, the more likely it will be successful and a glitch identified.

When a glitch is discovered, it is typically documented as a video with a voice-over tutorial that explains its replication. This is then uploaded onto a video-sharing website such as YouTube for distribution and eventual consumption by other glitchers and members of the public. For those interested in learning about new glitches, all they need do is search or view the latest releases from the glitch teams they subscribe to. Then, using the videos as guidance, the player can practice replicating the glitch and then use it within a game – that is, until the developer eventually patches it.

Glitches are entirely unpredictable and protean, with a huge range of uses ranging from those that offer competitive advantage to those that simply present an anomaly. It might show new visual and aural elements, change player navigation, make the player invulnerable, allow them to exit the play area, or offer new potent moves. Many glitches have profound potential for disrupting and dominating other players, such as attacking them invisibly from below the game map, which can be considered a classic malign glitch application often felt in *Call of Duty*'s multiplayer.

Glitches therefore can be used to disrupt, to antagonize, or simply to offer the player new insight into the game, and each glitch offers varying levels of advantage and visibility. Glitching communities therefore exist both hidden within the network of interpersonal communication and in the plain view of mainstream video-sharing websites. This allows them space to develop glitches in secrecy and then to communicate them to the widest possible audience on release. It is simultaneously the dark ambiguity to develop counterplay and then the way of loudly calling for a response. As part of the research for this book, I spent significant time with glitchers and within glitching communities.

I received an e-mail from one of the players with whom I had previously played *Call of Duty: Modern Warfare 2* (2009) and *Battlefield Bad Company 2* (2010) and to whom I had explained my research interests while waiting for matches to start. The e-mail offered to introduce me to the glitching group chaoticPERFECTION, which, he felt, would be particularly receptive. It transpired much later that the team had already discussed assisting me and had done background research to ascertain my credibility. The e-mail presented chaoticPERFECTION as "a very famous glitching clan on Xbox LIVE, they find ranges of glitches and just love f***ing the hell out of the bugs in the code". While I had occasionally encountered glitching on multiplayer games and had made use of glitches myself in single-player games such as the *Elder Scrolls IV: Oblivion* (2006) duplication glitch, I had little understanding of how they were identified or the structures and communities that coalesced around these counterplay forms. Instead I had viewed them as isolated acts.

Glitching can be broadly understood as a type of play in which, instead of observing the game rules and goals, the aim is to find, document, share, and ultimately exploit weaknesses in the game code. The glitcher is preoccupied with the exposure and utilization of any inconsistencies, contradictions, and flaws within the digital ecosystem. Unlike illicit modding or hacking, practices we will explore later, glitching is conducted with the commercial game as is. The software and hardware are almost always unmodified and therefore the glitch should be repeatable on any commercial game system. Glitchers demonstrate extreme understanding and awareness of the game-space and its processes, exposing flaws that have been missed by Quality Assurance teams and other institutional checks. In turn, these exploits or glitches are used to entertain and for more instrumental competitive advantage, at the same time building the reputation of the glitchers and clans of which they may be members.

Glitchers – those who willingly identify and align with this counterplay activity or those who have been labelled as such by the normalizing gaze of the playerbase, – are often seen moving beyond the conventional playspaces of the games, floating in the air, protruding from walls, becoming invulnerable, invisible, or engaging and interacting with the game-space in ways that mark them as other. The problem is there is no easy way of distinguishing between those who use and those who identify glitches. For the observer, they are one and the same.

Glitchers are generally considered deviant and illegitimate player groups and their presence is often treated with hostility by players and developers alike. This is not unwarranted as their behaviour or the outcome of their exploits have the potential to significantly damage the equilibrium of a game through radically altering the balance and equality of a competitive multiplayer first-person shooter, by introducing large numbers of high-value items within an MMO economic system, or simply by allowing pragmatic dominant strategies within a game.

As a result, the player base, developers, and game operators vigilantly look for examples of glitching that manifest themselves on the multiplayer aspects of video-game releases, particularly during the months immediately following their release when functionality and stability are commercially crucial. In comparison, single-player glitches, due to their reduced visibility and impact on other players, receive far less attention and are often never patched unless they are particularly severe in their repercussions or occur randomly during normal play. Developers encourage players to report any glitching they encounter, which, if substantiated, is negated by the release of mandatory software patches, warnings to any perpetrators, and the occasional high-profile invalidation of player accounts through the swinging of the "banhammer". These are the ways in which the game ecosystem safeguards against glitching, through intelligence-gathering, counter-insurgency work, the expulsion of violators, and jubilant reporting of the victory to the playerbase.

While the grief-play examples presented a playerbase that was generally silent and reticent about responding to counterplay out of a mix of fear of escalation and the ineffectualness of reporting, there are other players who intentionally go out of their way to identify and name counterplayers and encourage others to submit co-ordinated misconduct reports. One example of this, partly a community-led defence against counterplay and also a way to create an attractive and entertaining YouTube channel and identity, is Booster Busters, who submit videos across the gamut of counterplay and who not only document and report but openly troll and harass counterplayers who are playing inappropriately. The channel, which boasts over six million views, explains its vigilante role both emotively and effectively:

> Exposing and humiliating boosters, hackers and cheaters since 2010. ... This channel is for all the legit gamers out there. We are the center of all booster busting and will lead the fight against all the Cheaters/Booster/Bully/Hacker out there.
>
> (Booster Busters 2014)

While Booster Busters shows the playerbase responding to counterplay, including glitching, there are other situations where publishers are seen to exert control, whether illusorily or not. In November 2014, the Machinima game video channel warned its members that Activision was "issuing strikes on videos showing glitches. If you post videos highlighting these glitches, your channel may be liable to receive a copyright strike" (Campbell 2014). This was later contested by Activision, which stated: "Occasionally, some folks post videos that promote cheating and unfair exploits. As always, we keep an eye out for these videos. Our level of video claims hasn't changed" (Campbell 2014). While it is difficult to ascertain what the state of affairs was, especially considering the scale of glitches discovered for the recently released *Call of Duty: Advanced Warfare* (2014), both messages illustrate how the identification and sharing of glitching are regarded and handled. Despite these player and publisher interventions, glitches and glitchers are still commonplace, unified by the humble glitch tutorial video.

DUKE NUKEM FOREVER: OUT AND UNDER HIGHWAY BATTLE

I click on the glitch video on the chaoticPERFECTION YouTube channel. It opens with a slick animation introducing the team: "BRINGING YOU

GLITCHES AND TRICKS WITH VOICE AND TEXT TUTORIALS ... chaoticPERFECTION". It acknowledges the glitcher who found and documented the glitch, in this case Nickncs, before fading to black. The opening melody of Noah and the Whale's "L.I.F.E.G.O.E.S.O.N" strikes up, the *Duke Nukem Forever* (2011) loading screen is displayed briefly, and as the lyrics begin, we watch as Duke drives his monster truck through a Midwestern desert. The truck smashes headlong into a rock face but abruptly flips up and over it instead of being stopped. The solid-rock walls flicker as the monster truck passes through them and the player leaves the conventionally playable game area and enters the strangely rendered space beyond the boundaries of the game. As the video continues, the area outside the level is explored further. The player walks up to and begins shooting at a piece of scenery, drawing the viewer's attention to it. On closer inspection, the scenery appears to have "Fake Background" clearly written on it. The player continues to explore, focusing on interesting and striking objects. After a few minutes of this, the music and images fade and the video finishes.

I click on another video, this time on the mapMonkeys website. A small video window opens.

> Hey mapMonkeys, it's your boy Sewerwaste here ... on Dome you're going to come to this part of the map. ... You're going to do this kind of strafe-jump up there ... then you've got to jump around the corner and crouch at the same time. ... I recommend being on default button layout because you've got to crouch immediately after. ... Once you're up here you can just hang about, climb all over the dome ... stand on those little red bars. ... It's a good spot for infection if you guys play that.

These two glitch videos offer insight into some of the range of contemporary glitcher outputs, the first, produced by chaoticPERFECTION, is a sophisticated and professional-looking sequence that carefully encapsulates the glitch with motion-graphics, fair-use copyright statements, soundtracks, and branding, while the second, produced by Sewerwaste, a prominent mapMonkeys member, plainly explains what to do, where, and why.

The chaoticPERFECTION glitch, devised for the single-player *Duke Nukem Forever* campaign, offers no competitive advantage but instead allows the glitcher to explore the materiality of the game-space – for example, seeing the curious fake background texture – and, as a corollary, to learn something about the construction of the game. The chaoticPERFECTION glitcher acts as something between a tour guide and an archaeologist, digging into digital terrain and showing the viewer the fascinating constructions and beauty beneath. In contrast, the mapMonkeys glitch prioritizes the operation of the game itself, presenting a method of accessing a specific location on a multiplayer map that has competitive advantage. This may be conducted like the chaoticPERFECTION glitch, to explore, but as it takes place on a multiplayer environment, it constitutes an unexpected vantage point with strategic advantage and is therefore likely to be used to help beat other players.

Both of these videos were eventually uploaded onto YouTube as public listings. In eighteen months, the chaoticPERFECTION video had been viewed just over a thousand times while the mapMonkeys glitch generated 120,000 views in just over a year. The difference in views may be attributed to the relative popularity of the games and the utility of the glitch in question, with *Duke Nukem Forever* generally regarded as a poor game that generated low sales figures. By contrast, *Call of Duty: Modern Warfare 3* (2011) is one of the most popular and best-selling releases on the Xbox 360 platform and had a large and dedicated multiplayer following. The first glitch allows a player to explore, while the second allows not only exploration but offers an advantage in multiplayer games to partially dominate the opposition. *Call of Duty* is not only relevant to more players on account of sales figures but also for the genuine usefulness of what it does.

When considered in relation to the other counterplay activities explored so far, glitching is a hybrid productive form. It creates artefacts such as tutorial videos that invite others to act but it also refers to the act of using exploits. As a practice it is heavily reliant on video-sharing websites for documentation, articulation, and distribution, a prevalent activity from 2006 onwards with the release of YouTube as a platform. Both chaoticPERFEC-TION and mapMonkeys were formed as glitching entities in 2006 but represent divergent social structures. chaoticPERFECTION is a glitching team that focuses on the creation of high-end releases by verified team members "as a form of education and entertainment" (Ryan350 2011). mapMonkeys evolved from a glitching community site that enabled members to submit, catalogue, and share their own glitches, and was described by one of the founders as "one of the very few places you could actually find glitches on the internet" (Rezzzo 2011). chaoticPERFECTION's primary remit differs to that of mapMonkeys, seeking to engage with the widest possible audience, whether glitchers or members of the public, while mapMonkeys was steadfastly created by glitchers for glitchers. chaoticPERFECTION primarily utilized YouTube and social-media tools to host and publicize their glitches while mapMonkeys initially developed its own website, platform, and database to allow glitchers to share their output. This was eventually replaced by YouTube delivery in early 2012 after six years of use.

> mapMonkeys are a community of gamers who have become infatuated with discovering and sharing glitches, exploits, tricks, and strategies found in the video games they play.
>
> (Rezzzo 2011)

mapMonkeys (www.mapmonkeys.com) can be considered a glitching community site, differing from chaoticPERFECTION in the sense that it is not a team with a managed identity producing specific branded releases but instead is a place for glitchers to meet, converse, and share expertise. The mapMonkeys site had three core elements: the archive of videos; the forum where members post comments and discuss; and the instant-messaging chat system, which was invoked privately in a pop-up window on screen, used to co-ordinate events and also as an outlet for banter and ritual laughter.

Of these components it was the 3,500-strong glitch video archive that acted as the main attraction for new members, only accessible after registration, offering in-depth instructions and tutorials, supplemented with text and often voice-overs. Initially, videos that were deemed particularly powerful or attractive were restricted for premium members who paid a monthly or annual subscription, but this policy proved both unpopular and ineffective as it simply pushed these glitches onto other websites and distribution points. While mapMonkeys produced glitches for almost all mainstream video-game releases, its predominant focus was on the *Call of Duty* franchise.

I first joined the mapMonkeys community site in June 2011, roughly nine months before its content was moved onto YouTube and the website slowly wound down. By late 2012, uploading onto the mapMonkeys YouTube channel ceased as core members, Rezzzo in particular, moved onto other interests and projects. At this point mapMonkeys.com hosted more than 3,500 glitching videos and supported a community of more than 130,000 members, 1,600 of whom were "premium", paid-for subscriptions. They were the only members able to upload content onto the servers. The member information implies that just over one percent of the members were active glitch-producers who supported a much larger community wishing to view and utilize the glitches. However, there appeared to be a small, active population of around two hundred to three hundred regular and active contributors who tended to interact via the forum area and group real-time chats. During the time I spent on mapMonkeys, the video-posting frequency was particularly low, at around four per week, something to which the members paid special attention. This was partly as a result of being the seasonal glitching lull. Glitching is subject to the same annual release cycle as normative play. Without any new games being released there is little to glitch. September to February was viewed as the core glitch season, and the glitches produced outside this window were largely for game DLC or in direct response to new vulnerabilities introduced through updates and patches. What this lack of posts also betrayed was the gradual fracturing of the original mapMonkeys community, the transition from community site to YouTube distribution, and the wider churn and evolution of glitching sources. Now, while there are many glitch videos they are often hosted on the YouTube channels of individual glitchers and represent a fracturing or an individualization of the glitching scene.

The mapMonkeys video-archive section was carefully organized by the title of the game for major releases and then subcategorized by the game map on which it took place. Each video contained attribution of both discovery and the performers who contributed to its documentation, alongside a description and comments box in which viewers would update the status of the glitch. Comments would often include congratulations or evaluation of the glitch by others, announcing it had been patched, some contesting the originality and ownership of the glitch, and those who offered modifications to the technique. In addition the glitches were further categorized by type, such whether they could be conducted individually, what specific game mode they were conducted on, or whether they had been invalidated through software updates. Videos ranged in duration, but typically lasted between twenty to sixty seconds, and took the form of Sewerwaste's *Modern Warfare 3* example.

In May 2012 the mapMonkeys website was deleted and YouTube became its sole deployment platform. In doing so it lost some of the close-knit nature of a membership-only community and the relative anonymity and security of discussion. However, its move to YouTube also increased its visibility enormously. On the YouTube channel, views and those commenting appear largely transitory, but the level of interaction has increased. As of October 31, 2012, the mapMonkeys YouTube channel had over 45,000 subscribers, and hosted ninety-three videos, which have been viewed over nineteen million times. In contrast, the mapMonkeysDB channel, which contains 1,365 of the glitch videos that had previously been hosted on mapMonkeys.com, has only generated thirteen subscribers and 5,500 video views, of which a significant proportion can be attributed to my research. mapMonkeys, at least in its community site form, supported a cacophony of voices and contributions of varying utility and quality of production, but it was one of the places that enabled the creation and organization of glitching as a player activity. It was a community that facilitated and documented glitching. While the move to YouTube alters this relationship, and in particular its relationship with the public, it may have done so at the expense of the fostering of community. However, many of the original mapMonkeys members felt the move to YouTube had come at a natural transition and used it as a point to separate from glitching as an activity. Glitching appeared a typically male and adolescent activity, and by 2013, a number of the members were no longer especially active. They were now in higher education or had the pressures of careers and young families. Often they would laugh about not having glitched or even played gamesfor months, yet remained on mapMonkeys and its YouTube channel for the community and friendships it fostered.

CHAOTICPERFECTION CONSIDERED

In contrast to mapMonkeys, chaoticPERFECTION utilized YouTube to distribute its work, but this created different affordances, interactions, and difficulties. Its insistence on including copyrighted music in its glitching videos without prior permission had resulted in its YouTube channel being subject to repeated copyright claims, leading to three previous accounts being banned entirely. This was seen by its members as a major point of frustration, damaging the visibility of chaoticPERFECTION and undermining its considerable efforts.

> All of the videos, fans and views were lost including the 12,554 subscribers we earned over the years as well. Our reputation went with the channel and we became unknown overnight. So we decided to count our losses and get back up on our feet with another channel which we recently lost, although there is word that YouTube has looked over our channel and has removed the problems on it.
>
> (Ryan350 2011)

The videos were reinstated in late 2011 but this discontinuity undermined the development of a subscription base and made it difficult to reach the widest audience possible since on reinstatement, all the video subscriptions had been reset. The current chaoticPERFECTION YouTube channel, active since May 2010, hosts 277 videos, has 3,500 subscribers, and has generated more than two million views. As a result of the copyright claims against it, each video now clearly includes copyright information within its comments field and more often than not within the video itself, asserting a fair-use copyright disclaimer. Like mapMonkeys, the most popular videos on chaoticPERFECTION's channel are those that relate to competitive multiplayer glitches and "triple A" titles such as the *Call of Duty*, *Gears of War*, and *Battlefield* franchises.

chaoticPERFECTION consists of a small team of five glitchers, distributed throughout North America and Europe. Despite this geographic distribution, chaoticPERFECTION consistently finds glitches for almost every major game release, uploading a series of videos within the first week of a title's release. The videos tend to share the same production values and style as seen in the *Duke Nukem Forever* video. Its videos are longer than those found on mapMonkeys, lasting three to four minutes, and develop the distinct identities of team members with voice-over styles and differentiated animated introduction and ending videos. chaoticPERFECTION also actively engages with its viewers through the comments fields, and often recognizes other glitching teams and community members in the voice-over shout-outs at the end of the video. An equivalent would be to think about chaoticPERFECTION team members as radio hosts. There is a consistency and continuity across the channel but each member has their own style and identity that is embraced in the glitches they produce.

Despite the popularity of competitively advantageous "utilitarian glitches", in particular with the public, glitchers display a completist approach, documenting, archiving, and sharing less immediately useful glitches. This partially exposes the difference between two groups defined by glitchers: *glitchers* identify and document glitches while the public only utilizes the glitches. The distinction between the two is nebulous and indeterminate to the observer. They both appear to be glitching and they are referred to as such, but is clearer to those engaged in the identification of glitching. Identification becomes a mark of distinction used by glitchers to differentiate themselves from the subordinate public mode of consumption. Yet the identification of glitches, like other counterplay acts, is intentionally done out of sight and is something that has received little critical attention within academia. The popular understanding of a glitcher is somebody who utilizes glitches, often damaging the balance and play experience of a game. While I had made use of single-player glitches myself, I lacked any notion of how glitches were actually identified. What processes enabled somebody to repeatedly find exploits that Quality Assurance teams had missed? Video games are sophisticated entertainment products with so many opportunities for interaction and layers of complexity that the chance of encountering a glitch, let alone being able to reliably duplicate one – at least in the eyes of a neophyte like myself – must be an almost impossible occurrence. How does a glitcher discover that a specific point on a map is susceptible to that particular vulnerability? Do they systematically test every surface and interaction for each weakness? As we shall see, the most honest answer is pretty much, yes.

Each glitcher I asked about the process, even those on mapMonkeys.com and chaoticPERFECTION, was either unwilling or unable to articulate the process of glitch identification in detail. Responses and discussion were generally unclear, offering allusions of an approach but not specifics from which I could build understanding. Responses were typified by the following:

> I think, hmmm can I get up there? I use rockets … and partners … and spend hours doing it. It's trial and error my friend. … (LARS_SKYNYRD)

> If we aren't working in pairs of two we normally work in groups of six or seven all in one party, some working and others observing and vice versa. It's the best way to get things done. … We Tag Teamed for weeks, everyday we would get on working on something, we threw out ideas and messed around until we found this really cool glitch. …
> (Ryan350 2011)

While these responses suggested something of the approach, timescales, and orientation, it frustratingly said little about how glitching occurred. Fortunately, following extensive correspondence with chaoticPERFECTION, during which I repeatedly explained I didn't fully grasp how glitching took place, I was eventually invited to join some of the team on a "mammoth glitching session" for the *Rezurrection DLC* (2011) package for *Call of Duty: Black Ops*. Building on the franchise's popular "Nazi Zombie" mode, *Rezurrection* relocates to a Cold War moon base where, taking the role of Richard Nixon, Robert McNamara, John F. Kennedy, or Fidel Castro, players must co-operate to survive successive waves of Nazi zombies. I was asked to join members of chaoticPERFECTION as an active observer, able to learn the processes involved while hopefully being useful and contributing to the identification of new glitches.

A NOTE ON GAME BARRIERS

Before I joined the mammoth glitching session, which was to focus on the idea of overcoming the barriers of the game-space, the boundaries, and walls that restrict the player, I was given a short description of the different barriers that a glitcher saw. In addition to the conventional game barrier, which opposed movement within a 3D space, there were others that corralled the player in different ways, required different approaches, and offered different opportunities.

- **Permeable barrier**: a barrier that is generally invisible and does not resist the progression of a game object in any direction. It may be used to mark progress into an area or trigger events, such as loading new sections of the game, or "deloading" those sections that have already been passed, replacing them with lower-fidelity equivalents that often contain more vulnerabilities. I was told to watch for signs of crossing a barrier and what processes they appeared to cause;
- **Semi-permeable barrier**: a barrier that restricts progress in one direction but not another. It is commonly used to drive linear progression in a game map. I was told to note where these occurred;
- **Death barrier**: a barrier that destroys a game element on contact, such as an avatar, projectile, or object. These generally surround game maps in order to preserve system resources by preventing the rendering and calculations associated with elements outside the game-space. If a player touches a death barrier they are usually respawned immediately within the play area of the map. I was told these should be avoided at all costs, especially in the *Rezurrection* game mode. In other glitching sessions these were carefully mapped looking for ways they could be bridged or traced in reference to other static objects;
- **Timed death barrier**: a barrier that works in the same manner as a death barrier but the element is destroyed after a set duration. This is frequently combined with an on-screen notification and is used to encourage players to return to the conventional play area. I was told to avoid these but was assured that in many games, the timed death barrier was psychological instead of real. Many could be passed through and exited before the time ran out, but invariably players complied with the warning. Unfortunately, there was simply no way of determining whether a barrier was illusory or real without experimentation.

While this represented the smallest of pointers in order to prevent me from undermining the session and to allow me some idea of terminology, it offers some insight into the way glitchers understand game-space and the subtle differences in approach they adopt. I felt this was especially evident with their attitude towards timed death barriers.

I was instructed to download the *Rezurrection DLC* immediately on its release in the UK and to wait on Xbox LIVE for other members of chaoticPERFECTION to join and begin glitching. On meeting with the chaotic-PERFECTION members online, the specific nature of the game provided a role where I could contribute: assisting with the creation of a safe "beachhead" to enable glitching. I was to become the zombie herder. In a match of *Call of Duty Rezurrection*, players must dispatch zombies that spawn in waves. Once a specific number have been disposed of a stronger "boss zombie" enters the arena and no more weaker zombies appear. If the last weak zombie within a wave is destroyed, however, a new wave starts and scores of enemies invade the space.

It became my responsibility to ensure all zombies had been destroyed, bar one that I had decided was slower than others – a runt zombie. I was then to lure the runt zombie away from the other glitchers who were herding the boss zombie into a specific location. I had to remain close enough to the runt zombie to maintain its attention, leading it to locations it would then find difficult to navigate, such as staircases or areas littered with boxes, and once the zombie was there I would sprint back to observe and help with the glitching.

Through discussion it was agreed the boss zombie might become instrumental in glitching because it exploded when destroyed, and in the low moon gravity, the blast would send any players in its vicinity flying high into the air, hopefully enabling them to overcome barriers. It was hoped this process could be utilized to overcome the barriers that surrounded the playable area and allow the glitcher to get "Out of Map" (OOM), a highly desirable kind of glitch. In order to do this, it was essential that four states were managed:

1   That no new zombies entered the stage and interfered with proceedings;
2   That no player was killed;
3   That nobody killed the final runt zombie of the wave, triggering more zombies, and;
4   That nobody killed the exploding boss zombie until it was in just the right place to conduct the glitch.

GLITCHING TECHNIQUE

The luring process was slow and inexact and therefore it was easier if only one player herded the boss or runt. The others would stay well clear of its sphere of detection, spending the time exploring the map and looking for evidence of inconsistency (proto-glitches) until called back to observe and participate in the boss-zombie glitch. While away, the glitchers moved around the game-space, exploring potential lines of exploit, constantly communicating and reporting to their peers. They (we) looked for anything that immediately appeared anomalous or out of place: inconsistently shaped scenery or objects, different kinds of walls, barriers, floors, handrails, and other objects that might offer a foothold, and places where the player felt something odd happen, such as their avatar "sticking" or catching while moving. As a result of these techniques, three anomalies were detected in the first fifteen minutes, even before we first tested the boss-zombie hypothesis: a death barrier marked by an open cliff side in an exterior section of the map; a point where the player model appeared to get stuck on the level scenery, giving the impression of a pirouetting astronaut; and lastly an exterior staircase flanked by a tantalizingly low barrier wall. It was decided this boss zombie would be lured onto the stairs, at which point it would be killed and the resulting explosion would send the glitchers soaring over the game barrier and onto a ledge or send the player Out of Map.

Through careful manoeuvring, the zombies were separated and the boss zombie lured onto the steps and detonated. The resulting explosion launched the players into the air, but at the wrong angles. One slammed into the doorway in front of me and ended up wedged into the corner of the walkway, while the other arced gently over the bottom steps and brushed against the wall, too low to confirm whether a barrier existed above the wall or not. This process had taken twenty minutes and five restarts of the map to prepare, as each time previously one of the four states mentioned earlier was violated through confusion, miscommunication, or misfortune.

We continued this process until the prototypical glitch we were investigating was conducted perfectly, with the glitcher sailing high above the visible wall. Unfortunately, it merely confirmed an invisible barrier did exist beyond it and that particular location was not susceptible to that glitch under those circumstances. Undeterred, we split and each went looking for other places where a glitch might expose itself. To explore, we jumped against barriers, rubbed against walls, constantly calling for other glitchers to observe and offer advice as we repeated the potential proto-glitch. After we had done this for around fifteen minutes, we returned to the boss-zombie plan in a different location. We persisted in this mode for around three hours, at which point I had to leave the session.

While this glitching session was largely unsuccessful, it at least offered insight into the techniques and processes utilized when glitching multiplayer spaces. It is based on hypothesis generation, repetition, observation, and most of all perseverance, all of which is done within a social and highly communicative environment. While we were challenging the boundaries of the game-space, I was assured the same process applied to other types of glitch, such as those based on movement, animation, or affordances. In addition to this example, I was fortunate to be invited to participate in other glitching sessions by chaoticPERFECTION and mapMonkeys members, both within a diagnostic capacity, as with this *Rezurrection* example, and a documenting capacity, creating the glitch video artefact.

A SUCCESSFUL ZOMBIE GLITCH

While our *Rezurrection* glitching session was unsuccessful, other glitchers found success by using a similar hypothesis in a different location, discovering a "ledge" (a foothold) and a "spot" (a strategically significant location), the use of which placed the glitcher (FinalKilla) far beyond the reach of the zombie hordes. The glitch was uploaded onto YouTube on August 26, only three days after *Rezurrection* had been released, and people using this glitch saw themselves rocket to the top of the game leader boards – not that this was their core aim but an amusing secondary outcome.

Later, within the same tutorial, video a new technique is presented. Instead of using the conventional boss-explosion process, it shows that performing a running jump and laying "prone" while in the air (a "dolphin dive"), the player is able to reach the same spot directly. This illustrates the progressive and iterative nature of glitching. Even within a single video, a strategy may be developed, tested, and then improved on, offering progressively more sophisticated and refined ways of navigating and manipulating the space and undermining the game.

These two examples highlight a general process shared by many glitches:

- The identification of a safe beachhead in which the game settings are adjusted or managed to create an environment conducive to glitching;
- The development of focused and coherent hypothesises that are systematically tested and developed;
- Open communication and reporting between glitchers within the game and in extended groups, a kind of community knowledge that is maintained across glitch sessions with different practitioners;
- A systematic process of documentation and distribution, focused on notions of originality, attribution, and ownership, which in turn can be seen as establishing a broader set of community knowledge.

HOMEFRONT EXAMPLE: DOCUMENTING A GLITCH

Following the *Rezurrection* session, I was invited to glitch Epic Games' *Bulletstorm* (2011), *Gear of War 3* (2011), and then later to assist with the recording and documentation of a glitch on THQ's *Homefront* (2011). The *Homefront* glitch recording session offered some insight into the process of documenting a glitch for "education and entertainment". As with the *Rezur-rection* session, I was instructed to get onto Xbox LIVE and wait for the team to get together. This was to be a three-person video, with Ryan350, Nickncs, and myself. Nickncs joined early and we spent time casually playing the multiplayer game and discussing its merits while waiting for Ryan350, who was going record the glitch. When Ryan350 joined, we created a private multiplayer match and Ryan led us through the glitch.

This glitch allowed players to get out of the map and was reliant on the multiple occupancy vehicles that can be used in *Homefront*'s multiplayer game and the specific rules that surround respawning in a match. If a team-mate is in a vehicle, it is possible to spawn directly into a vacant seat. This spawn mechanism can be repurposed to effectively reset and overcome the timed death-barrier countdown that gives the player five seconds to return to the game-space or be respawned. By spawning into the vehicle a second before the timed death-barrier countdown ends, the original player is killed but the newly spawned one is not. One assumes there is a rule that states a player is invulnerable immediately after respawing to prevent being imme-diately killed by other players and this overrides the command to kill them sent by a timed death barrier. On conducting the glitch, the counter remains at zero without killing the vehicle's occupant, who can then freely explore the space beyond the map, in vehicle or on foot, and alternatively attack their foes, who are still subject to the boundaries of the space.

As previously, we each had specific roles but they were even more rigid in this session. Ryan350 was the recorder. His point of view was the camera, being captured via his personal video recorder. Nickncs and I were the actors. We were instructed where to stand, where to move to, and significant time was taken to ensure the composition was aesthetically pleasing. The glitch video would eventually consist of two elements, both of which were to be recorded in this session: the voice tutorial, during which Ryan350 detailed how to conduct the glitch as Nickncs and I demonstrated it, and a montage section in which the spectacle of the glitch and its potential were emphasized.

We rehearsed the glitch and then did two full takes. As previously, where we made errors of timing, location, or dexterity, we would restart from an appropriate point with Ryan350 directing the proceedings, taking note of locations and movement to ensure continuity. The initial tutorial run-through took approximately forty minutes to record, at which point Ryan350 left the match to record the voice-over separately and edit the introduction section. While this was being done, Nickncs and I were tasked with identifying interesting or spectacular points on the map, made acces-sible through the glitch that would be used in the second part of the video.

After just over an hour, Ryan350 returned and we conducted the mon-tage elements. In this section the recorder had to perform the glitch in order to get out of the map and into the space beyond the barriers. Nickncs and I took it in turn to perform the glitch with Ryan350, visiting the areas we had identified, such as where we had found the final edge of the ground on

Figure 4.2 Glitching, exploring beyond the game barriers in Homefront.

Figure 4.3 Glitching, exploring beneath the game map in Homefront.

the game map, which naturally we parked next to, explored, and then leapt off into oblivion. After less than an hour of recording we decided we had enough material and we ended the glitching session. By this point it was the early morning and I went to sleep. When I awoke and checked YouTube, the finished video had been uploaded and was already generating views.

Naturally, all glitch tutorials are different, taking different forms for different audiences, and therefore the highly polished video tutorial of chaoticPERFECTION is just one model. However, even with text-based glitch tutorials similar themes and important practices can be traced, particularly the development of individual or group identity (the glitcher claiming ownership of the glitch), and recognition (making it clear who assisted with the development of the glitch or what techniques it built on). It appears important within glitching communities to find new glitches and to develop a reputation through this, which is something I then attempted myself.

GOING SOLO: BARRIER-BREAKING BATTLEFIELD 3

Following my experiences of glitching with chaoticPERFECTION, map-Monkeys, and others, I decided to replicate the process and attempt to glitch the single-player element of EA Games' *Battlefield 3* (2011). I purchased the game on its European release date (October 28, 2011) and began testing the boundaries by rubbing against and working on the walls, game barriers, and, where possible, racing into the timed death barriers on open maps. Over the course of three days, glitching for around four hours each day, I identified three map glitches. I found the process mesmerizing. I would play the single-player game at a snail's pace, clearing a section of enemies and then systematically testing all the barrier edges. In some instances I would get stuck and have to restart that section, but the eventual satisfaction of discovering a glitch that I believed had not been found by somebody else was euphoric, if only because of the long period of time spent without finding a glitch.

However, when I enthusiastically announced my discoveries on the map-Monkeys message boards, I was swiftly assured that other glitchers had already identified two of the three. What is interesting about this is not my ineptitude as a glitcher but the fault lines between appropriate and inappropriate glitching that this uncovered: the wider issues of consumption and appropriation, such as video-game piracy, the distribution of pre-release game-image files, and the use of hacked consoles.

The first glitch I identified was an "up and over" Out of Map that uses objects to leap over a boundary. In an urban combat environment, I vaulted onto a refuse skip and used it as a platform to jump a barrier wall and into the space beyond and outside the map. This was almost identical to one already uploaded. Another glitcher had simply beaten me to it, the only difference being that their version used a running jump instead of jumping off the trash dumpster. The second glitch was more interesting. At one point on a map an earthquake spectacularly takes place, levelling buildings and entirely redrawing the anticipated level route. I found that after the earthquake, I was able to simply walk up some rubble, mash the jump button until I got traction, leap onto a partially buried first-storey garage roof, and by running across it get outside the conventional game-space and into the void beyond.

This time, having done a little more research and not finding any evidence of the glitch elsewhere, I performed the glitch and recorded a video. I then once again announced my discovery to the glitchers on mapMonkeys, presenting a link to the video on YouTube as evidence. Almost immediately I received a message: "I uploaded it on a different account on October 22, keep trying LOL" and was provided with a link to an unlisted video that was almost exactly the same as the one I had discovered. While I have to admit I was annoyed, the video's timestamp was October 22, and this intrigued me. This was three days before the game's North American release date and six days before the European release, when I was able to obtain it. Somehow the glitcher either had access to pre-release game discs, had altered the YouTube timestamp, or was using a hacked Xbox 360 and was playing with illegally shared game rips, known as ISOs, from which the *Battlefield 3* file had been leaked online in mid-October.

It became apparent that the use of hacked consoles, JTAGs, RGHs, flashed consoles, and other hardware modifications was a highly contentious issue within glitching circles, and there was a hushed suspicion that some of the most rapid glitch discoveries were enabled through these activities. This accusation was sometimes traceable in the comments threads that accompanied a video release, but more often than not the comments were robustly defended against, shouted down, or simply ignored. The implication was the really dedicated glitchers were using leaked pre-release game ISOs to give themselves a head start on other glitchers, and when they found glitches, they could be recorded and prepared ready to be published on the game's release date. I was never able to get a real sense of the extent to which ISOs were used, but suffice to say that accusations of hardware hacks being used while never quite central to the discussion was always somewhere in the periphery, exposing itself when glitchers argued or on random negative posts. It became clear the majority of glitchers felt glitching from the release date was an important dynamic of glitching, alongside playing unmodified code, but this was at odds with the demand to quickly identify glitches.

The final glitch I identified was as simple as taking an abrupt right-hand turn, vaulting over yet another refuse skip, and dashing through the timed death barrier until no longer within its restrictive boundaries and therefore Out of Map. While I am not claiming it is a particularly novel or important glitch in itself, what it demonstrates is the point at which I understood enough about glitching to identify them myself.

My understanding of the glitching process only really extended to the discovery of boundary-related glitches and from my experience of previously using duplication glitches on *Elder Scrolls IV: Oblivion* (2006). By looking at the range of videos on mapMonkeys and chaoticPERFECTION I was conscious there are many other glitch types. I therefore began to use the video databases as a way of attempting to understand this scope and to offer an introductory typology of glitches, thinking of their interrelations and the status or meaning conferred to them in glitching communities.

A TYPOLOGY OF GLITCHES

For those unfamiliar with the practice of glitching, even a cursory look at the range of glitches available, such as those on mapMonkeys, chaoticPERFECTION, or YouTube more generally, is likely to appear as a bewildering, apparently random diversity. Glitches are unexpected interactions and outcomes of code. They are not fundamentally illogical but are simply the result of code that has been written in error, that interacts with other functions in unanticipated ways, or goes beyond the functional capabilities of the hardware. As a result there is almost infinite scope for what a glitch may do and what form it may take. However, if they were utterly random outcomes of code it would be impossible to develop coherent and replicable ways of finding them. Fortunately video games, and certainly the popular commercial releases found on home consoles, are not free expressions of the potential of software code and hardware mechanisms but are generic software constructions. Their scope is restricted by the models that define the expected form of the games, such as first-person shooter, and by the specific capabilities and range of interactions, such as input types, of the hardware product and its application framework, such as the software engine used to render the game. Video games therefore have similarities of form, context, and operation between releases within the same genre that offer coherence for the consumer, but while these structures create the foundation for correct or normal play, they also provide the potential for glitches.

As a result, the kinds of games explored by glitchers on the Xbox 360 platform, predominantly action-orientated first-person and third-person military shooters, offer a distinct range of glitches on account of the affordances, focus, and operations of the genre. These games generally prioritize the exploration and navigation of simulated 3D space – looking, aiming, and attacking – and the management of finite resources such as ammunition or health. It is therefore rational that glitches also tend to work on these lines of activity – the practices that the code simulates and models but also the very practices that enable a player to progress within the game i.e. the lusory means and pre-lusory goal. While there are inevitably some wild-card glitches that are the unpredictable outcome of the potential of code, most fall along the lines of the affordances of the generic constructs they are conducted on – movement, boundaries, aiming, and resource management – and the engines used: Unreal, Frostbite, etc.

On the mapMonkeys and chaoticPERFECTION databases, it is possible to identify glitches that focus on the following aspects of video-game interaction:

- the way the game environment looks and all things within it;
- the way the game-space is defined;
- the way the player looks around the space;
- the way the player navigates the space;
- the potency of the player;
- the way in-game objects and items are interacted with, consumed, accumulated, or destroyed;
- the way the game logic behaves;
- and the rules that restrict access and setup.

On closer inspection it is evident these categories cover the majority of potential interactions on an action-orientated console game. They also provide the beginnings of a framework that offers order over the apparent chaos. Glitches are protean in their nature in the sense that many of them can be viewed simultaneously as a method – a tool for uncovering additional glitches or that is combined in sequence to reach an outcome – and an outcome: the final situated purpose of the glitch, such as accessing a specific point or augmenting the damage of a weapon. This dual reading makes categorization problematic and presents significant challenges when first confronted by a profusion of glitches.

The following typology of glitches is built on sustained interaction with glitching communities and textual analysis of extensive glitching archives containing in excess of 3,500 individual glitching videos. It is meant to offer insight into the vocabulary of glitching and the various ways in which glitches enable the transformation of the experience of space, game, and time within a video-game environment. It is not implied that this represents a comprehensive overview of glitching but it offers a preliminary sketching out of the boundaries based on the body of data and interactions available. The 3,500 or more glitches observed on mapMonkeys and chaoticPERFECTION therefore can be categorized by whether they are graphical, navigational, barrier-based, process-based, logic-based, or affordance-based.

Table 4.1 Types of glitches.

Graphical Glitches	Glitches that identify or instigate errors in the way that the game is visually presented, how the game looks.
Navigation Glitches	Glitches that instigate changes to the way that the player is able to move around the space, how movement feels.
Barrier Glitches	Glitches that instigate changes to the way that the gamespace is defined and configured, the boundaries and scope of the gamespace.
Process Glitches	Glitches that instigate or utilize vulnerabilities caused by processes and functions of the game system and application framework, the processes that allow the game to be executed.
Logic Glitches	Glitches that exploit the logic of the game, exposing anomalies in the system or by predicting causality.
Affordance Glitches	Glitches that alter the capabilities of the player within the game directly. These are the most powerful, unpredictable and versatile glitches generally coming out of the combination and interruption of game routines, exposing anomalies in the system or by predicting causality.

Additionally glitches can be further differentiated by their perception within the player population, the extent to which they are visible or observable, and the amount of advantage or deviation from the anticipated order of the game that they offer. While not entirely consistent, this way of mapping out glitches offers some insight into how a glitch is understood, the response it elicits, and the accommodation of a range of different subtypes or glitch examples. Those that offer high levels of advantage and visibility are most likely to be regarded as "game-breakers" and are therefore treated with disdain by players and game operators, necessitating security updates and sanctions on perpetrators while conferring significant status on the glitcher(s) who identify them. In contrast, glitches that offer low levels of advantage and visibility are likely to be viewed as trivial diversions, of little interest to the public, and largely ignored. Despite this, any glitch is of note to a true glitcher.

The visibility continuum reflects the extent to which the glitch is perceived or seen by conventional players. It expresses the visibility of the glitch from low, effectively invisible glitches through to highly conspicuous glitches. The advantage continuum expresses the extent to which the glitch alters or interrupts the conventional function of the game-space and forces players to alter their behaviour. A broad definition of the differences between levels of glitch visibility and advantage can be found below.

Table 4.2 Glitch visibility continuum.

Value	Characteristics
Low	The glitch is rarely detected and/or identified as anomalous activity by the playerbase / game operators. It may or may not have directly observable characteristics, these will be of a minor nature. The glitch may be so difficult to conduct, or restricted to highly specific circumstances, that it is rarely witnessed or identified in ongoing gameplay.
Medium	The glitch is occasionally detected and/or identified as anomalous activity by the playerbase / game operators. It has observable characteristics but it may be relatively difficult to conduct or restricted to limiting circumstances so that it is visible in few aspects or elements of gameplay.
High	The glitch is frequently detected and/or identified as anomalous activity by the playerbase / game operators. It has observable characteristics that may be conspicuous in their manifestation. The glitch may be relatively easy to perform and/or unrestricted in its invocation and therefore seen in many aspects or elements of gameplay.

Table 4.3 Glitch advantage continuum.

Value	Characteristics
Low	The glitch is perceived to have little or no impact upon the core functions of gameplay, the game continues as normal for almost all players. It may influence peripheral game functions but this does not confer any competitive advantage or force others to adjust their play.

(Continued)

Value	Characteristics
Medium	The glitch is perceived to impact upon the functions of gameplay, but the impact upon core functions is limited, it can still be played conventionally by most players, but the experience may be altered for some. It may offer competitive advantage, but players are able to limit and/or neutralise the impact of the advantage by altering their behaviour in a way that does not radically alter core play mechanics.
High	The glitch is perceived to impact significantly upon the core functions of gameplay and the game cannot be played in its conventional manner by many players. It offers competitive advantage that is difficult or impossible to neutralise and forces players to alter their behaviour to attempt to escape its impact.

Glitches that are highly visible but have limited or minor advantage, such as those that can be easily conducted and countered, are likely to be regarded as alternate strategies or undisclosed functions available to the player. Those that confer a significant advantage but are sufficiently difficult to perform or can only be done in limited circumstances are viewed as glitches. These definitions also have a bearing on the ways the protagonist is perceived by the public.

Game-breakers mark a temporary descent into chaos and are conducted by a large proportion of the population, not simply glitchers but those who are juvenile, mischievous, bored, or intrigued. While all who conduct game-breakers are likely to be treated with censure, the high visibility of the act means many will be reconciled back into the playerbase. The act will be configured as poor judgement instead of identity and often key protagonists or the originators are penalized. Glitches are instrumental in forming identity. Their power to subvert, combined with the small number of protagonists, enable them to be used as a point of distinction against a group i.e. glitchers, who are treated with widespread derision. Strategies are viewed as alternate but semi-legitimate play styles. They are odd but not necessarily perceived as oppositional. Instead they are viewed as the mark of different or deviant groups, such as expert players or power-gamers. They are the practices of those who care about the game too much. Finally, novelty glitches are rarely perceived by the playerbase, and when they are, the lack of advantage and visibility makes them of scant interest to players generally.

GLITCHING PURPOSES

In addition to the glitch type, its level of visibility, and advantage, it is also possible to make a general observation about the more abstract purposes of the deployment of these glitches. These can be thought of as the benefit offered by the glitch, what it enables the glitcher to do with the game that they were unable to do previously, and where the pleasures may be found. Many players utilized glitches for competitive advantage, such as attacking their foes from beneath the ground, while others used them to marvel at the subverted and sublime vistas they offered.

Figure 4.4 Glitching, admiring the sublime beauty of a glitching game engine in
    The Elder Scrolls V: Skyrim.

Table 4.4 Glitch purposes schema.

Purpose	*Description*	*Associated glitch types*
Exploration	Where glitches enable the ability to explore and interact with the video game text at a deeper level. It can be considered an outcome motivated by wishing to understand and experience as much of the game as possible. It extends from the aesthetic appreciation of the spectacle of a glitched game environment to an awareness of the actual construction of game levels. Glitchers who are motivated by this kind of attitude approach the game environment as detectives, archaeologists, or media historians – performing close critical readings, slowly working through concentric layers of the game, paying close attention to the appearance and feel of the spaces. In doing so they develop an increasingly intimate understanding of the game, and become 'closer' to the game.	Graphical glitches, Navigation glitches, and Barrier glitches.
Productivity	Where glitches enable the reappropriation of a game environment for purposes other than those set out by the game, such as the development of new game modes and the creation of machinima. This purpose often makes use of glitches that alter the appearance or available interactions with the space, presenting new vistas and game objects. Examples include glitched animations where the player models look and behave differently to normal, or the use of navigation glitches to enter previously inaccessible game areas for use in a "Mike Myers" game subtype.	Graphical glitches, Navigational glitches, and Barrier glitches.

(*Continued*)

Purpose	*Description*	*Associated glitch types*
Renegotiation	Where glitches are used to alter the range and nature of interactions with the game, but in a way that recognises and aligns with some of the pre-lusory goals. The glitches allow the player to access a game element that may be unavailable to them at that point in the game or as a result of the requirement of temporal investment or skill. These kind of glitches align closely with the notion of cheating and frequently occur on single-player games where the capacity to perceive inequality is largely removed e.g. glitches that enable progression, duplicate items or enable invulnerability.	Navigational glitches, Barrier glitches, Logic glitches and Affordance glitches.
Domination	Where glitches are used to explicitly alter the balance of multiplayer play in the favor of the glitcher. This may manifest itself as: indirect domination such as the deployment of more efficient means than others e.g. the use of speed glitches to access key locations before teammates; or more explicitly, such as with the use of glitches to attack players without being seen or the deployment of weapon glitches that make the glitcher powerful.	Barrier glitches, Process glitches, Logic glitches, Affordance glitches

Following my experiences glitching with others and conducting glitches myself, I became interested in the motivations and reasons for glitching. Why were some players willing to spend such lengths of time scrutinizing a game to identify a small number of glitches that would then likely be patched and removed from the game a few weeks later? What pleasures and purposes might be attributed to this – and as a corollary, what might their relationship be with the discourses that compete to rationalize these events? I began to interview and discuss this with glitchers. Rezzzo, the leader of mapMonkeys, and Ryan350 saw a clear distinction between two groups of glitcher.

> Those who do it for fun and enjoyment, and those who do it to gain unfair advantage over other players" (2011). "There are two main reasons why people glitch. ... to show off and brag about how cool they are when and if they find something" [while others] "enjoy doing the unintentional, they find a satisfaction in launching above the map more than they do staying inside the boundaries that the developers intend them to do.
>
> (Ryan350 2011)

This reputational aspect of Ryan350's comment resonated with the perspectives of many other glitchers with whom I spoke. It appeared that within the dedicated or professional glitching communities, glitchers were playing a metagame in which the chief goal was to identify, claim, and distribute an exploit before others. The act of discovering a glitch and its use, while enjoyable in itself, is contextualized by the way it enables glitchers to clamour status in a hierarchy, to form individual and group identity, and to open up the specific pleasurable purposes of the glitch: exploration, productivity, renegotiation, or domination.

Therefore the pleasures are additionally for many not restricted to the implicit joy of conducting a glitch but the response it elicits when presented to others. Their responses will offer varying meaning to the glitch, dependent on the observer's ideological perspective and the visibility and advantage it confers. Curiously, many glitchers felt happy with any recognition, negative or positive, which was attributed to the recognition of a "good glitch" by fellow glitchers, as a terrible exploit by those fearful of the impact to the conventional game, or even where developers instigate software security patches to remove the glitch.

Glitchers also approached glitches with an additional perspective of how difficult they may have been to identify. They, too, like members of the public and developers, primarily judged glitches by what they enabled along the axis of visibility and advantage. The interaction of the severity or significance, and the eventual visibility of a glitch, in turn define the type of response and the status given to the glitcher. The more visible a glitch, the more people become aware of it, and the greater the advantage, the greater the status attributed to those who find it. For teams like chaoticPERFECTION, this appeared a primary driver for its mode of production, but also the importance of attributing contribution towards the glitch and how it was presented.

> A single big glitch, something crazy like a "No Clip (GOD Mode)" that would spread around the world while giving me a big rep boost. ... So the biggest things are glitch credit, reputation and coming off as professional to the public.
>
> (Ryan350 2011)

Glitches have their own hierarchy of authenticity and significance. A good glitch is measured by different criteria according to an individual's predilections but it may be determined by the utility or universality of the glitch and the advantages they confer.

> If your intentions are to exploit it in an online match then it's probably considered good depending on how much of an advantage it gives you to other players. If your intentions are just for fun then it is seen good depending on how universal it is and where it gets you to. If it gets you on a high roof or out of a map, then it's most likely seen as good, but if it just gets you on a small shed or in a small tree, then it's not seen to be as good.
>
> (Ryan350 2011)

Once more, everyone is watching and judging the play of others.

AUTHENTIC GLITCHING AND SUB-WHORES

These dynamics express the motivations for finding glitches: the glitcher engages with an enjoyable act in which they feel they are doing something novel and authentic. In turn, by documenting and distributing the glitch, they gain status and reputation within glitching circles, have their techniques adopted by the public, and potentially become more visible to the developers. As the idealized model of glitching from a glitcher's perspective, this is the mark of authentic or appropriate glitching. However, by defining an ideal form, it becomes vulnerable to subversion and manipulation. There are inauthentic ways of glitching.

Many glitchers were critical of those who packaged the wrong kind of glitches into too-slick video sequences with animated intros and idents, labelling this as "sub whoring", where glitchers cared primarily about driving viewers and subscriptions to their YouTube channels in the hope of generating revenue and celebrity rather than actually glitching. For example, glitchers who made excessive references to their YouTube channels in forums, who claimed false ownership of previously identified glitches, or whose glitch videos were so full of bombast yet so lean in glitch quality (measured by advantage and visibility) were dismissed and ridiculed. This was how most serious glitchers viewed appropriate glitching, but while those who violated these principles were subject to ridicule, finding themselves overlooked when glitching sessions were being recruited, and, in extreme cases, ostracized entirely from glitching communities, the democratic nature of glitching, where knowledge is shared with the public, meant that even though they might be considered inauthentic glitchers they still had access to the specific exploits. For those who cared about being part of glitching communities and assisting with group-based glitch identification sessions, adhering to these principles was important but beyond this, anybody could do anything.

The release and utilization of glitches were also the subject of notions of authenticity. For example, it was the general consensus that while members of the public knew no better but to abuse glitches once they became aware of them, authentic glitchers used them with taste and restraint. Glitches were typically to be used while among other glitchers, at least until they had reached wide adoption, and never primarily to inflate or confer advantage in competitive games. Glitching was therefore seen as a separate, more sophisticated way of playing games, requiring greater patience and understanding than most members of the public would have, and equally suggested glitchers were likely to be more skillful than other players at the conventional game anyway, so would never have to resort to glitching for progression. Here you can see that notions of authenticity simultaneously police the boundary between true glitchers and the public while immunizing glitchers from many of the criticisms levelled against their practices: true glitchers don't use glitches competitively, they do it because they understand the game more, and then they benevolently share the information to players and developers alike. By contrast, the public is unable to efficiently detect glitches, abuses them when they become aware of them, and sub-whores do whatever they can to try to build a YouTube following. Even when glitchers admit to violating some of these principles, it is justified through a higher purpose such as pure carnivalesque enjoyment.

> I must admit it is sometimes fun to go into online lobbies and glitch to see people's reactions, which by doing that I am glitching to gain advantage over other players, but I'm not using it to boost my Kill/Death ratio or to get higher on the leader boards, I'm doing it for pure enjoyment.
>
> (Rezzzo 2011)

To the observer, Rezzzo would have been glitching for competitive advantage, glitching in order to progress, while his primary motivation was an experience of the glitch: glitching to glitch. When glitches are adopted by the public they can become part of the repertoire of play, providing they do not challenge the game too strongly. In multiplayer games they are often patched with relative haste and removed from the game, especially if they are visible and confer advantage. Examples of glitches that are retained are those regarded as strategies or novelties: rocket-jumping and the *Gears of War* Kung Fu Flip, found by the founder of chaoticPERFECTION, xJediP-iMPx: "that glitch was used by everyone as a new form of getting to certain places faster. If there was a flight of stairs, you could choose to take the time to walk up the stairs or to flip up in the air and land upstairs faster. ... It became a part of the game as a new feature." (Ryan350,2011).

Authentic glitching conducted with other glitchers manifests itself in new play types or modes, becoming part of the gaming repertoire, such as the "Mike Myers" and "Secret Room" games for the *Call of Duty* franchise. Rezzzo explains how each of these work:

> "Michael Myers" is where one player can only use his knife to kill everyone on the other team. The other team can't shoot at him, can only run away and jump to places, which most people get to using glitches since they usually require some skill to get into. Other games developed around glitches usually pertain to what the glitch is, like if you find a secret room then the game is usually one team has to be in the secret room protecting one of the players, and the other team's job is to infiltrate the room and kill the player being protected.
>
> (Rezzzo 2011)

The adoption as player repertoire and alternate game modes can be considered the benign utilization of glitches. However, glitchers were well aware of the radical nature of those glitches that were both powerful and visible and therefore incurred the wrath of the developers. As a result some glitchers entertained withholding game-breaking glitches from release and the general public. The Javelin glitch on *Modern Warfare 2* was a highly conspicuous example: easy to conduct, immensely powerful, and therefore a prime example of a game-breaker.

OF JAVELINS AND GAME-BREAKERS

The Javelin glitch was first posted on YouTube on November 29, 2009. News of it spread quickly and it was replicated by players within the game almost immediately. It was then further clarified by glitchers including mapMonkeys. The mapMonkeys Javelin glitch video, posted two days after its discovery, has been viewed in excess of 1.3 million times, while the original video has less than 350,000 viewers. The Javelin glitch disrupted the normal operation of the majority of public matches within hours of its documentation and Activision was put under pressure from a vocal and irritated playerbase. There was the perception that the game was now unplayable in its conventional sense, and forums and message boards were flooded with comments similar to the following, but perhaps without the self reflection.

> I LITERALLY cannot go into a single game without at least one person using it. ... I used it at the beginning of yesterday back when I was like the only one using it – showed it to my friend, it gave us a lot of laughs. I know, I know, I helped to perpetuate the bullshit in this game [it's] ... impossible to enjoy any match of MP anymore.
>
> (Metal Ninja Cake 2009)

This also illustrates the speed at which a game-breaker can take hold. The glitch necessitated a mandatory security update that was deployed on December 10, 2009, with an announcement from Xbox LIVE's Director of Programming, Larry Hryb. The glitch was removed and play returned to its normal state. This process cost Activision $40,000 in Microsoft patch-verification fees alone (Stuart 2012), and while this is a small fee for a franchise as commercially successful as *Call of Duty*, it still stresses the direct financial implications of glitching. Following the appearance of the exploit, in an attempt to enforce rule and placate players after its patching, Microsoft and Activision began to develop a much more stringent and clear glitching policy leading to the "game abuse" definition, and retrospectively banned many deemed to have glitched *Call of Duty* multiplayer games.

Rezzzo, one of the glitchers who had contributed to the adoption of the glitch (his version of the glitch video was the one viewed in excess of a million times), acknowledged that "sometimes sharing these glitches can be very destructive to the game. ... It was fun to do but it ruined the game for some" (2011). Yet Rezzzo did not see the release of the glitch as especially negative or damaging and felt no culpability. Instead he viewed the sharing of the glitch technique as a service to players and game developers alike, whom he regarded as core members of the glitching audience. The developers were members of the public. This was an apparently counterintuitive perspective but one shared by the majority of glitchers I spoke with that in turn exposed some of the initially hidden motivations for glitching.

Many glitchers saw any response from the developers, such as patching a glitch, as recognition of glitching handiwork and a tacit challenge from developers to glitchers to attempt to discover further exploits. Glitchers therefore saw themselves as being engaged in a symbolic dialogue with developers and system-holders through their counterplay interactions with the games and their systems. By releasing a game-breaker, the glitcher pointed out a major flaw in the game missed by Quality Assurance that was then recognized and responded to by the developer, even though glitchers were quite aware glitching was forbidden in the code of conduct. This symbolic dialogue motivated releases, while the openness with which the glitch was shared was felt to remove any sense of negativity of opposition. To document and share a glitch is simply an act or sharing information. It is the (over)use of information that constituted a negative act.

> If a game developer asks me how to do it, I don't try to hide it from them. I'm perfectly willing to show them how to do a glitch so they can be patched. That's how other glitches are eventually found, if big glitches weren't patched, then no one would be going out and looking for other newer glitches.
>
> (Rezzzo 2011)

However, other situations questioned this benign sharing of information, such as when glitchers identified exploits and flaws within beta releases or early game demos but withheld sharing them in anticipation of the eventual game release. If the exploits were available in the final commercial version they would be adopted by more members of the public, become more visible, attribute more status, and, of course, cause more damage. Other glitchers were more circumspect about the relationship with game-breakers.

> I do my best not to release glitches that have the potential to be Game-breakers because they will absolutely be abused without question, thus ruining the game for others and making the company that made the game lose money by paying people to patch. … I hate it when I try and play the game for real in public or ranked matches and see a glitch that I found being used as an advantage to somebody else.
>
> (Ryan350 2011)

While chaoticPERFECTION's small team membership enabled them to restrict access to the glitches they discovered, within a larger, more diffuse community such as mapMonkeys it is particularly difficult to maintain secrecy about a glitch or prevent it from being utilized on account of the many community connections, the relative anonymity, and negligible accountability. Beyond this, the recruitment of other glitchers to identify glitches and even the pressures to find them first meant that withholding was a precarious strategy, and many felt it better to benefit immediately from the exploits. As Rezzzo explains:

> I didn't want the glitches I was finding to get out to the public, but the more I thought about it the more I realized it would eventually be found by someone else, so if I were to post it on the website then there would be proof that I was the first to find a glitch.
>
> (Rezzzo 2011)

Ryan350 suggested that despite the positive impacts of releasing a game-breaker, in terms of visibility and reputation chaoticPERFECTION had decided to withhold a number of major glitches in the past and had presented them in a way that would reduce their exploitation by the public. This can be seen in the following example from the *Gears of War 3* beta (2011).

During the three-week pre-release beta period, chaoticPERFECTION identified a number of major glitches and attempted to contact Epic Games to alert it to the issues. chaoticPERFECTION then uploaded a video onto YouTube for the attention of Epic titled "Gears of War 3 Beta Glitches – Can't Reach Ya (Message 2 EPIC GAMES)" (chaoticPERFECTION 2011). The video presented a glitch that enabled the player to levitate into the air and become invulnerable. The introductory voice-over presented the video as assistance for Epic Games and for information only. It also adopted an unusual authoritarian tone, warning the public considering utilizing the glitch.

> This is actually us trying to get a message out to Epic Games. …We don't want what's gonna happen now to happen in the finalised game, also Epic released a notice saying that if you're caught glitching in a match in the beta that you'll be banned and all the retail unlocks that you've earned will be taken away. … This is just a fair warning to those thinking of abusing the information that you're going to receive.
>
> (chaoticPERFECTION 2011)

Unlike conventional glitch videos, there is no tutorial element, but a relatively accustomed *Gears of War* player, and certainly anyone who had used chaoticPERFECTION glitches in the past, would likely be able to repeat the process with a little trial and error. The video implied chaoticPERFEC-TION was working in collaboration with Epic Games, but also placed it in strange relation to the developer's position on glitching. Was it anticipating it would have its accounts banned? Was it assuming its openness would be treated generously? In retrospect, this seems like a miss-step on the part of chaoticPERFECTION but at the time of production, the intent was genuine (chaoticPERFECTION shared the full detail of the glitches with me at the time, with the assurance I would not distribute them further). It also illustrates the apparently contradictory motivation of some glitchers. Unfortunately for chaoticPERFECTION, despite its attempts at placating Epic Games, all of the players visible in the video had their gamertags invalidated on *Gears of War 3*'s commercial release date. Irrespective of withholding or obscuring the means to glitch and any attempts to reach out to Epic Games, they were glitchers and, as prophesized in the video, Epic Games was true to its word.

The relationship between glitchers, the public, and developers is an interesting one. Glitchers appear to glitch for the implicit enjoyment of the act and the reputation and status these acts confer, but their actions also have a secondary value. If a glitch is presented to the public and then adopted, there is the chance (or at least the perception) the glitcher may become recognized by a games developer, a profession many found enormously desirable. It transpired that for many, this was yet another aspect of the motivation to glitch. It was perceived to offer a valuable skill the developers required on account of the evident fallibility of their Quality Assurance testing teams.

> We understand how the testers and developers don't find the stuff we do because they don't look for the stuff in the right way. We work cooperatively while they have solo assigned places and areas and weapons to test. ... It just isn't flexible enough. I think, given the opportunity to work with the developers for a week or so, especially if they are working on a well known game, would be something any glitcher would accept, whether paid or not.
>
> (Ryan350 2011)

The urge to be recognized and potentially recruited by developers appeared to be part of the motivation to become part of a larger institutionalized glitching team or clan, as it could guarantee the skill of members and present a more professional face when interacting with developers – like a recruitment company of a mercenary corporation. This wasn't an entirely unmerited assumption, as a team of professional mapMonkeys glitchers, led by Rezzzo, had already been recruited to do Quality Assurance testing on *Call of Duty: World at War* (2008) and *Modern Warfare 2* (2009), and were in the process of arranging the same for *Modern Warfare 3* while I was part of the mapMonkeys community. Activision was planning to pay for four mapMonkeys glitchers to go to Los Angeles to work from Infinity Ward's studios, and unsurprisingly, there was significant demand from the community to participate. As a result it was necessary to instigate a recruitment process to ensure the spare places went to the most skillful glitchers. This try-out process was a point of significant contention within the mapMonkeys community but reflected common practice within glitching teams and clans, and can be understood as the professionalization of glitching.

To select who would be going to Infinity Ward's studios, mapMonkeys members were asked to nominate the best glitchers, who would be invited to present supporting evidence such as links to recent glitches. Rezzzo and mapMonkey (in this case the name of the site's founding member) would then review the presentations and make the final selections. A week after the submission notices, Rezzzo announced:

> Four members of MapMonkeys are being flown out to California on Sunday, July 10th, to test MW3, including mapMonkey, IM Budd88, skatebin, and myself! We've been flown out to test other games in the past (Such as World at War and Modern Warfare 2), but we only had 2 or 3 days to test the game and find glitches, which wasn't nearly enough time. This time, Infinity Ward is keeping us there an entire week so we can find more bugs and glitches than ever before!
>
> (Rezzzo 2011)

This announcement inevitably caused significant consternation over the selection of team members, with some questioning just how active and prodigious they were, and the extent to which they were considered "true glitchers" and represented the best of mapMonkeys. While this was occurring, popular gaming website Computer and Video Games (CVG) reported mapMonkeys glitchers were going to work on *Modern Warfare 3*, which was then corroborated by Robert Bowling, Infinity Ward's creative strategist:

> These guys focus specifically on exploits that can potentially be used to an unfair advantage. … They're a great addition to an already rigorous Quality Assurance process that the internal team here at Infinity Ward/Sledgehammer and additionally at Activision have been doing since development began.
>
> (Ivan 2011)

The issue here is that glitching is counterplay. It can be destructive and if it became public knowledge, as it did, that glitchers were being recruited for Quality Assurance purposes, poachers turned gatekeepers, hundreds of thousands of willing players would begin rubbing against walls and looking for exploits hoping this would be a golden ticket to their dream careers. For many, the announcement of glitcher recruitment was tacit approval of glitching as a practice, and new members flooded onto the website.

While mapMonkeys' work on the *Call of Duty* franchise is an illustration of where developers might make use of glitchers' skills, this is a rare and perhaps foolish occurrence, and even this example is further contextualized by conflicting attitudes and animosity. Despite utilizing the mapMonkeys team and publicly complimenting their skills, less than three months later, Robert Bowling was forced to strongly denounce both the practice of glitching and those who conduct it as a result of an upsurge of counterplay on the game.

Any attempt to cheat, hack, or glitch in #MW3 will not be tolerated. 1600+ bans issued. ... Every ban unique to the level of douchiness of the offense. The greater the douche the greater the length. PermaDouche possible.

(Bowling 2011a, 2011b)

It is perhaps no surprise then that Infinity Ward's creative strategist announced the company was taking a hard stance when responding to cheaters, hackers, and glitchers, and over "1600 douches (of various levels)" had been banned from the PC, Xbox LIVE, and PlayStation Network game-servers. Bowling was no longer complimenting glitchers but articulating a negative and pejorative attitude. Glitchers are "douches" whose offensive behaviour is anathema to compliant play. As a result they are not to be matter of factly ejected and banned but to be derided and made the subject of a public company tweet. *Modern Warfare 3*'s banning policy states the company takes "action on player behavior that violates the spirit of the game", explicitly defining the separate offenses of glitching, hacking, cheating, boosting, offensive behaviour, and offensive playertags (effectively offensive user-generated-content) as "game abuse", which have a penalty of from forty-eight hours to 5,000 days of banning from the game systems (Activision 2011).

To an observer, this change in stance is so emphatic – from congratulation to censure – that it feels duplicitous or exposes a latent distrust of glitching. This is not particularly surprising, considering the potential damage to reputation and operation, but what is curious is that Activision ever thought it prudent to use the mapMonkeys, a self-identifying glitching group, as Quality Assurance testers. Certainly the Quality Assurance support would have been world class, but at what risk? The announcement is contextualized by a spate of glitches being utilized, perversely, some of which were identified and distributed by mapMonkeys, once again with the perception of game-breakers damaging the game steps needed to be taken. The discourse of pathogen and the humiliation of douchey-glitchers served to reinforce the boundaries of normative play. This illustrates the complex and often contradictory relationships between glitcher and developer, perhaps even more clearly displayed when I raised the sense of duplicity over Activision's change of stance to the mapMonkeys community. Nobody I spoke with recognized this, let alone saw it as an issue.

Instead, there was consensus that bans were necessary to protect the games they loved, and glitches were being abused by the public. Any prior engagement with Infinity Ward was an individual transaction that was unrelated to glitching as fun. The Quality Assurance work was seen as a professional commercial service, like consultancy. Other glitchers reminded me glitching had always been a divisive and objectionable activity, especially when abused, and it was this exploitation by the public, rather than by glitchers, to which the Activision and Infinity Ward messages were attributed. From this perspective it is logical and necessary for the developer to intervene aggressively. This is simply seen as part of the oppositional context of glitching, and inevitably it is this that marks its illicit thrill.

What I found curious was the general passivity of glitchers and the spiralling contradictions in their stance. The majority expressed a deep love or seduction with games as texts. "I myself love the games I glitch in, otherwise I wouldn't be playing them and finding glitches in them" (Rezzzo 2011). By contrast, some admitted to knowing glitchers who held more hostile attitudes to developers as companies but interestingly, not to the games they produced.

> One could love the game and hate the developer. Depending on how the developers react to glitches/glitchers, but also the way that they treat the gaming community. ... This determines feelings towards the developers.
>
> (Rezzzo 2011)

These are precisely the apparently contradictory approaches explored within the biopolitical empire and postmodern approaches to resistance and identity in particular. Other glitchers, who wished to remain anonymous, suggested glitching as a more directly overt and active form of resistant counterplay, arguing "there are some amongst us who dislike a gaming company so much that we will buy the game just to intentionally break it". One of the motivations for this resistance was the statement from David Vonderhaar, Treyarch's game designer director, prior to the release of *Call of Duty: Black Ops*, which once again diminished glitchers in a familiar "douchey" fashion.

> We are disinterested in making mini-celebrities out of douche-bags. You better think twice before you glitch. You never know who in your game doesn't like glitchers who reports you and saves the game in their File Share and tells us about it.
>
> (Vonderhaar in Nicholson 2010)

It transpired that Vonderhaar's statement was interpreted by some as an open challenge and insult to glitchers, who felt sufficiently slighted to motivate retaliation. As a result, I was told, "The company got nailed with hundreds of glitch videos spreading across the internet from campaign glitches to multiplayer glitches and to the famous zombies glitches. They went quiet after that show of force".

This highlights the ambiguous and tenuous relationship between glitcher, developer, and public: the strained relations, respect, and deference. Some glitchers feel motivated to intentionally break games as a statement of ill-defined resistance against a developer, while others fought to assist with Quality Assurance testing on the same franchise. The resistance was not in relation to the limiting nature of the games, Aarseth's tyranny of the game (2007), nor a rejection of its annual mode of production but against a perceived slight and diffuse dislike for a corporation – but not its product? This is most definitely the terrain of postmodern biopower. Others ride rough-shod over modes of consumption, engaging in practices of piracy not through a rejection of the economic model, due to a lack of funds or even a sense of entitlement, but motivated by the need to obtain the game earlier than others, to glitch it first. and release videos before their peers. I was assured there were glitchers who went to these troubles to get pre-release ISOs only to glitch and never play the game conventionally. The pleasures for these glitchers were, as Rezzzo described, a "scavenger hunt" seeking the "shock value of everyone's reaction" (Rezzzo 2011). The ludic quality of the games, their playability or quality, was utterly peripheral. All that mattered was they offered fresh pastures on which to find more glitches.

From such a perspective it is understandable we approach glitching in a reductive way. It is tempting to simply see it as deviant, negative, trivial, hostile behaviour – a fundamentally "douche" activity. Yet this perspective is at odds with the lived experiences of those engaged in glitching and, to some degree, in the values attributed to it by some developers. Despite the negative perception of their activity, many glitchers still spend their time playing video games with the sole aim of exposing, documenting, and sharing game exploits and glitches, yet many more played games conventionally and compliantly in this mode. These activities are motivated by an urge to become closer to the game, to discover more about it, to be seen as being a masterful expert: to somehow contribute to its production, create new game experiences, and also occasionally instigate chaos and watch a game experience fall apart.

Yet while glitching is certainly a counterplay activity – it works against game rules, contexts, and expectations of the player, is antagonistic towards the intended lusory means and prelusory goals, and roles of authorship and consumption – I found it difficult to trace a substantive thread of resistance or direct opposition when talking to glitchers. In fact, far from seeing attempts to undermine and challenge games as in counter-mobilization, even in the face of developer ridicule and douchiness, glitchers appeared seduced by the games rather than in opposition to them. The game is broken out of love. The developers might be resisted out of defence for the product or an expectation that finding flaws in their games is secretly appreciated, and destructive practices are distributed just to elicit recognition from the thing they love. Once again, contradiction and ambiguity are rife. However, there were also cases where glitchers seemed to believe the same rules simply did not apply to them, such as was seen with chaoticPERFECTION's attempts to engage with Epic Games. It was so convinced of the value of its practices that it was shocked and disappointed when Epic Games remained true to its word and did what it always said it would. It appears to me that in the noise and excitement of glitching, in the urgent energy that drives glitchers to be the very first to find the next glitch, rules and boundaries fade away, becoming less pressing besides the illicit tingle as they are broken. This is not necessarily done out of overt resistance but out of something that resonates more with the discourses of identity, mastery, and, every now and then, carnival.

Glitching, much like grief-play, easily fits into the discourse of pathogen. It has the capacity to significantly undermine game-play, particularly with the widespread introduction of game-breakers such as the Javelin glitch. However, while the Javelin is an important example of the radical potential of a glitch, and one that has received public attention, this chapter illustrates that glitching is a practice that offers a far greater range of outputs than game-breakers. What might be a more balanced way of approaching the acts is that the abuse of glitches, their over-use, is the thing that determines the pathogenic aspect of the glitch. However, the public and developers/publishers are unlikely to be able to make this distinction, nor are they particularly concerned to do so. The point is that some glitching activity can be significantly damaging to a game. It also became apparent that glitchers were generally oblivious to the pejorative language and negative way in which they were perceived by the general playerbase, or directly oppositional to that reading, arguing that people, members of the public, were highly receptive to glitches, although they cared little for who had originally discovered them. Instead of resistance, glitching appears to be an implicitly enjoyable process, an utilization of the space as opposed to an act invoked to change the order of things.

Much like grief-play, mastery seems to be a significant discourse for the glitcher. The process of glitching is one of seeking out the occasions in which the game can be temporarily mastered or the power-structures temporarily inverted. Yet outside the identification of the glitches that allow some degree of mastery, the glitcher is hedged in by rules and often deeply observant of them. This is also illustrated in their deference to the game developers, their preparedness to share and collaborate under the assumption the inversions they expose will be fleeting and eventually patched. Despite the initial reading that the glitcher becomes the master of the game, this is hard to support. They are so constricted by the repercussions of their activities and so seduced by the games themselves that their activities might at best be thought of as temporary diversions.

Yet the pleasure of the glitch discovery revolves around the moments when the prevailing order is suddenly subverted, the testing of thousands of interactions over hours of play that result in an anomalous outcome. What this says to the glitcher is that the authority of the space has shifted on some level and for a while that glitcher understands more about the game than even those who created it. The relationship between the dominant and subordinate has altered. This is mastery with a small m, mastery as expertise. In addition, the relationship to game production articulates mastery. The glitcher is more masterful than the Quality Assurance tester but they remain deferent to the developer. Instead of claiming superiority to the creators of the game, the majority of glitchers I spoke to articulated a yearning to be viewed as peers and hoped to enter the industry in some capacity. In these instances the display of mastery takes on the role of a resumé or curriculum vitae. There is an assumption – actually a desire – for the glitches to be patched and order to be reinstated. This is recognition that fuels further glitching and reinvigorates the act.

In terms of identity, the glitcher asserts technicity that offers both identity and status. They demonstrate expertise within the game, which distinguishes them from the public in their ability to find glitches and to use them sparingly, and if glitchers eventually deploy these glitches, they are once more differentiated by their new strategies. The demand to demonstrate authentic modes of glitching expertise and to display dominance of the game and other glitchers can be so compelling that some are prepared to subvert the glitching norms, such as through the use of ISO downloads to break release dates. This, though, is carefully hidden lest it impact on the developing identity of the arch glitcher. For some, the implicit pleasures of the glitch are subordinate to the status associated with being first to a glitch, but unlike grief-play, the creation of identity is largely related to the community of glitchers and, by extension, developers as opposed to members of the public.

The released glitch has an implicit pleasure associated with its discovery, has varying levels of pleasure associated with its utility, and confers status on the glitcher. From its release it becomes a vicarious pleasure, where the glitcher watches how the glitch performs, mutates, and what impact this eventually has on the game. Through this process the glitcher is able to develop aspects of identity that some found even more pertinent: the configuration as a professional glitcher, generating subscriptions and income through YouTube or perhaps leading to recruitment in a team or the ability to enter video-games development in some capacity.

Glitching resonates strongly with the discourse of the carnivalesque. Aside from the identity-formation aspects of technicity deployed by those identifying the glitches, their release within public channels results in glitch adoption by conventional players and glitch abuse. In this sense, the release of a glitch is an egalitarian invitation to misrule, and as the glitch is developed, repurposed, and appropriated by other players, its ownership shifts to the collective, anonymous mass of the public. Glitches have the capacity to offer a range of outcomes, from novelty trough to the utilitarian domination of a game-breaker, but they are utilized without restriction. Players use them as they wish and against whom they wish and as such, they share the universal antagonism of the carnival. The glitch becomes a gift to the baying crowd, who utilize it as they wish.

What is particularly interesting to me is the extent to which glitchers appear deferent to the game developers and the degree to which they institutionalise (form teams) and professionalise (adopt branding strategies), in order to interact and work in games development. Glitching is seen as a means of entering the industry or, for some, is done out of resignation.

Unsure or separated from means to enter the video-game industry, they interact with games as if they were already within it. This is seen particularly with the formation of glitching teams and the high-quality videos in chaoticPERFECTION. It is perhaps worth adding that Ryan350 of chaotic-PERFECTION was eventually recruited as a permanent Quality Assurance role at Respawn Games, working extensively on the development of *Titanfall* (2014) and featuring quite often with his mohawk during E3 press coverage and in Xbox One promotional videos. For Ryan350 this was a dream come true and testament to his hard work and dedication, but his story, and the other voices traced through this chapter, challenge the conventional pathogenic reading of the glitcher as simply attempting to break the game to ruin play. Instead, this breaking of the game is an expression of a seduction with the text and the entire milieu. This is counterplay motivated by love.

GAMEOGRAPHY

Battlefield 3. 2011. Electronic Arts. EA Digital Illusions CE.
Battlefield Bad Company 2. 2010. Electronic Arts. EA Digital Illusions CE.
Bulletstorm. 2011. Electronic Arts. Epic Games.
Call of Duty: Advanced Warfare. 2014. Activision. Sledgehammer Games.
Call of Duty: Black Ops. 2010. Activision. Treyarch.
Call of Duty: Black Ops 2. 2012. Activision. Treyarch.
Call of Duty: Black Ops Rezurrection. 2011. Activision. Treyarch.
Call of Duty: Ghosts. 2013. Activision. Sledgehammer Games.
Call of Duty: Modern Warfare. 2007. Activision. Infinity Ward.
Call of Duty: Modern Warfare 2. 2009. Activision. Infinity Ward.
Call of Duty: Modern Warfare 3. 2011. Activision. Infinity Ward / Sledgehammer Games.
Call of Duty: World at War. 2008. Activision. Treyarch.
Destiny. 2014. Activision. Bungie.
Duke Nukem Forever. 2011. 2K Games. Gearbox Software.
Elder Scrolls IV: Oblivion. 2006. ZeniMax Media. Bethesda Softworks.
Elder Scrolls V: Skyrim. 2011. ZeniMax Media. Bethesda Softworks.
Gears of War. 2006. Microsoft Studios. Epic Games.
Gears of War 3. 2011. Microsoft Studios. Epic Games.
Homefront. 2011. THQ. Kaos Studios.
Titanfall. 2014. Electronic Arts. Respawn Entertainment.

REFERENCES

Aarseth, E. 2007. "I Fought the Law: Transgressive Play and The Implied Player." *Situated Play, Proceedings of DiGRA 2007 Conference*, 130–133.
Boosters Hotline, The. 2008–2014. http://bhlgaming.com/. Accessed November 28, 2014.
Booster Busters. 2014. https://www.youtube.com/user/XboosterBustersX. Accessed December 1, 2014.

Bowling, R. 2011a. @fourtwozero. https://twitter.com/fourzerotwo/status/137327656420122624. Accessed November 20, 2012.

Bowling, R. 2011b. @fourtwozero. http://twitter.com/#!/fourzerotwo/status/137733006310903809. Accessed November 20, 2012.

Candyslexia. 2014. Ghosts online code of conduct. http://community.callofduty.com/thread/200790395. Accessed December 3, 2014.

Campbell, C. 2014. "Activision declares war on 'cheating and unfair exploits.'" YouTube. http://www.polygon.com/2014/11/24/7276911/activision-declares-war-on-cheating-and-unfair-exploits-youtube-videos. Accessed December 3, 2014.

chaoticPERFECTION. 2006–2014. http://www.chaoticPERFECTION.info. Accessed November 17, 2014.

chaoticPERFECTION. 2011. *Gears of War 3 Beta Glitches – Can't Reach Ya.* Message 2 EPIC GAMES. https://www.youtube.com/watch?v=LDtVyM484H0. Accessed February 6, 2012.

Destiny Dev Team. 2014a. Destiny Dev Notes. http://www.bungie.net/7_Destiny-Dev-Notes/en/News/News?aid=12188. Accessed September 27, 2014.

Destiny Dev Team. 2014b. Hot Fix – 09/25/2014. http://www.bungie.net/7_Hot-Fix—09252014/en/News/News?aid=12190. Accessed September 30, 2014.

Ivan, T. 2011. *Infinity Ward talks up 'rigorous' Modern Warfare 3 QA process.* Available at: http://www.computerandvideogames.com/311399/infinity-ward-talks-up-rigorous-modern-warfare-3-qa-process/. Accessed July 2, 2012.

mapMonkeys. 2006–2012. http://www.mapmonkeys.com. Accessed September 3, 2012.

Metal Ninja Cake. 2009. Activision Community Forums. http://community.activision.com/message/203217684?tstart=0. Accessed November 10, 2012.

Nicholson, B. 2010. "Treyarch Says You Should Think Twice Before You Glitch In Black Ops." http://www.giantbomb.com/call-of-duty-black-ops/3030-26423/forums/treyarch-says-you-should-think-twice-before-you-gl-465541/. Accessed November 5, 2012.

Stuart, K. 2012. "Schafer's Millions." http://www.hookshotinc.com/interview-schafers-millions/. Accessed October 28, 2012.

5   Hardware-Hacking

So far we have touched on a range of counterplay activities, defined by their violation of rule or edict, but as appears to be becoming apparent, not necessarily an expressly antagonistic approach to rules or the systems of production and consumption. What's more, we have explored situations, notably Ocelot's discussion of lag-switch usage, Zakhaev's deployment of derank lobbies, and the implied glitcher utilization of game ISOs, which allude to the fact that sometimes players alter the hardware on which they play in order to engage in counterplay. However, when certain changes are made to video-game-related hardware, such as game consoles, these acts constitute violation of law. Counterplay in these circumstances goes beyond the offensive, the unfair, and transgressive into the territory of criminal acts.

This book generally uses console-based video games as its context, and these hardware systems can be considered closed, never intended to be widely upgraded or serviced by the user but also closed in the sense the majority of the system processes, and by extension network connections, are hidden from the user and should remain under the full control of the platform holders and developers. This means that for those interested in altering or changing what occurs on and within these systems, they must first open them up and overcome any restrictions that are built into them. This kind of hardware modification can take many forms, including utterly benign and licit hardware changes such as sticking self-adhesive crosshair stickers onto a television to increase from-the-hip firing accuracy on a first-person shooter, the installation of longer controller thumb sticks to allow for greater accuracy of movement, the cosmetic installation of the ubiquitous blue neon LEDs into console hardware, through to the addition of extra autofire buttons on a controller. Beyond this are the more problematic forms, from the interruption of network traffic through lag switches to the full-scale alteration and replacement of console components to overcome copyright protection and allow software that lacks authentic verification details from the platform-holder to be executed.

While hardware-hacking is an interesting and loaded practice, in itself it plays an important role within the manifestation of other counterplay forms, primarily illicit modding but, as we have already seen as a corollary, in grief-play and glitching. It is a facilitating counterplay process in terms of how it enables other counterplay forms to take place, but as a result of this, it is subject to strong restriction and censure. What follows is a brief overview of console hardware-hacking, its key manifestations on the Xbox 360, and the social structures and practices that have formed around it. Ultimately the aim of this relatively short chapter is to present hardware-hacking as a discreet counterplay practice, with its own legacy, significance, and motivations, but also to then allow us to explore the other practices it enables, such as illicit modding.

My experiences with hacked hardware began while I was playing *Call of Duty: World at War* on the Xbox 360 in early December 2008. I'd contracted the flu and had been ordered to bed. Not missing the opportunity, I set up a console in my room, had plenty of medicated lemon drinks ready, and began to play the multiplayer in earnest. On the Courtyard map, based in the grounds of Shuri Castle, Okinawa, which slowly smoulders in the distance, I found myself repeatedly devoured by attack dogs and every time I'd encounter one player, they would kill me. It wasn't especially notable that I was being beaten at the game, more so in my weakened state, but what was conspicuous was that it was the same opponent and despite us both having the same weapon, a Gewehr 43 semi-automatic rifle, I'd rapidly mash the trigger, taking about ten seconds to empty the magazine, while my opponent would do the same in about two seconds. It was not that I was being dominated, but how it was taking place that bothered me.

I continued to play as my opponent ended up at the top of the match leaderboards time and time again. When I was finally certain something was amiss, I sent a message to my foe asking how it was done. He eventually left the game, but twenty minutes later I received a response: "It's a modded controller. You should get one noob. LOL".

And so it began. I started looking for ways to modify Xbox 360 controllers, opening them up and adding new resistors and switches, and found many. While there were a number of companies that offered willing customers off-the-peg modified controllers, such as Evil Controllers, there were many guides that explained how to do the same yourself. Evil Controllers boast they create "controllers with gameplay enhancements" but also modify controllers to make video games more accessible for those with limited mobility (Evil Controllers 2014a). They sell a range of controllers specifically for *Call of Duty* multiplayer, including the $150 "master mod" version that includes "rapid fire, adjustable rapid fire, auto scope, auto run, quick knife, drop shot, fast reload, left-trigger rapid fire, and auto aim" enhancements (Evil Controllers 2014a). These controllers consist of Xbox 360 and PlayStation 3 controllers that have new PCBs and switches added to them to automate certain functions, such as automatically triggering the prone button after a jump, as used by Finalkilla in the successful *Resurrection* glitch. This is normally a relatively unnatural movement on the controller, requiring dexterity and practice, but one that significantly reduces the size of the player from an opponent's perspective and thus makes them much less likely to hit. Some of the existing buttons have new functionality added to them while new buttons are added to the controller, such as a separate auto-fire switch.

These kind of modified controllers are designed with specific games in mind, the *Call of Duty* franchise in particular, and represent an entrepreneurial approach in which companies assist players to meet the expectations of appropriate play – for a profit. Companies such as Evil Controllers simply respond to customer demand and create unapproved peripherals that offer advantage. It should be noted that as the controllers are not subject to any technological security countermeasures (bar the shape of the screws that hold the shell together) and the act of creating a modified controller does not violate the DMCA, Evil Controllers can be regarded as yet another third-party peripheral manufacturer the products of which have a compelling selling point.

Beyond the rapid-fire modifications, Evil Controllers also offer a gamut of hardware modifications that sit within the rule of copyright law. For $4.99 you can buy smaller, convex-topped Evil-Sticks or, for $9.99, a customer can purchase a set of Evil Scope stickers, "placed on to the center of your television screen. The Evil Scope will assist your aim and give you deadly accuracy without having to pull on the Left Trigger. ... This is a ridiculous advantage" (Evil Controllers 2014c).

However, for those unwilling to pay $150 for the advantage service there are many websites that offer comprehensive guides, including Se7ensins. com, TheTechGame.com, or Nextgenupdate.com. These three websites are pivotal to counterplay practices on the Xbox 360 and PlayStation 3 and will be discussed repeatedly in this chapter and the next. These sites also to some degree support grief-play, glitching, hardware-hacking, and illicit modding. What's more, these sites, being primarily gaming fan sites and platforms as opposed to selling products, are much more able to drift beyond the legal and into the illicit or, rather, they are able to distance themselves from the occasionally illicit actions of their members. It is here that we find instructions to conduct our own rapid-fire controller hacks – I attempted two, but despite only requiring a few components, both failed on account of my poor soldering skills – but also lag switches and, if we look closely, details about hacked consoles and modding frameworks. These latter examples are more interesting for a discussion of counterplay because they constitute the facilitating technologies and are in violation of either the DMCA and computer-misuse acts. While difficult to detect, the use of lag switches could be considered an intentional interruption of service data at the client end, while the hacked console expressly violates and circumvents successful technological security measures. These are counterplay through not just their oppositional attitude towards play or the rules they violate but against the law.

While a modded controller introduces new components to an existing peripheral, a lag switch is built from a stretch of CAT-5 networking cable and a normally closed push switch. The network cable is spliced and connected through the push switch and then, when connected into the console, all the player need do is depress the switch with their foot for a second or so in order to temporarily interrupt their connection with the game-servers. Games, designed to be resilient towards momentary networking errors, make predictions of the whereabouts of the player until the network communication recommences and the location of the player is synchronized. Providing the player uses the lag switch judiciously and is aware of any individual settings that control the duration of dropped communications until the player is kicked from the game, they can travel across game-spaces without being seen or touched by their foes. In a competitive multiplayer game, a lag switch, a modified controller, and even a little sticker on the television offer incremental advantage, and these mean the player has more strategies at their disposal and are more likely to win.

This was what I was up against when I was sitting in my room with the flu. I was playing against counterplayers who were deploying hardware modifications and it was dispiriting stuff. But while hardware hacks that alter the peripherals and systems the consoles connect to are certainly unfair and confer advantage to the user, it is the hacks done to the console platforms themselves that are truly protean and pave the way for a range of interesting and highly illicit counterplay activities.

HACKING CONSOLES

Generally speaking, console hardware-hacking can be understood as the circumvention of security functions on the video-game hardware, allowing users to execute unsigned software code including pirated game ISO files, "homebrew" applications, and edited instances of commercial releases. While each of these activities is relatively easy to do on an open platform such as a regular Windows PC (as opposed to a predominantly closed Apple Mac I'm writing this on), on an intentionally closed video-games console the same activities necessitate not just the alteration of code but negation and/ or circumvention of inbuilt hardware restrictions. Both the Xbox 360 and PlayStation 3 have been subject to the perpetual development of hardware-hacking processes since their launch, and this has been one of the most contentious and damaging counterplay dynamics within this generation of gaming platform.

In late 2010, the PlayStation 3 was subject to the development and public release of a "private key" package that, if used correctly, enabled the calculation of the security passcode that policed the execution of software on the system, in effect presenting a digital skeleton key and turning the PlayStation 3 into a genuinely open system (Chaos Computer Club 2010).

In the closing days of 2010, in a modernist conference centre a stone's throw from Alexanderplatz, Berlin, the Chaos Communication Congress was underway. For those unfamiliar with the hacking and technological counterculture event, the Chaos Communication Congress focuses specifically on the sophisticated alternative uses of computing technology, including hardware, software, and network hacking. The event, running since 1984, attracts thousands of artists, hackers, computer scientists, and technologists each year, and is considered the pre-eminent conference for novel and counter-cultural uses of technology in Europe. At the 2010 event, a hacking group known as Fail0verflow took the stage to present what it billed as a "PlayStation 3 epic fail". What they presented was instrumental in the circumvention of the PlayStation 3 security measures and its opening up as a system.

> We promised epic fail so ... we've got a private key without even having to know most of the curve parameters or anything. ... These signatures are every bit as valid as Sony's official signatures, they are indistinguishable. ... They botched their public key crypto so that's epic fail ... pretty much botched the entire thing.
>
> (Fail0verflow 2010)

Fail0verflow, one of many hardware-hacking groups at the event, had identified a way to obtain the private key – the other half of encryption hidden somewhere in the PlayStation 3 that authorized the execution of code – without having to physically open the system or interrogate its parts. It had found a weakness in Sony's security system and as a result had opened the system up for alternate usage. At this point, the private key wasn't able to execute game code, but another hacker, George Hotz, known as Geohot, and famous for developing the iPhone jailbreak process in 2007, utilized Fail0verflow's discoveries to complete a PlayStation 3 jailbreak he had abandoned earlier in 2010. By combining his process and that of Fail0verflow, Geohot created a package that could enable any interested individual to jail break their PlayStation 3, allowing it to run unsigned code including pirated and homebrew applications. In early January 2011, Geohot posted the method and related files onto his website and they were rapidly and widely adopted. Simultaneously, another hardware hacker, Graf_Chokolo, released a software package that reinstated the OtherOS feature Sony had removed from the PlayStation 3 after release, which had allowed previously owners to install operating systems such as Linux on their Sony consoles.

Following the releases by Fail0verflow, Geohot, and Graf_Chokolo, Sony instigated a number of punitive measures. On January 11, 2011 a court order was filed against Geohot, Fail0verflow members, and other hardware hackers under violation of the DMCA and computer fraud, and on February 23, 2011, Graf_Chokolo's German home was raided by police, who seized all his hacking-related equipment and data. Subsequently Graf_Chokolo released all of his hacking work to the public domain, which had been stored on remote servers, likely violating the terms of the police investigation and escalating the severity of the case against him. In addition, Sony forced Internet Service Providers to disclose the details of individuals who had accessed and downloaded the private root-key package from a number of websites.

The release of the PlayStation 3 private key enabled users to open their consoles by copying data onto a USB drive and connecting it to the system. Sony patched out the vulnerability through a major security update released on March10, 2011. However, ever since there have been occasional developments of new jail breaks that utilize the same general process, such as the release of the JB2/TrueBlue dongle in October 2011 and the LV0 key exploit by "The Three Tuskateers" in October 2012. It appears to be the case that once any closed computing platform becomes established within the market, attempts are made to eventually force open the system with jail-breaking hacks.

While the immediate effects of Sony jail-break hacks were hugely problematic, one assumes leading to a profusion of the use of copied game code and unauthorized software on their systems and jeopardizing their business model, what became more of an issue was the way in which hackers and hactivist groups responded to their legal injunctions against Geohot and Graf_Chokolo and the demands for web-user data. On April 4, 2011, Anonymous, a loosely associated network of hacktivist and activist entities, posted the following message to Sony on AnonNews.org, its central communication point.

> You now have now received the undivided attention of Anonymous. Your recent legal action against our fellow hackers, Geohot and Graf_ Chokolo, has not only alarmed us, it has been deemed wholly unforgivable. You have now abused the judicial system in an attempt to censor information on how your products work. You have victimised your own customers merely for possessing and sharing information, and continue to target every person who seeks this information. In doing so you have violated the privacy of thousands. ... The very same information you wish to suppress for sake of corporate greed and complete control of the users.
>
> (Anonops 2011)

This announced the beginning of Opsony, in which Anonymous would do whatever it could to disrupt and undermine Sony's potential to operate. Opsony took the form of a number of high-profile Distributed-Denial-of-Service attacks and database hacks, both crimes under the UK Computer Misuse Act, resulting in user-data breaches, including passwords and credit-card information. Inevitably the attacks exposed the vulnerability of Sony's network and systems, resulting in criminal elements joining the attacks in order to capitalize on the credit-card data. Due to the urgent need to protect users, Sony began to isolate services and turn off systems. Eventually Sony suspended its entire PlayStation network gaming and transaction system globally, and nobody could play online while Sony frantically developed new security countermeasures. The service remained off for twenty-four days in the US and Europe, and for seventy-seven days in Japan. This meant more than fifty million PlayStation network accounts unable to access the system, resulting in an estimated $171-million of direct damages and lost revenue for the company and its affiliates in the US alone (Schreier 2011). As a result, Sony's stock price tumbled twenty-two percent from 31.42 on April 4 to 24.28 on June 20 (Yahoo Finance 2011). The intrusions between April 26 and May 2, 2011 resulted in the breach of 101.6 million users' data, including my own (Yau 2011). While the assumption is the majority of those who make use of hacked consoles do so to obtain games without having to pay for them, modify games, and attempt to generate income through offering access to new experiences and services, the associated activities result in major financial loss and disruption to video-game services.

Opsony illustrated the vulnerability of video-game-related servers and the potential availability of valuable credit-card data. Following this, a large number of other video-game platform-holders and developers were targeted. Although this was not done under the aegis of Opsony, it can be indirectly linked nonetheless. Following the Sony attacks, Nintendo (Osawa 2011), Codemasters (Porter 2011), Epic Games (Sweeney 2011), Bethesda Softworks (Gstaff 2011), Microsoft (Plunkett 2011), Bioware (Pakinkis 2011), *Eve Online, Minecraft*, and *League of Legends* (Gaston, 2011), and others were subject to attacks and/or data breaches. Whether conducted by criminals sensing lucrative targets or as a genuine rebellion by players is impossible to ascertain. Perhaps it is best to simply say that hacking and system attacks have become part of the lexicon of counterplay, part of oppositional gaming culture.

THE ORIGINS OF HACKING

While the gaming technologies and services being hacked are relatively new, hacking as a computing-related concept has existed for nearly fifty years. Steven Levy (2001) is considered the most reliable chronicler of the emergent or early days of hacking. Centering on the activities of MIT's Tech Model Railroad Club, Levy details the ways in which elegant or sophisticated technological hacks ostensibly used to increase the functionality of model railway dioramas and received considerable kudos from the other members of the group. Over time this objectification and appreciation of elegant technological innovation created a culture in which hacking as an activity became revered and hackers jockeyed for status within a group.

Hacking at MIT became closely associated with other forms of technological disobedience including phone-phreaking and pranks, both of which were activities central to American university culture. Slowly, hacking developed as a discreet practice describing the use of a range of technologies including phone networks, computer hardware, electronics, and an ideology that prioritized access to information as a way to justify transgression. This eventually became understood as hacker ethics.

- All information should be free;
- Mistrust Authority – Promote Decentralization;
- Hackers should be judged by their hacking, not bogus criteria such as degrees, age, race, or position;
- You can create art and beauty on a computer;
- Computers can change your life for the better. (Levy 2001, 40–45)

Paul Taylor suggests these ethics prioritized and emphasized three qualities of the hack:

- Simplicity: the act has to be simple but impressive;
- Mastery: the act involves sophisticated technical knowledge;
- Illicitness: the act is "against the rules". (Taylor 1999, 15)

However, the hands-on imperative and the distrust for authority, twinned with a competitive dynamic, motivated diverse interpretations of what was appropriate. Invariably some hackers sought out their pleasures in ways that violated the law, especially as computing became a more overtly commercial discipline. Manufacturers started to produce closed systems and intellectual-property laws were more aggressively defended. As Taylor succinctly puts it, "The main bone of contention in these differing interpretations is the extent to which the ingenuity of the hack should be made subordinate to its legality" (Taylor 1999, 15). The hardware hacks of Fail0verflow, Geohot, Graf_Chokolo, or indeed Tmbnc are demonstrably interpretations in which the ingenuity of the hack takes dominance and, as a result, these hackers find themselves at odds with the legal contexts of consumption and play. Yet once more we should show restraint, unless we assume these hacks were developed in direct opposition to the game systems. Instead we should consider they come from a genuine interest in the hardware as platforms and the potential they offer. In addition to individuals who develop the hacks, there are many others who wish to use them or see opportunities for their creation and distribution, not entirely dissimilar to Evil Controller's cornering of the hacked peripheral market but expressly within the realms of illegality.

In late September 2014, a team of hackers known as the Xbox Underground was found guilty of a range of violations related to hardware-hacking and network attacks against video-game developers. The group's exploits included accusation of the theft of:

> … more than $100-million in intellectual property and other proprietary data. Two of the charged members have already pleaded guilty. The alleged cyber theft included software and data related to the

Xbox One gaming console and Xbox LIVE online gaming system ... a pre-release version of Epic's video game, "Gears of War 3;" and a pre-release version of Activision's video game, "Call of Duty: Modern Warfare 3." The defendants also allegedly conspired to use, share and sell the stolen information.

(US Department of Justice 2014)

The DMCA and European Directive 2001/29/EC that protect copyright, and the UK Computer Misuse Act and the US Computer Fraud and Abuse Act, if interpreted to the letter, may result in five years incarceration per offense. To offer some indication of the kind of potential sentences associated with hackers, Hector Xavier Monsegur, known as Sabu and one of the leaders of Lulzsec who piggy-backed onto the OpSony attacks, was sentenced for attacks on more than 250 public and private entities. According to official guidelines, he had been facing more than twenty-six years' imprisonment. However, due to radical co-operation with the FBI working as a federal informant, this was reduced to seven months incarceration and a year's supervised release (Pilkington 2014). This brief discussion of the legal restrictions of counterplay offers greater context to the counterplay acts this study explores, and in turn exposes that very few of the counterplayers are aware of the full risks and implications that bind their counterplay.

An illustration of the potential implications of such violation can be seen in the 2009 case of Matthew Crippen, an American student who was accused of violating the DMCA on two counts as the result of being caught on covert video while performing Xbox 360 hacks for $60. The USA vs. Crippen case represents the first time a DMCA violation related to video-game hacking has reached a court of law, with the accused facing a penalty of up to five years' imprisonment for each violation. This case served as a crucial test case, defining the literal interpretation of the DMCA in relation to hardware-hacking. Fortunately for Crippen, the prosecution abandoned the indictment "based on fairness and justice" (Kravets 2010), after it became known the evidence had been obtained illegally. The case failed not because Crippen was found innocent but because the specifics of the evidence precluded a fair trial. Despite the implicit risk, there are many who are prepared to sell and buy hacked consoles.

Despite their major impact on the operation of video-game platforms, hardware hacks have received relatively little scholarly attention. Those that have explored this territory include Greg Lastowka, who offers a comprehensive exploration of the legal contexts of video-game-hacking (Lastowka 2010, 144–166), Mirko Schäfer, who discusses the development of mod-chips and the creation of the Xbox Media Centre (XBMC) software hack that circumvented security protection on the original Xbox (Schäfer 2011, 83–94), and Andrew "Bunnie" Huang's *Hacking the Xbox: An Introduction to Reverse Engineering* that offers a hacker's-eye view of the same development (Huang 2003). Many justify the use of hardware hacks to open systems as a means of utilizing and developing homebrew software, which is seen as non-parasitical on the financial operation of the video-games industry. The suggestion is that a hacker purchases the console legitimately but then uses it in a way that does not affect its original context of use. The hacked console is taken out of the gaming ecosystem and becomes used for homebrew. In turn, its use is read as a breach of copyright under the fair-use defence, for intellectual, academic, or transformative purposes. The issue here is the hacked console has the capacity to still be used in ways that have bearing on the expected context of consumption, such as allowing users to play pirated game ISOs, to alter commercial code, or, with a bit of research and development, to connect the hacked system to multiplayer servers and affect the experience of other players.

Hardware hacking and illicit modding are overlapping practices, and the websites and communities that focus on them reflect this. There are two general types of website: those that predominantly focus on hardware hacking such as XboxHacker.org (2006–2012) and Free60.org (2006–2014), and those that focus on the use of hardware hacks to produce illicit game modifications such as TheTechGame.com (2009–2014), NextGenUpdate.com (2008–2014), and Se7ensins.com (2010–2014). While the distinction is not entirely discreet – for example, the XboxHacker.org forum has threads discussing game modifications and NextGenUpdate.com includes comprehensive instructions on how to perform hardware hacks – the motivation and focus for each category of site are different. The former is preoccupied with the opening up of game consoles as systems while the latter is concerned with the opening up and alteration of games and systems as structures.

AN INTRODUCTION TO XBOX 360 HARDWARE-HACKING

Currently there are three core modified Xbox 360 consoles: the JTAG, the RGH (Reset Glitch Hack), and the Flashed Console. Each represents a different technique for the creation of open devices from the closed Xbox 360, which is essentially a heavily restricted, inexpensive personal computer. The move towards the sale of closed devices by manufacturers, making use of many levels of black-boxing obscurification, and the efforts of hackers to open these systems can be seen as a particular example of contemporary dynamics in consumption and the contestation of ownership and use. Seen within the context of the legal (in the US) act of jail-breaking and opening of the Apple iPhone, the modification of Xbox 360 consoles into JTAGs, RGHs, and Flashed Consoles shares the same emotive justifications and compelling arguments about piracy and misuse. The following section will contextualize some of these practices by exploring the background of the three hardware hacks and the practices they enable. Following this, we will explore specific instances of their use on a range of video games for a number of purposes.

JTAGs and RGHs are based around the same kind of hack: a circumvention of the security checks that ensure an Xbox 360 is executing software from an appropriate Microsoft-verified game disc or software source such as a game demo file downloaded from Xbox LIVE. The core difference between the two systems is that the JTAG utilizes a small number of rudimentary components soldered directly onto the Xbox 360 circuit board. However, when the vulnerabilities that it exploited were eventually removed through hardware manufacturing revisions, an alternate method of invoking the same hack was necessary. This was eventually discovered through using a reset glitch, where small electrical pulses are sent to the Xbox 360's processor. These pulses partially reset the CPU or rather, reset the security processes, enabling the hack to be conducted. The RGH console, as it became known, is then reliant on the addition of a small micro-controller (called a Coolrunner board) that piggybacks on the chip and provides the necessary reset pulses. Both the JTAG and RGH allow the execution of unsigned code and therefore simply enable the same versatile functionality through different methods.

In contrast, the Flashed Console also requires a modification but this is only to the disc drive built into the Xbox 360. Once hacked, the drive provides a false positive to disc media checks that look for the special markers of a legitimate Microsoft disc. As a result of its lack of versatility, the Flashed Console is generally only used for video-game piracy, often hidden under the aegis of enabling game backups i.e. copied game disc ISO files. While the Flashed Console can facilitate some modification of game data, its lack of versatility makes this largely untenable.

In contrast, the JTAG and RGH consoles are capable of running any correctly compiled software and therefore represent a radical and versatile opening up of the system. They can be used to execute pirated code from any source, they are able to execute code that has had its contents altered, irrespective of the file size, and can be used to executed bogus game patches and updates. The JTAG and RGH therefore facilitate total modification of game code. They are platforms that, in addition to piracy, facilitate extensive video-game modding and the use of alternate software.

ORIGINS OF XBOX HACKS

The Xbox 360 JTAG and RGH hardware hacks originated from two communities: XboxHacker.org, which served as the discussion point and developmental locus for hardware exploitation and hacking; and Free60.org, which documented and presented the finalized hacks and modifications. The hacks were initially developed "towards porting GNU/Linux, BSD, Darwin and related open-source operating systems to the Microsoft Xbox 360 video game console" – essentially attempting to use the Xbox 360 as an inexpensive Linux computer (Free60.org 2012). While this aim was achieved with relative ease, the opening of the system and circumvention of security it necessitated enabled other less noble uses for the platform, notably piracy and the creation of illicit game modifications. The hacks were initially instigated along the lines of the hands-on imperative, where infraction was rationalized as a learning process. Simultaneously, the sites that supported the Linux project became attractive to those wishing to utilize the hacks for entrepreneurial purposes, as a method of saving money, and, as we shall see, making money.

The Xbox 360 hacks were developed by the communities who had successfully produced the 2003 Xbox Media Centre (XBMC) hack and software for Microsoft's original Xbox, which turned the console into a powerful "open source (GPL) software media player and entertainment hub" (XBMC 2012). Since the original Xbox, like its successor, was a closed device, the act of developing the XBMC necessitated the opening and deciphering of the console hardware and software, a process extensively documented by Huang (2003). Huang, who was part of the XBMC team, argued the very motivation for developing the XBMC was the "unbreakable monopoly over computer hardware and software" that the closed system represented (2003, 9) and this stance justified the process of deconstruction, architecture-deciphering, security circumvention, reverse-engineering, and eventual homebrew development. It was precisely this process that the Free60.org and XboxHacker.org members were keen to replicate on the Xbox 360.

Following the release of the Xbox 360, the XBMC team attempted to do this, building on expertise obtained with the development of the original Xbox, which was facilitated through the creation of the Free60.org wiki, and the repurposing of the XboxHacker forum for the development of Xbox 360 hacks. The public discussion and development of the exploits eventually led to the JTAG and RGH and enabled others than those wishing to port Linux to the system to join and utilize the modifications. It is this egalitarian and open nature of the development cycle that enabled their illicit uses.

FROM PETER JACKSON'S KING KONG TO JTAG

In late 2006, Free60.org and XboxHacker.com members identified the Xbox 360 version of *Peter Jackson's King Kong* (2005) contained an exploitable susceptibility that could enable other applications to be executed from within the game. This was swiftly adopted to execute a recompiled version of Linux known as the Xenon Linux Loader (XELL), achieving the core aims of Free60.org and receiving extensive plaudits from the hacking communities. The King Kong hack, or SMC hack, as it became known, represented the first major circumvention of Xbox 360 security. However it required the use of a King Kong game disc to execute new code. Despite the fact this achieved the core aims of Free60.org, there was the need to develop and synthesize the hack into a more stable variant that would not be dependent on a game disc.

Following the publication of the SMC hack, Microsoft introduced hardware and software revisions to overcome the vulnerability, patching it by early 2007. The SMC hack had proved memory address-based exploits were viable on the system and indicated ways in which the Xbox 360 could be modified to re-enable the exploit in the future, but also potential ways of developing an autonomous loader. Following the system patches, hackers found ways of reintroducing the exploit and performing the hack, such as through downgrading the console firmware. These activities represent the beginning of a hostile relationship between hackers and security professionals, where susceptibilities are identified, exploited, patched, and new forms developed, much like the symbolic dialogue between glitchers and developers: the dialectical process of identification, documentation, abuse, patching, and repetition that forms the development of the relationship between counterplayers and producers.

While those identifying and developing the hacks were focused on the deployment of Linux, the creation of new software, and the opening up of the Xbox 360, there were others keen to utilize the developments to obtain free games and to alter commercial releases. The JTAG hack was developed in August 2009 by Tmbnc, after the King Kong/SMC hacks had been invalidated by Microsoft. The JTAG replicated the King Kong hack without the need for the King Kong disc and instead relied on the reprogramming of hardware components through an interrogation process known as Joint Test Action Group IEEE 1149.1 or its catchier acronym, JTAG, which was adopted when giving the hack its name. In addition to reprogramming components, the JTAG necessitated some minor hardware modifications such as the addition of new capacitors on the circuit board. In doing so, the JTAG circumvented all the Xbox 360 security checks, providing each with a false-positive.

In addition to this entrepreneurialism, the hacks that followed the JTAG, such as the Flashed Console and the RGH, necessitated the use of bespoke hardware components (microcontrollers and firmware adapters), on account of Microsoft's escalating security countermeasures. The production of these hacking and modding components in turn allow a wider audience to conduct and utilize the hacks and therefore represent another layer of entrepreneurialism. These are not the act of commercialization by entrepreneurial individuals who are prepared to hack equipment for a fee but the creation of hacking hardware on a literally industrial scale. Companies such as Team Matrix, Team Squirt, or Team Xecutor, which creates the Coolrunner microprocessor that facilitates the RGH, are key example of this industrial level of commercialization.

HACKED CONSOLE TRADE

The process of obtaining an RGH/JTAG for those without the willingness or skill to conduct the modification themselves is problematic and fraught with the concerns associated with buying any illicit product. Hacked consoles are controlled items in the sense they are automatically removed from auction sites or online retailers. Any reference to RGH, JTAG, or Flashed Console in item descriptions are likely to result in the listing being removed from sale and the seller issued a warning. Those wishing to purchase a modified console through these sources must search for euphemisms including "Special Consoles" and "Limited Edition Consoles". The use of these terms introduces uncertainty and suspicion over the credentials of hacked-console purchases and many listings of this kind invite potential buyers to contact the seller before purchasing or simply the ominous instruction of "don't bid if you don't know what this is".

As a result of this ambiguity and uncertainty, many of the transactions take place on separate trade sections of websites such as Se7ensins. com where, operating as a safehouse, hacked consoles are at least openly discussed and not subject to the same level of censure as elsewhere. This enables a potential purchaser to quiz the seller and clearly ascertain what is purportedly up for sale. Yet even in the open marketplace of the modding website, the illicit nature of the item means few are confident of the guarantees offered by payment systems such as PayPal, and scams and reneged deals are relatively common, or at least occur so vocally on forums that buyers inevitably have to take this risk into account.

Websites that support trading between members generally adopt common policies about item advertising. They normally require sellers to provide photographic evidence of their product or service, including a date and forum username within the image, to ensure the items actually exist and allow potential buyers to seek advice about the reputation of the seller. Additional restrictions are placed on the point at which sellers are allowed to post an advert, requiring a certain number of posts or another marker of community engagement before approval. Buyers are occasionally subject to similar cross-examination, but on the basis of a payment-before-dispatch policy, this occurs much less frequently. The suspicion and expectation of proof firmly rest with the seller. Despite these recommendations and checks, all that the selling are really placing at stake is their reputation within the counterplay community, balanced against any reasonable likelihood of legal or vigilante retaliation. As a result, if someone intends to scam others they are likely to develop and maintain multiple online identities specifically for this purpose and to carefully distance their online personas from their real ones, much like the grief-players and trolls explored earlier.

When this is contextualized with the cost of the items involved (in late 2012, RGH consoles commanded around £150 per unit) it is no surprise there are frequent purchases that never arrive or are botched or defective on delivery. Despite these risks there appears to be considerable demand for hacked consoles, and sites such as these – and local independent video-game shops of the less salubrious nature – are among the only ways of obtaining a hacked console unless a person is willing to do the modifications directly.

Those who build a reputation as reliable sellers are treated with significant status within hacking- and modding-orientated communities, receive frequent referrals, and are able to command premiums for their handiwork.

INTERVIEWING A SUPPLIER

While my attempts to make contact with representatives from Team Xecutor, Team Matrix, and Team Squirt, the manufacturers of the components used to conduct RGH hacks, were unsuccessful, I was able to enter into dialogue with a number of sellers who produced Xbox 360 hacks for profit. While most were only willing to offer limited responses, one, who we will call Bob, was not only considered a major hacked-console seller on TheTechGame.com but was also prepared to discuss his experiences and perspectives with me.

Bob had started modifying consoles after being asked to fix broken Xbox 360 consoles by his friends. An electronics hobbyist and a further education student at a large city college, he had an aptitude for soldering, access to useful facilities, and also many fellow students who were potential customers. Using tutorials from XboxHacker.com and Se7ensins.com to assist with Xbox 360 repairs (namely a soldering process called reflowing), Bob quickly built a reputation as being able to fix problems including the extensively documented Xbox 360 hardware fault, the ring of red. In addition, Bob said there was a demand for refurbished consoles and, seeing a commercial opportunity, he began to cheaply purchase broken Xbox 360s speculatively and sell them on if and when he had fixed them. This proved lucrative and Bob frequently returned to Se7ensins.com and XboxHacker.com to learn of other fixes and other processes such as the JTAG hack, which also widened his customer base beyond his college friends.

It transpired that once repaired, one of the broken consoles he had purchased had been inoperable or disconnected from the Xbox LIVE servers for so long as to never have had major security updates applied and "was on an exploitable dashboard version for the JTAG hack". Having a console that was running a sufficiently decrepit version of the Xbox 360 dashboard operating system that it was vulnerable to the JTAG hack, Bob's interest was piqued, and using the equipment he had amassed for repairs he conducted the hack "with some trial and error" out of curiosity. When he told others what he had done, he found they not only knew what the JTAG was but were keen to buy it, offering significantly higher sums than a standard refurbished console. Ever the entrepreneur, Bob saw an opportunity, sold the system, and whenever the age of a broken console's dashboard allowed, he conducted the hack and began to advertise the "upgrade" as a service in addition to standard reflow repairs. As he became more confident and RGH hacks became more affordable to conduct, he moved into that as well.

Over the course of a year and a half, Bob's Xbox 360 hacks became professionalized as a shop and existed on a single forum post on NextGenUpdate.

com, Se7ensins.com, and TheTechGame.com, which was updated with new posts as stock became available. By ensuring the quality of his products (partly due to his expertise in electronics), Bob's reputation as a hardware hacker on the websites grew and as of mid-2012, he was considered one of the most reliable hardware providers on the scene, producing highly finished, reliable machines that commanded a premium.

Bob suggested that over a period of two years, he had performed in excess of forty JTAG and RGH hacks, 150 Flashed Console updates, and over 100 Xbox 360 console repairs, making in excess of £3,000 profit from the console flashing services alone. As demand for his services outstripped supply, he was then able to vet buyers to avoid the complication of unreliable customers and had the flexibility to conduct commercial modifications as and when he needed the money. He used this as a convenient supplementary income until he eventually wound the service down when his priorities changed and demand dwindled with the announcement of the approaching release of the PlayStation 4 and the Xbox One.

Despite becoming quite central to the delivery of hacked consoles, within the UK at least, and within the contexts of these websites and the time period he was operating in, Bob voiced a disinterest with the wider hacking- and modding-orientated communities. "I try to stay out of online groups as they are a waste of time". He was simply interested in them to the extent they supported his entrepreneurial commercial services. Fortunately, the disinterest allowed Bob to detach himself from having to consider the eventual uses of the consoles he hacked and therefore the legal and ethical implications this raised, such as copyright circumvention, piracy, and the subversion of commercial game spaces. Bob was clear he separated himself from the process. "I get paid for the service I do on the console and then the customer gets to choose what they want to do with their newly modified console".

By seeing his actions as a service Bob distanced himself from the implications of his actions, and displayed either a genuine uncertainty or a willful ignorance about the legal significance of his actions, considering his behaviour was precisely what Crippen had been prosecuted for but on a much wider scale.

> I never do anything that involves anything illegal. Just providing a service to modify the console that you totally own and it is down to the customer what they do with it. ... It's not a business in my eyes, just a service that responds to demand.

Once more we see that under the right kind of conditions and pressures, individuals are prepared to conduct hardware hacks, whether the legal enhancements offered by Evil Controllers, the creation of lag switches, or the development and then reappropriation of techniques to open up hardware platforms. Additionally, in the face of stiff demand for these services, we see companies and individuals systemizing the hacks as services. Ultimately, though, we must remember these hacks are conducted to do things, and that is the value that contextualizes the transactions. The hacker gains reputation or payment for their services and the player using the hacks appears a better, dominant, rapid-firing player in *Call of Duty*, a player of illegally shared game ISOs, more able to discover game glitches, or, as we shall see in the next chapter, modify commercial software and interfere with network systems – and even be recognized as one of the few hundred individuals worldwide who challenge developers, publishers, and platform-holders with their counterplay acts.

I spoke with Tmbnc, one of the XBMC developers and originator of the Xbox 360 JTAG exploit, about the relationship between the hacker-ethic approach to hardware modification and those using them for other purposes such as illicit modding and piracy.

> The topics of piracy and cheating were the main reasons why I lost interest in Xbox hacking – I didn't want to work on stuff anymore that's constantly abused (in my eyes) for cheating and piracy. When I worked on the console hacks I've done so far, my true and only focus was homebrew development – replacing as much code as possible with own code. It was not for a better world, it was just because it was fun for me. ... Pirates and cheaters ... are abusing the "benign" hacks for their crap. Except that I have to admit that most hacks are not benign at all, even if they have been made with a good intention.

Tmbnc's questioning of the benign nature of hacks is stark, and resonates throughout the counterplay practices explored so far. The benign nature of grief-play as game mode or the benign glitch as developer assistance are questionable. This alludes to the realization that, irrespective of the legitimizing discourses that may be attributed to an act or the lack of culpability felt as a result of warning others of the risks and implications of misuse, the apparently justified counterplay act holds an oppositional aspect. The glitch is shared with the assumption of exploitation, the game mode will be used to bully, or the hack will be repurposed for piracy and chaos.

The original motivations for the hardware hacks align strongly with a discourse of resistance. They were conducted in part in response to the perceived restriction of a potentially powerful and egalitarian product: a low-cost personal computer. This is seen with Huang's vocalization of his objection to the Microsoft monopoly, and the subsequent XBMC and then later the Free60.org community, or Graf_Chokolo's urgency to reinstate a lost function of the PlayStation 3. Despite the motivation of the facilitating technologies and processes articulated by Huang in particular, discussion with hackers demonstrates a much less resistant approach. Their actions, such as Tmbnc's development of the JTAG hack, appear not to come from an attempt to change but through a masterful assumption of access and authority – simply engaging with the system and technology as they wish, irrespective of restrictions placed on access and interaction. The hardware hackers I spoke with were often rather non-assuming, to the extent of not appreciating the negative potential of their actions or attempting to persuade me the damage was minimal, as seen with Tmbnc's critique of apparently benign hacks. Yet within the hacker communities, meritocracy ensured hackers received status and recognition, and inevitably, whether acknowledged or not, part of this was based on the illicit or malign capacity of the hack.

Hardware hackers might well approach the Xbox 360 from this perspective, changing it from an entertainment device into a personal computer. It fundamentally rejects all of its core affordances. The very notion of player and of consumer becomes irrelevant in relation to the hardware hack, providing it is used for a different purpose. The value is created through what the player is able to do, what they don't have to pay for, or what profit can be made as a corollary. There are authentic and inauthentic ways of hardware-hacking (piracy vs. productivity, botched processes vs. excellence of production, unreliable trader vs. extended aftercare support). Yet for other hacking-orientated groups, selling hacked consoles for profit is appropriate, provided they are sufficiently reliable and the seller trustworthy. Identities certainly spiral out of a counterplayer's relationship with hardware-hacking, but as this is a facilitating counterplay process, the real complexity comes from reflecting on what is done with these hacked consoles. This is precisely what we will explore in the next chapter.

GAMEOGRAPHY

Call of Duty: Advanced Warfare. 2014. Activision. Sledgehammer Games.
Call of Duty: Black Ops. 2010. Activision. Treyarch.
Call of Duty: Black Ops 2. 2012. Activision. Treyarch.
Call of Duty: Black Ops Rezurrection. 2011. Activision. Treyarch.
Call of Duty: Ghosts. 2013. Activision. Sledgehammer Games.
Call of Duty: Modern Warfare. 2007. Activision. Infinity Ward.
Call of Duty: Modern Warfare 2. 2009. Activision. Infinity Ward.
Call of Duty: Modern Warfare 3. 2011. Activision. Infinity Ward/Sledgehammer Games.
Call of Duty: World at War. 2008. Activision. Treyarch.
Peter Jackson's King Kong. 2005. Ubisoft.

REFERENCES

Chaos Computer Club. 2010. Chaos Communication Congress, December 27–30, Berlin Congress Center, Berlin, Germany. http://events.ccc.de/congress/2010/wiki/Welcome. Accessed December 1, 2014.
Evil Controllers. 2014a. *Evil Controllers.* http://www.evilcontrollers.com/. Accessed November 25, 2014.
Evil Controllers. 2014b. *Call of Duty: Ghosts Themed Master Mod.* http://www.evil-controllers.com/call-of-duty-ghosts-themed-master-mod.html. Accessed November 25, 2014.
Evil Controllers. 2014c. *Evil Scope 2 Inch 5 Pack.* http://www.evilcontrollers.com/evil-scope-2-inch-5-pack.html. Accessed November 25, 2014.
FailOverflow. 2010. "Console Hacking 2010 – PS3 Epic Fail Part 3." http://www.youtube.com/watch?v=btDiX319P4w. Accessed November 20, 2014.

Free60.org. 2006–2014. http://www.free60.org/Main_Page. Accessed November 27, 2014.

Gaston, M. 2011. "*Minecraft, EVE Online,* and *League of Legends* hacked." http://www.videogamer.com/news/minecraft_eve_online_and_league_of_legends_hacked.html. Accessed November 24, 2014.

Gstaff. 2011. "Please Read: Hack attempts against our websites and forums." http://bethblog.com/index.php/2011/06/13/please-read-hack-attempts-against-our-websites-and-forums/. Accessed November 6, 2012.

Huang, A. 2003. *Hacking the Xbox.* San Francisco: No Starch Press.

Kravets, D. 2010. "Prosecutors Dismiss Xbox-Modding Case Mid-Trial." http://www.wired.com/threatlevel/2010/12/crippen-dismissed/. Accessed December 4, 2010.

Levy, S. 2001. *Hackers: Heroes of the Computer Revolution.* London: Penguin.

NextGenUpdate. 2008–2014. http://www.nextgenupdate.com/. Accessed November 28, 2014.

Osawa, J. 2011. "Hackers Attack Nintendo." http://online.wsj.com/article/SB10001424052702304474804576366802876217440.html. Accessed November 6, 2012.

Pakinkis, T. 2011. "Hackers hit BioWare in latest attack 18,000 Neverwinter Nights forum accounts compromised." http://www.computerandvideogames.com/307483/news/hackers-hit-bioware-in-latest-attack/?attr=CVG-General-RSS&cid=OTC-RSS. Accessed November 6, 2012.

Pilkington, E. 2014. "LulzSec hacker 'Sabu' released after 'extraordinary' FBI cooperation." http://www.theguardian.com/technology/2014/may/27/hacker-sabu-walks-free-sentenced-time-served. Accessed May 24, 2014.

Plunkett, L. (2011). *Microsoft is (Not) Helping an Xbox Live Hacker "Develop His Talent" [Update].* Available at: http://kotaku.com/5805742/microsoft-is-helping-an-xbox-live-hacker-develop-his-talent.

Porter, W. 2011. "Codemasters hacked, personal information stolen." http://www.computerandvideogames.com/306764/news/codemasters-hacked-personal-information-stolen/. Accessed November 6, 2012.

Schäfer, M. 2011. *Bastard Culture! How User Participation Transforms Cultural Production.* Amsterdam: Amsterdam University Press.

Schreier, J. 2011. "Business Sony estimates $171 million loss from PSN hack." http://www.wired.co.uk/news/archive/2011–05/24/sony-psn-hack-losses.

Se7ensins. 2010–2014. http://www.se7ensins.com/. Accessed January 15, 2011.

Sweeney, T. 2011. "Epic Games hacked." http://gears3blog.com/2011/06/epic-games-hacked/. Accessed November 5, 2012.

Taylor, P. A. 1999. *Hackers.* London: Routledge.

The Tech Game. 2009–2014. http://www.thetechgame.com/. Accessed January 15, 2011.

US Department of Justice. (2014). "Four Members of International Computer Hacking Ring Indicted for Stealing Gaming Technology, Apache Helicopter Training Software." http://www.justice.gov/opa/pr/four-members-international-computer-hacking-ring-indicted-stealing-gaming-technology-apache. Accessed October 8, 2014.

XboxHacker. 2006–2012. http://www.xboxhacker.org/. Accessed October 31, 2012.

XBMC. 2012. "Xbmc About." http://xbmc.org/about/. Accessed October 31, 2012.

Yahoo Finance. 2011. "Sony Corporation Common Stock Share Price Chart." http://uk.finance.yahoo.com/echarts?s=SNE#symbol=sne;range=20110404,20110620;compare=;indicator=volume;charttype=area;crosshair=on;ohlcvalues=0;logscale=off;source=;. Accessed November 8, 2012.

Yau, N. 2011. "Largest Data Breaches of All Time." http://flowingdata.com/2011/06/13/largest-data-breaches-of-all-time/. Accessed November 6, 2012.

6   Illicit Modding

I ignore the insults and posturing challenges coming over the voice chat, instead focusing on where I'll position myself once the game starts. I decide on one of the bunkers that'll give me good visibility over the dusty Afghan battleground. I've got my custom load-out, a holographic scoped assault rifle and a stock of claymore mines to use to cover my back as I look out over the wreckage of the downed transport plane for insurgents. The game starts and I spawn on the south end of the map. I sprint past the Humvees, watching out for potential hiding spots in the wrecked fuselage, and pause, scanning the ridge to the north for the silhouette of enemy snipers. Finding nothing, I break back into a sprint across the poppy fields, seconds away from the entrance to the bunker. ... Then it all goes wrong. Rockets rain down from the sky and I am killed in a plume of smoke, dust, and debris. I spawn somewhere else on the map and die almost instantaneously. Each of my attempts to escape the rockets fails, but my opponents aren't on the ridge, nor in the wreckage of the plane. Instead they are hovering in the air, firing streams of missiles that would normally be restricted to one or two per spawn. It is clear the rules of the game have been ruptured and subverted and the game has been modded. After perhaps sixty seconds more, a klaxon sounds, a towering mushroom cloud erupts on the edge of the screen, and the map is engulfed in flames as the match comes to its jarring conclusion.

For those unfamiliar with the *Call of Duty* franchise or its sixth iteration, *Modern Warfare 2* (2009) in particular, I should stress the match described was atypical. It had been modified without the consent of the developers through the use of hacked Xbox 360 consoles and the execution of unsigned code. While some research has already been done exploring some of the significance of PC modding communities, their relationship to intellectual property, and notions of resistance, such as the body of work by Hector Postigo (2007, 2008, 2010) and Olli Sotamaa (2007a, 2007b), this has tended to revolve around cultures that utilize sanctioned modding tools – more akin to incendiary user-generated content. While Postigo and Sotamaa have explored ways in which sanctioned modding tools may be used in illicit ways, such as through the unauthorized recreation of copyrighted content, the practice explored here is different.

By contrast, illicit modding is where individuals modify video-game software without the approval of the developers or publishers, using unauthorized modification tools. Their activity necessitates the use of hacked console hardware, the extraction and decompilation of code, its alteration, recompilation, distribution, and eventual execution. One assumes that due to the illicit and potentially litigious nature of their chosen activity, modders are relatively cautious, relying on the use of pseudonyms and alternate personas, yet paradoxically, examples of illicit mods and information about how to produce them are widely available on the web. Modders tend to aggregate on a number of websites relating to the practices, including those already introduced such as Se7ensins.com, and in turn the mods they produce are often viewed, commented on, and even iteratively developed by their peers.

Much like the hardware hacks, illicit mods are also in direct violation of rules and law, including the game's end-user license agreement (EULA), the consoles' terms of service (TOS), the US 1998 Digital Millennium Copyright Act, and the European Directive 2001/29/EC. This radically subverted play experience is an example of one of the potential uses of a hacked console, in this case a JTAG. The example of the specific modification for *Call of Duty: Modern Warfare 2* on the Xbox 360 is a "modded lobby".

The JTAG modded lobby is produced by connecting a hacked console containing modified game code directly to Microsoft's Xbox LIVE system, eventually invalidating the console but briefly allowing players to play in remediated game-spaces. Before we explore the development of these modding techniques, the process of creation, and eventual deployment, we should first discuss the specific context of their use in *Call of Duty*. Each *Call of Duty* release has included both a single and multiplayer component. However, the fourth, *Modern Warfare* (2007), introduced elements of avatar development and persistence unseen within multiplayer first-person shooter gaming. It rewarded players with experience points that unlocked increasingly potent weapons and skills that remained persistent across the matches they played. In addition to the weapons the player unlocks as experience is gained, progress is marked with military rank and medals that are displayed when playing in multiplayer matches, indicating a detailed service-record profile. In the journey from the first rank, Private First Class, through to Commander (level 70), the player accrues all the weapons and perks in the game, typically taking a player around sixty hours of online play to achieve. This focus on long-term goals shifted the temporal focus and social significance of multiplayer console gaming from a short blast of competitive fun against faceless opponents to a long-term process of accrual in a culture of competition, much more akin to traditional MMO "grind" mechanics.

Yet after sixty-odd hours, the grind ends, and players who reach Commander rank have no more weapons, perks, or attachments left available to unlock. It would be entirely logical for players to simply play using the most effective weapons and unlocks, dominating other players until the game became boring and they leave. Alternatively it could be the case that after reaching Commander rank, equilibrium would establish itself or the game would shift into something different that no longer focuses on progression, attainment, and status, or at least not on the terms offered by the game itself. However, efforts have been made to avoid such stagnation through the introduction of "prestige status". Once a player reaches Commander rank, a menu option becomes available and the game challenges the players to "trade all your accomplishments for a bit of prestige ..." and "Prestige has a price. ... There's no going back" (Activision 2009).

By going prestige, the players abandon their accumulated weapons, perks, and experience points, starting as if new to the game in exchange for a "prestige emblem" visible in multiplayer matches. This process can be repeated up to fifteen times – although most *Call of Duty* games enable you to do this ten times, getting "10th prestige" – with a more desirable emblem awarded each time. By going prestige the player indicates their mastery of the multiplayer game to their peers, it becomes an act of asceticism, a rite of passage in which the powerful veteran warrior renounces all accumulations in order to start their battle again. For a group of players so orientated towards the notion of mastery and dominance, the invitation to go prestige takes on a powerful significance. It becomes another mark of legitimate play.

Modded lobbies like the one described at the opening of this chapter are part of the way in which the playerbase responds to the pressures and demands of this legitimate play, particularly with the creation of "prestige lobbies", modded versions of the *Call of Duty* multiplayer game executed on hacked consoles, designed to rapidly give players experience points necessary to repeatedly prestige and thus respect within the community without having actually had to play for sixty-plus hours. Within a prestige lobby, killing an opponent or performing another predetermined action, such as committing suicide with a grenade, rewards the player with hugely inflated experience points, often the maximum within the game, which is unable to be displayed correctly in the interface and instead shows as +2.674E+006. This typically allows the player to accrue sufficient experience points to reach rank seventy with one kill. During the intermission between games, the player goes prestige and then repeats the process when the game recommences. If they repeat this process ten times, they have reached tenth prestige. The player then leaves the lobby (or is booted by the host), carrying the experience points and the relevant prestige icon into all the subsequent games they play.

The actual process of running a modded prestige lobby requires significant co-ordination, interaction, and transaction between hardware hackers, software modders, and players wishing to obtain prestige through subterfuge. This complex relationship is illustrated by considering the process in depth. In order to produce an illicit mod, such as a prestige lobby, the player first needs access to a hacked console, a JTAG or RGH, through the means discussed previously.

Figure 6.1 Modding, awarding a player maximum experience points in a Call of
Duty: Modern Warfare 2 prestige lobby.

The modder typically uses the hacked console to rip the game data into an
ISO file onto an attached portable hard disc drive, or copies an ISO obtained
from another source such as peer-to-peer sharing. They then connect the
hard disc drive to a computer and begin to alter the code directly, or create
patch files to be applied to the game. Changes are guided through reference
to "managed code" lists and patch-making tutorials on modding-orientated
websites. The managed code list consists of snippets of game code and a cor-
responding explanation of the impact that modifying this has on the *Call of
Duty* game environment, including entries for "Wallhack, God Mode, Auto
Aim, Spawn Projectiles, Invisibility" and those related to prestige: "Complete All Challenges without Challenge Progression and Experience". These
desired changes are compiled into an illegitimate game update – a "patch
file", which is placed onto the hard disc drive and the game restarted. The
patch is automatically applied and the new modified game settings overwrite
what was previously there. Once the patch has been applied to the game code
installed on the JTAG, the hacked *Call of Duty* lobby is ready to be played.
This can be used offline if modifications have been made to the single-player
game component, allowing players to experience manipulated code such as
rapid fire or invulnerability, but if they wish to accrue experience points, gain
unlocks, or prestige, the hacked console must be connected to Xbox LIVE.

That a patch applied to a lone JTAG console, perhaps in a different con-
tinent, has any bearing on other players in a multiplayer match is due to
the specific architecture of the Xbox LIVE system and the design of *Call of
Duty*. *Call of Duty* multiplayer matches utilize a dynamic hosting system
in which the player determined to have the highest quality connection and
least latency, or who instigates a private match, becomes the host for the

match. This host's hardware co-ordinates the match with all other players, communicating with them invisibly and copying any settings to the other systems joining. Crucially, this synchronization includes specific game settings such as weapon damage and the experience conferred for each kill, which, if modified, can be made utterly at odds with those in a conventional public match. In addition, a modification can be made that controls which console hosts the games and therefore what rules control the match, ensuring the modder's rules are applied, irrespective of how good their connection is. However, joining Xbox LIVE with a JTAG brings repercussions.

When a player connects a JTAG directly to Xbox LIVE, as if it were a conventional console, it is detected as illegitimate and instigates an automated process that takes three to five hours to process and results in the console hardware and the player profile using it being permanently banned from the system. The JTAG's unique hardware identification number, its "keyvault", seen by Xbox LIVE, is eventually placed in an ever-expanding blacklist that is referred to when a system attempts to join the network. Despite being invalidated for online play, the banned JTAG is still operable offline and therefore retains some residual value for people wishing to use its functionality, such as executing homebrew software or, much more frequently, to play pirated ISO game files. Banned JTAGs command around half the fee of unbanned ones, at around £70, although this naturally fluctuates according to supply and demand. However, if its owner is willing to go through a complicated process, they can overwrite a new keyvault onto the JTAG, taken from a virgin and entirely legitimate console, a process known as "keyvaulting". This enables the JTAG to be resurrected and used online once more. A prestige lobby designed specifically for multiplayer and online play therefore has a typical operational window of four hours per keyvault. As a result, the modder must ensure they recoup the cost of a new keyvault or the differential between the value of a banned and unbanned JTAG or face financial loss. At least initially, these financial pressures determined how hacked consoles were used and the form of counterplay on the Xbox 360 and *Call of Duty*.

In addition to the relatively toothless threats of gamertag and console "permabans", circumvented by alts and keyvaulting, there is the risk of legal challenge. For example, players are warned that Microsoft "may take any legal action it deems appropriate against users who violate Microsoft's systems or network security". This was enforced in 2008 with Matthew Crippen's case. While the production of a JTAG appears in violation of the DMCA, so too are extraction, manipulation, and recompilation of Xbox 360 software on a JTAG required to deploy an illicit mod.

PAYING FOR THE PLEASURE: ACCESSING A MODDED LOBBY

Modders advertise the availability of prestige lobbies and their respective entrance fees on various auction websites, bulletin boards, and specific gaming forums. At their peak in 2010, access to *Modern Warfare* 2 JTAG prestige lobbies cost between $6.99 and $14.99. Websites, such as those that sprang up to specifically offer modded lobbies as a service, such as 10thprestige.com (2010) and Xbox360xperts.com (2010–2014), charge higher rates: between $30 and $50. In comparison, modding community sites such as TheTechGame.com (2009–2014), Se7ensins.com (2010–2014), and NextGenUpdate.com offer a wide range of price points largely based on the reputation of the modder and the swiftness of service, varying from around $25 to $75 (and the occasional gratis version) for lobbies run by "verified" sellers.

In addition to the variation in price, other ways of using a JTAG lobby have developed, such as lobby rental services, where players are free to use the modified game however they wish for a set period of time. Lobby rentals vary from as little as $23 per thirty minutes to $150 for four hours. One assumes these prices are largely calculated around the cost and effort needed to keyvault a banned console and, of course, what the market is prepared to pay at the time. Lobby rentals allow the player to adopt the model used by Internet hosting resellers, buying modded lobby access in bulk and then inviting other users to join for fun or profit. This shows the costs involved in accessing a modded lobby fluctuate significantly, largely based on supply and demand and the reputation of the modder, much like the way a hardware hacker's reputation affects the price of their wares. However, unlike hacked consoles, the modded lobby is immaterial and the customer is effectively paying for an invitation into a multiplayer game. These are both intangible transactions and illicit acts, and the customer has little recompense if the modder does not deliver. This has led to the development of processes that reassure customers of the reliability of the seller and the legitimacy of the mods.

The anxieties that surround non-existent prestige lobbies can be seen on a relatively minor Xbox 360 modding-related websites, Xbox360xperts.com forum's "shout box", on which customers publicly communicate directly with site administrators. Over the course of fifteen minutes on January 4, 2011, I watched as three customers posted questions to the administrators, asking when the prestige packages they had paid for would eventually take place. Nobody responded and the customers became increasingly agitated but still contrite, lest they annoy the people they'd paid. I never ascertained whether they eventually experienced the modded lobby or whether they had been scammed.

I spoke with Bob, the hacked-console supplier, about the scale of prestige lobby use, as he had naturally built strong links with modders needing hardware for revenue generation. At the time of my interviews with Bob, the original JTAG lobby method had been superseded by the second type known as "infection lobbies", which we will discuss later, but he suggested it was quite reasonable for a typical JTAG prestige lobby run by a verified modder to generate £3,000 during peak demand before it was invalidated, especially if the modding-orientated community sites were utilized properly to co-ordinate custom. In subsequent releases, after the JTAG prestige and infection lobbies had been invalidated due to improved security, the few modders who had developed ways of still running lobbies due to their technical ability could command even greater premiums than the JTAG equivalents.

> High traffic sites such as TheTechGame.com and Se7ensins.com can lure in many customers when they are noted as "legit" and "verified". E.g. Charging £60 a go for Modern Warfare 3 prestige lobbies, makes £6000 from 100 people, which is easily reached with a site with 500,000 members and lots of new traffic and clicks every day.

The fact there have been continual development modding deployment processes, and players are willing to pay considerable sums of money in rather risky circumstances to use them, illustrates the demand for prestige within the playerbase. This demand and the technologies that met it determined the prices and availability of lobbies and eventually, players' attitudes towards the *Call of Duty* multiplayer component generally. Bob later admitted to having hosted his own modded lobbies, but he provided them at a much lower cost than others as he already had access to a large stock of hacked consoles.

> I can tell you I ran too many to really count – although I'd estimate I did about 150. ... Realistically the most I ever charged anyone for a slot in one of my lobbies was £10. I saw that as fair.

Bob didn't specify how many customers he had served, the period of time they were run, or his total profits, but it is possible to make a conservative estimate. On the basis that Bob's lobbies were less than one-third full (five out of a maximum of eighteen players), 150 lobbies would have generated £7,500. Once the cost of retooling, by purchasing replacement keyvaults at £50 every ten lobbies, is factored into Bob's figures, the overall profit would be in the area of £6,750. It should be stressed that this is a crude estimation. There is no way the number of lobbies nor the number of paying customers nor the veracity of Bob's suggestion for that matter can be confirmed, but it is offered as a way to contextualize the practice and shows that under the right circumstances, feeding players' demand for prestige could be financially rewarding. Bob assured me that the 150 lobbies he ran were sporadic and a paltry figure compared to others who had realized the lucrative potential of modded lobbies and who systematized and cornered the market.

Those who fully embraced the deployment of modded lobbies, and therefore sought to offer a consistent and reliable product, adopted other management systems in order to overcome the problems of orchestration that Bob found so tiresome. While he never went as far as to make the link between conventional organized crime and the verified sellers, Bob described systems of operation similar to drug-dealing or prostitution, with "bosses" investing capital to facilitate the lobbies and subordinates doing the day-to-day operation and organization, paid through a percentage of profits and free access to lobbies whenever they wished. Bob alleged this system also recognized the importance of the websites within the system, offering the verification legitimization process, which also received payment in exchange for reassuring potential customers and served as combined advert and shop front for the verified sellers and their lobbies. Verified sellers were careful to accentuate the quality and service they offered, even adding consistent branding to their adverts, posts, and modded lobby interfaces, and once they had established reputations, they demanded premiums justified through reliability and convenience. According to Bob:

> I always thought the prices the verified sellers chose was really expensive, but after looking behind the scenes it was logical. They were always online and hosted lobbies sometimes all day long ... making a big profit to give a percentage to the site owner, as well as for themselves.

We have finally reached the point at which we can return to the example of the modded lobby, first introduced in the open paragraphs of this chapter. One begins to ask the question: If a modded lobby is such a contentious and legally precarious event, why would a modder ever take the risk of exposing this to the public? Why allow mods to spill out into the normal game? Why not simply ensure customers solely populate the lobbies and control access more discriminately? This is something that is also possible through modding, in which code can be added to allow the host to kick players at will from the match. Drawing modded lobbies into the public realm not only raises awareness of their existence but increases the chances of reporting and developer-led intervention and, ultimately, for the modding to cease. The reality is that the modded lobby described at the opening of this chapter serves two purposes. It was part of a process instigated to demonstrate the skills of the modders, leading to increased reputation and increasing the likelihood of them running viable commercial lobbies, and secondly, it acknowledges another use and pleasure of modding: it is enjoyable to spread chaos and meddle with things. We will explore more of the former, related to the financial operation of lobbies, and then move to the latter, the use of lobbies for alternate reasons.

BRANDED LOBBIES AND VERIFIED SELLERS

If the modder has set up prestige lobbies as a serious commercial concern, they will need to replace any invalidated JTAGs with functioning equivalents and seek new customers. If conducted effectively, repeat trade is relatively unlikely, at least until the next iteration of the *Call of Duty* franchise a year later, and as a result the modder must find ways to maximize the visibility and perceived integrity of their services. The offering must remain coherent and distinct across the few sporadic hours during which a lobby is operational, while the proposition must appear sophisticated, authentic, discrete, and good value for money. To complicate matters further, this must all be done anonymously if the modder is to mitigate any legal censure or social response. In effect, the modder is engaged in the process of the creation of an illicit brand, complete with its own recognizable product name and unique features that can be advertised across a set of forum-post shop fronts and YouTube videos. Instead of Evil Controllers, we encounter GODx's Mega GUN Game, Team XEX's Mod, or Mofos Modz, each of which includes branding within the modded lobby interface and serves as the touchstone that allows a potential customer to ascertain a modder's reputation before purchase. These videos are simultaneously used as advertisements, assertions of status within the modding communities, and as way in which the modder establishes an identity across the disparate and apparently unrelated modded lobbies that spring up from time to time on Xbox LIVE. The video becomes an advert, a résumé, a business card. Add to this the verification offered by an impartial senior member of the modding website forum and the product is persuasive.

What this leads to is a curious replication of advertising and copyright in which modders heavily brand the user interfaces of the lobbies they create and simultaneously cast aspersions on other modders deemed inauthentic imposters or competitors. The modded lobby becomes a rhetorical device that attempts to persuade players of the merits of the mod, the status, technical ability, and reliability of the modder, and also says things about the right way to mod.

While the modder must record video of the lobby in action as evidence to drive future income, they daren't risk implicating any paying customers on their matches via their gamertags. In effect they need to populate a modded lobby with marks, players in which the modder has no real interest and no concern whether or not they receive censure or reprimand from their peers. This is done by offering free access, which can backfire on account of devaluing the lobby and infuriating any players who have recently paid for the service. Instead, the modder often simply places the lobby online in the public matches, and conventional players inadvertently experience the mod. The modder ideally does this once a list of paying customers has been exhausted but the JTAG and gamertag hosting have not yet been invalidated. By enabling a "force host" parameter in the modded code and joining general public matches, unsuspecting players around the world enter the modded lobby and are governed by its rules. In this situation the modder needs to prove the functionality of the mod, but as the code related to experience accrual is well known and rather dull to watch, there is a motivation to make the lobby, and its video, as spectacular as possible. Why not make players fly and have them shoot rockets as well as giving the host the experience settings? This brings us back to the events described in the opening paragraph.

Figure 6.2 Modding, a Call of Duty: Modern Warfare 2 illicit mod user interface.

Figure 6.3 Modding, a Call of Duty: Modern Warfare 2 illicit mod user interface with square overlays displaying opponent location through cover.

The unsuspecting players who are in the match suddenly find they and their teammates can fly through the air, shoot missiles for bullets, release unlimited numbers of attack helicopters, and, if the modder has enabled it, accrue experience. Understandably, seduced by the power now randomly conferred on them, players tend to experiment and revel in the fleeting omnipotence, all the while playing an unwitting role in a calculated, secret marketing campaign. This continues until that JTAG is finally banned and the lobby ceases to exist, at which point the modded lobby becomes net-lore in the eyes of the players and the modder uses the video as evidence of their skills to better support running more lobbies.

It should be stressed that JTAG and prestige lobbies are simply one commercial application of modding within the context of a specific platform and video-game franchise, although the same changes to code also worked on the PlayStation 3 version of the game. Modders also use hacked consoles for a wide range of other purposes and on different games. Even within the same franchise, the development of new methods of deploying mods has led to new uses and manifestations, as can be seen with the modding practices that came from the widespread use of "infection lobbies", the modding method that immediately followed the JTAG deployment of *Call of Duty* mods.

THE INFECTIOUS PLEASURES OF INFECTION LOBBIES

In late 2009, a few short weeks after the release of *Call of Duty: Modern Warfare 2*, players on the Xbox 360 and PlayStation 3 began experiencing jarring corruptions of the multiplayer game space. Players joining public multiplayer matches found they suddenly had unlimited ammunition and had no need to reload, which encouraged unconventional ways of playing the game. Instead of deliberate use of cover, an emphasis on well-aimed shots, and a conservative approach to ammunition, multiplayer games became spaces riddled with bullets, rockets, and grenades in which survival was determined largely by luck rather than judgement.

While the alterations represented a radical subversion of the expected experience of the *Call of Duty* franchise that many found enjoyable or novel, it also presented a troubling issue. Not all players experienced the altered settings, but those who did found the settings travelled with them into each subsequent game they entered. The modifications were the equivalent of a conventional software virus that used contact in multiplayer game lobbies and matches as the method of transmission. It soon became apparent that a latent game bug or glitch did not cause infection lobbies but that they were the result of player modifications, much like the prestige lobbies, and these mods quickly became known as infection lobbies.

THE SOURCE OF THE INFECTION

Following their first appearance on *Modern Warfare 2* in late 2009, infection lobbies became increasingly common, used to alter a wide range of game settings including those related to experience accumulation, weapon behaviour, movement, and match setup. After their arrival in *Modern Warfare 2*, the latest version of the *Call of Duty* franchise at the time, infection lobbies then began to appear in older releases such as *Modern Warfare* and *World at War*, which shared the same game engine and core code as *Modern Warfare 2*. Due to their increased visibility and the widespread perception that infection lobbies undermined the fundamental processes of the game, Activision instigated a series of mandatory title updates that attempted to minimize the settings that could be altered and ultimately to entirely immunize the system against infection lobbies. While these title updates were generally successful, modders responded with alternate ways of deploying infection lobbies, and in turn, this led to additional updates and patching. Eventually Activision released TU7 (title update 7), which effectively prevented JTAG lobbies from being hosted and infections temporarily became the only way to mod. To clarify, for a short time both JTAG and infection methods worked simultaneously, but the visibility of infections led to the security releases that prevented JTAGs from connecting.

Infection lobbies can be considered the second generation of illicit modified lobbies. Whereas the first generation was reliant on connecting JTAG consoles directly to Xbox LIVE, infection lobbies used a method in which an unhacked retail console is infected with the modifications by physically connecting it to a JTAG. Once the infection has taken hold on the retail console, it can be disconnected from the JTAG and then connected to Xbox LIVE. As the console has not been hacked, it is not invalidated or the keyvault blacklisted, and the modded lobby freely enters the multiplayer game network. By using an unmodified console as the undetectable vector to introduce the infection into the closed game system, the JTAG is never invalidated – banned JTAGs can even be used to run infections – and the on-going costs of deploying modded lobbies is greatly reduced.

By using the infection method, modified lobbies could be deployed in public servers and infect hundreds if not thousands of players as the settings spread throughout the system. In addition, no longer bound by the necessity of income generation, the infection lobby could be used in more esoteric or creative ways than its previous counterpart. The purpose of JTAG and infection lobbies remains largely the same. They generally offer competitive advantage within the game, introduce new and interesting game modes, or make locked game content available for use, such as weapons, insignia, or trophies that may hold cachet or "gamer capital" within the player community (Consalvo 2007). However, what is also significant about the infection lobby is that its mode of distribution is inherently democratic and expansive instead of the carefully controlled spaces the JTAG lobby represented. Due to financial prerogatives, the infection lobby costs next to nothing to deploy and could be utilized to spread infections to others in a more free-form manner. As a result, those who became infected could pass the settings on to others, and once this was understood, it allowed illicit modifications to be used in situated and individualistic ways. The infection lobby took the control and operation of illicit modifications from the hands of a relatively small number of entrepreneurs with resources and verified status and gave it to a wider group of modders who used infection lobbies for a range of purposes.

PLAYING AGAINST THE INFECTED

In August 2011, spending time on the Se7ensins.com website, it became apparent from a number of posts that *Call of Duty: World at War* had become the site of an outbreak of infection lobbies, following their gradual immunization by title update of more recent iterations of the *Call of Duty* franchise. Keen to see what this felt like, I got online and on joining my first public multiplayer match, I found myself playing against the infected. The expected user interface had been conspicuously altered and the play experience was radically different to the game I had last played two years previously. Multi-coloured text cascaded down the screen each time a game message, such as the death of a player, was announced, inviting me to sign up to a forum in order to access the modifications other players in the match were using. The text was so obtrusive that in effect, it appeared akin to the experience of a mobile phone app that urges you to upgrade to the full version in order to remove adverts.

> Sign Up To [URL] For Free Infections HexxR Runz XBL Bitches …
> IGotInfection's•10thFromYouTube.Com/[URL]

Figure 6.4 Modding, a Call of Duty: World at War infection lobby with a spurious and annoying wall of text.

It appeared that all the opposing teams were using a modification that made them invincible and there was nothing that I, nor my teammates, could do to kill them. When the match ended we had not obtained any points or kills and, had I been interested in maintaining the persistent statistical record that documents my skill, this match would have represented a significant setback. Within the *Call of Duty* franchise player statistics and the ratio of player kills to deaths (K/D) are used as additional ways of ascertaining player skill and expertise, especially now that so many players were suspected to have used modded lobbies. A good statistical profile betrays a skilled player, as opposed to somebody who has little skill but plays often or who has used prestige lobbies, and those who have good K/D ratios are frequently invited into games, clans, and treated with greater respect.

Despite its detrimental impact on my player profile, the visual obstruction the cascading text presented, and the subjectively "unfair" nature of the game, I was compelled to continue playing. In the following match, a number of my opponents and teammates had oddly unconventional animated gamertags that indicated they also had become infected but, more spectacularly, many of them appeared to be playing in entirely different ways. Instead of killing their weak opponents, many of the modders flew high above the map, exploring its periphery. They landed on rooftops, clipped through solid walls, hovered in the air, and even balanced on telegraph poles in the centre of the map. These modders appeared to be doing something else in the game-space, playing an entirely different game in the map we shared. Yet while many were content to explore, there were other infected players who persisted in the one-sided battle, and I was repeatedly killed from afar, often picked off even before I was able to locate my quarry.

Out of frustration I found myself intentionally obstructing the modders who ignored me. I got in their way, threw smoke grenades and signal flares in an attempt to break their concentration and provoke a response, even if it meant being killed. I felt frustrated and impotent, yet found pleasure in provoking a response. It felt like a small victory – like I was having some influence in the game from which their actions excluded me. After playing against the infected for around an hour, I powered off the system.

BECOMING INFECTED

Unlike the *World at War* public match example above, this infection lobby occurred in a private match on *Modern Warfare* that the player (who we will call Soap) was invited into by an unknown recent player. Private matches are pertinent, as they do not contribute to a player's statistical profile due to their suitability for collusion, manipulation, and boosting. Nothing was said to indicate the private match had been modified, yet once it began, it was evident it was a "speed lobby" variant where every action – aiming, reloading, and movement – occurs at an accelerated rate. It was evident the other players were already familiar with its operation, as betrayed by the strategies they immediately deployed, equipping grenade-launchers and firing projectiles into the open swamp area where most players were spawned. Soap appeared frustrated by being duped into joining an infection lobby, and for the way that it broke his concentration and represented a deviation from what he had originally been doing, producing videos that documented another kind of expertise, using a "quickscoping" affordance glitch where a sniper rifle could be made to partially auto-aim.

> I was a bit annoyed at first as my previous few games had boasted some pretty high K/D whilst quickscoping and now I was being bombarded by constant noob tubes [gun-mounted grenades] and RPGs. But once I knew what was going on I did join in for a little while as it is fun just firing under barrel grenades like bullets. ...

While in the speed lobby he began to alter his strategies and embrace the divergent play style. Instead of the staccato pace of a typical *Call of Duty* game, where a player moves from cover to cover, checking corners and known vantage points, he became focused on "finding a good camping spot where I could bombard the map without being reached easily myself". Yet "as fun as it was it got boring very quickly" and Soap left the lobby through "dashboarding", a process whereby the Xbox 360 is forced to its operating-system front screen or dashboard. Dashboarding immediately terminates any game processes in memory and disconnects the system from Xbox LIVE. If done during a multiplayer game, it presents any statistics related to the current match from being synchronized with the servers. Tthis could also be done by powering off the machine but the system restart takes longer to return to the game than dashboarding. While Soap was in a private match that would not influence his statistical profile, he still cautiously dashboarded through force of habit.

Soap said he dashboarded quite frequently, even if there were no explicit evidence of modding. He appeared to be suspicious of matches, judging their legitimacy on the "feel" of each individual game, whether a player or team was being particularly dominant, or certain weapons were being used more than others. If a game felt wrong he would dashboard immediately. This was something many other players concurred with, but as for determining the correct feel of a match, it so subjective that I would assume many perfectly normal matches would have been abandoned, and perhaps those playing in earnest would regard Soap's behaviour as inappropriate rage-quitting. Irrespective of this, when the choice to dashboard removes the risk of modded (or poor) games detrimentally impacting on a player's statistical record, there is an incentive to be especially cautious. The odd feeling might simply be attributed to a bad game, but dashboarding also enables players to only register games in which they perform well, positively distorting their profiles accordingly. Once again the disparities between apparently legitimate or wise ways of playing become apparent. Dashboarding to mitigate the damage caused by infection lobbies leads to a suspicious attitude towards the feel of matches. The same processes can be exploited to bolster a statistical profile by only recording good games, and observers may take umbrage at the dashboarding player, seeing them as unsportsmanlike rage-quitters. And as seen previously, this may well warrant retribution later.

CATCHING THE BUG: INFECTION FOR FUN

Zakhaev, whom we have already met in relation to his use of modded lobbies as grief-play, is a twenty-year-old British man who considered himself part of a group of active modders that tended to play multiplayer games together. In addition to playing *Call of Duty* at a "semi-professional" level, approaching the game in a dedicated and serious manner and carefully managing his statistical profile, he also deployed infection lobbies for retribution and to play within for pleasure, using alternate dummy accounts. Zakhaev suggested he and his friends had run forty to fifty infection lobbies across *Modern Warfare* and *Modern Warfare 2*, motivated by what he saw as frustration with the predictability of the multiplayer component:

> Sometimes we just play standard games but once you've got top rank there's pretty much no point playing standard games, you don't get xp [experience points], you're not levelling up, you've got all the titles and emblems. The only reason to play is to boost up your stats.

Instead of editing the game patch code required to deploy an infection lobby, the group downloaded and used pre-made infection lobby patch files that had been created and shared via websites including Se7ensins.com. They saw the appearance of a new patch in a similar way that one might an official game release or DLC.

> When a new glitch or mod is released we normally text one another saying that this has just come out. Everyone is like "get online". When a new patch is available ... [or] as soon as someone finds something new that shouldn't be there the word spreads in like ten minutes and then we're on.

The group used the infection lobby deployment process as a way of overcoming the fact that while not all of the group members had access to the requisite hardware and technical expertise to use mods, they still wished to play together and share the experience of modified game types. Once one member of the group had deployed the infection lobby, using their JTAG and retail console combination, they then invited their friends and passed the infection to them, enabling them all to play together. Only one friend in a group needed a hacked console to enable them all to play with mods. Once Zakhaev and his friends had become infected, they then invited other players to join their matches, topping up the numbers or filling the spaces when some friends eventually had other things to do. Getting people to join the lobbies was not a problem, as Zakhaev stressed there was extensive demand for lobbies.

> If we send out a message saying we're hosting a lobby people are like "yeah fine" and then they play with us instead. ... When people just leave it gets annoying. Our modded game types will fill up in seconds, quite a lot of people like playing something different that's not meant to be there.

In order to avoid any damage incurred to their statistical profiles if the modded games were taken onto public matchmaking, or indeed the minimal risk they would somehow be reported to Microsoft, Zakhaev and his friends each held multiple Xbox LIVE accounts they used for different purposes. They collected promotional Xbox LIVE short-term access scratch-cards, frequently bundled with new retail releases, and also took advantage of seasonal reductions and special offers to build a stock of multiple accounts. These inexpensive, or often free, accounts allowed them to host and play infection lobbies with relative anonymity and little personal risk. Yet it transpired they were fearful of potential retribution from other players and the retaliation that sometimes came with upsetting others, as opposed to a penalty from Microsoft, which Zakhaev "didn't see as much of a threat at all". Most of all, Zakhaev was fearful his activities as a modder (and grief-player) would become known and this would damage his reputation within the playerbase. Zakhaev enjoyed competitive conventional play, he enjoyed modding, enjoyed playing in chaotic scenarios with his friends, and enjoyed grief-playing those he targeted, but he did not want all of these activities to be associated with his repertoire of play. Instead he was happy if his play was seen as the unconnected behaviour of disparate individuals.

Zakhaev described some of the pleasures of infection lobbies, including one of his favourites, the "slow lobby", in which everything runs at a fraction of its normal speed.

> You'd see a rocket launcher coming at you from like 100 metres, but you'd just find it funny – maybe try and jump out of the way – nobody takes it very seriously and in a game mode like that it's purely just for fun. ... You can't take it seriously, there's no way you can get good stats on that.

For Zakhaev and his friends, infection lobbies were a refreshing way of extending the game offering but that also held an additional ambiguous, unserious, and anarchic tone. In subsequent correspondence, the ambiguous and antagonistic aspects of this anonymity became increasingly apparent. Alongside running matches that were filled with willing (and, one assumes, anonymous) participants, Zakhaev admitted to also running the games on public matches into which unwitting conventional players would be randomly placed, much like the JTAG prestige examples. Unless these players dashboarded or disconnected in time, their statistical profiles would have been corrupted and subsequent attempts to leave may have resulted in the modification travelling with them as an infection, exacerbating and extending the damage. Despite the unexpected rules of the match and the potential risk to those who care about their statistical profiles, Zakhaev assured me "about sixty percent of people enjoy joining a different lobby and stick around". But for those remaining forty percent, especially those unfamiliar with dashboarding and infections more generally, the experience of play would have been utterly undermined and the lobby would feel like grief-play.

THINKING ABOUT INFECTIONS

These examples detailing different perspectives of infection lobbies highlight not just their varied uses but a range of apparently contradictory or paradoxical intents. Each of these perspectives – playing against the infected, becoming infected, infection as extension, and, by extension, Zakhaev's grief-play infection as retribution – has a different meaning and resonance.

My experience of playing against the infected was profoundly frustrating. It was nearly impossible to orientate myself within the map and as a result, deaths were frequent and random, often without me even seeing my opponent. I still shot at other conventional players when I could and occasionally got kills, but this was the product of luck rather than strategy. These kills felt like hollow victories as it was clear the infected represented the real opponents. Instead I played in a skulking, furtive manner, conscious of the power imbalance and my inability to rectify it. I ran, I hid, I threw smoke grenades, I swore. I felt utterly subordinate.

The experience of playing against modders illustrated that the game was unplayable in its conventional manner. Aside from the experience of being constantly and unfairly defeated, there was a sense the modders were playing an alternate metagame from which the conventional players were excluded. Not understanding what they were doing or how it was being done was as frustrating as being defeated. I felt paradoxically both harassed and ignored.

The speed lobby deployed on the private match was egalitarian in the sense it had no impact on statistics and all players were subject to its (mis) rule. Soap did not articulate any intrinsic opposition to the notion of illicit modifications, and even found them enjoyable, but this was coupled by concern over their potential to undermine statistics and a cautious awareness of how to safely extricate himself when he did encounter them. In many ways Soap was an ideal *Call of Duty* player, dedicated to his statistical profile but also knowledgeable about glitches, mods, and the appropriate interactions, and thus able to negotiate the game-space with the minimum of visibility and fuss.

> In a private game environment I don't have a problem with them, but when the host player is roaming the public lobbies it gets annoying when all of a sudden the opposite team is invincible, leaping 30ft into the air.

For Soap, the problems of infection lobbies centred primarily around the ways in which they had the capacity to undermine achievement and, secondarily, around issues of openness and fairness. Providing there was an informed choice and the lobbies were confined to invite-only matches, he saw little reason for objection. Despite the negative implications of Zakhaev's public lobbies and the estimated forty percent of players who were opposed to them, he saw them as improving and adding value to a product that deeply seduced him. This is illustrated when challenged about the oppositional or hostile nature of his actions in relation to the authority of the designers and the experience of the game.

> No, it's not like that at all! Everyone who plays *Call of Duty* would love the people who created it – without them we'd have no game to play. These games are to extend, like an extra DLC that's free for everyone, and it's just different.

There was even scepticism over the intent of the designers and platform-holders, suggesting that on some level, there was tacit approval and the game was meant to be modded, but the logic of this argument was weak at best.

> They haven't made it any harder for us. The fact that we can actually do this means they've left it there for us to do. We'll find it and we'll change it.

While this smacks of all-to-familiar efforts to rationalize and justify illicit acts, if the sentiment is genuine (and I believe it was), it nevertheless illustrates significant differences in attitude and perception among player communities.

Lastly, Zakhaev's use of infection lobbies as retribution (as detailed in the grief-play chapter) exposes the antagonistic and protean nature of the infection lobby and "bad play" more generally. The issue is that irrespective of the intentions of the individual modders, whether they wanted to demonstrate their power or were simply playing with the space in their own way, the cumulative impact was an experience of victimization, isolation, and harassment by an inscrutable and what seemed at times like a co-ordinated group. Yet at the same time the experience was also exciting and novel, at least at first, and I found just being in radically subverted space had an enjoyable illicit charge. However, had I been concerned with my statistical profile, the experience would have had a much more negative meaning.

Modded lobbies may simultaneously be a tiresome articulation of inequality, an egalitarian play extension, a mischievous and damaging trap, and even utilized in extremes as a tool of retribution. The modification becomes reused as a method of repairing the perceived damage caused by other modifications, and this exposes either a dangerous vigilantism or fitting sense of homeostasis.

What translates from each of these readings of infection lobbies is the importance placed on "gamer capital" as manifested in *Call of Duty* in a comprehensive understanding of the processes associated with the game and a presentation of skill through statistics or unlocks. Being a good player by the conventional markers of the game is highly important, so much so that it motivates the black market in prestige lobbies, but this also drives the steps taken to create alternate accounts with which to dabble in modding and the frustrations felt around those who manipulate and unfairly display the markers of skill. As a corollary, what also becomes apparent is that for many players, encountered modifications represented an expanded part of the game environment and something many were either curious about or keen to experience. Additionally, understanding how to dashboard and other ways to navigate through modded lobbies with impunity become yet other expressions of expertise and skill alongside knowing how to navigate the maps and dominate opponents.

The message is clear. Learn to deal with infections, use alternate accounts to experience them, or dashboard when they are encountered in the wild or allow your reputation within the game community to be diminished. For those like me whose lack of manual dexterity has necessitated an ambivalence towards gaming leader boards and reputation, dedicated gamers' infection lobbies and other illicit modifications take on a genuinely attractive and amusing meaning. But for the many who care deeply for the goals and values designed into a game, this is not necessarily the case. However, we should remember that *Call of Duty* modded lobbies are just one example of illicit modification on console systems, and while lobbies are about making money, building reputations, and experiencing something chaotic and novel, mods are used for other altogether different purposes, such as in the case of "ISO modding" and the development of "trainers".

ISO MODDING AND TRAINERS

The YouTube video loads and a slick animated sequence fills the screen. The logo rotates left and right, accompanied by a rising orchestral score and powerful drum beats. The screen fades to black and we are presented with a video from Bioware's popular *Mass Effect 3* (2012). Commander Shepherd stands in a barren alien planet, taking up most of the bottom-left quadrant of the screen. The soundtrack is punchy dubstep, and debug data, co-ordinates, and commands are superimposed over the user interface in the top left. The player looks left at an architectural feature in the far distance, far beyond the limits of the playable game environment, aiming his weapon reticle at the column, and promptly flies through the air towards it. The player dives down through the column far beneath the game map before stopping, aiming, and teleporting to another point instantaneously. Using this method the player teleports around, scrutinizing various monolithic pieces of digital architecture far beyond the game map before dropping to the ground and sprinting towards the heavily armed alien foes in the distance. On entering combat, the player shoots an assault rifle that spews a laser-like stream of projectiles. There is no need to reload, no recoil, and no damage when Shepherd is flanked and lunged at by a robo-insectoid-xenomorph. The player then demonstrates a range of attacks and strategies: levitating high above the battlefield, slowing game speed to make progress simple, and where Commander Shepherd's 3D model grows perhaps twenty times larger than normal. The video fades to black and text appears, inviting us to download the mod file from a link provided and the video ends.

For those of you unfamiliar with the description, this is a modified instance of *Mass Effect 3*, a hugely popular science-fiction, action roleplaying game in which the player is tasked with saving planet Earth from an alien invasion force. The game is characterized by slow and protracted battles, with players using cover, the unique abilities of their colleagues, and tactical orders to carefully progress through the levels. Aggressive or hasty approaches to play in *Mass Effect 3* are generally met with failure.

The modded video appears to offer a rather radical subversion of the tools and abilities within the game. It undermines, or enhances, practically each of the game mechanics – movement, cover, timing, and resource management – and evidently destroys any narrative flow or sense of progression. It shares the same visual and aural resources but the game feels inherently subverted. This is a mod that is expressly meant to be shared with and used by others, but only a small audience on the basis that they will need access to a hacked console to run it. To be clear, this is a ISO mod on account of it being based around the editing of a ripped game-image file, and it is considered a "trainer" mod, changing the way the game is played in order to help the player become better at the game but also radically changing the relationship between player, game, and challenge.

Other examples of mods on the same YouTube channel present similar subversion and reinvention of the game experience. In a modification of *Homefront* (2011), a rather generic first-person shooter, the player, leaps into the air and flies around San Francisco's Golden Gate bridge, firing missiles and throwing an infinite stream of grenades. Then the player exposes the wireframe construction of the simulation, before intercepting the fighter jets that act as scenery, occasionally screaming across the game level, slowing time to a crawl and riddling them with bullets. Another mod for *Batman: Arkham City* (2011), a third-person action game, has the game shifted into a rudimentary flight simulator, with Batman levitating high into the air before gliding down through Arkham City using his Batcape. In a final example, in *Duke Nukem Forever* (2011) the only visible change to the game is that all the video screens display "Happy Birthday Lupo" instead of the expected video loops. The game-space is reappropriated as a greetings card.

While each of these mods are the product of one modder, a cursory YouTube search of almost any current generation game title and "Xbox 360 mods" indicates how prevalent these forms of counterplay appear to be: *Mass Effect* (2007, 11,700 hits), *Gears of War* (2006, 21,2000 hits); *Bioshock* (2007, 11,800 hits), and *Medal of Honor* (2010, 12,100 hits). Despite, or perhaps entirely because of, its illicit nature, thousands of individuals appear to find the creation and dissemination of console-based mods an engaging cultural practice, choosing to play with video games in this manner. I was able to spend time within the company of illicit modders who had produced a number of trainers and ISO mods, including those detailed above, and was able to explore the processes and motivations that underpinned their activity.

The interaction with modders, and particularly being shown the process of modification, challenged the reading of the mods as spectacular or dependent on sophisticated technical understanding. Instead it highlighted that the modifications were a rather mundane and repetitious product of the use of relatively few game-development platforms. It was not that these modders were actively having to decipher and develop processes afresh each time they modded a game but that they were applying the same set of debug commands and therefore triggering the same modifications: invulnerability, flight, no-clip, slow motion etc.

Video-game development is a highly competitive and financially demanding process. As a result, development studios are under pressure to consolidate and centralise production wherever possible. One instance where efficiency can be achieved is through the use of "middleware" production tools such as the Unreal Engine, which boast high levels of portability, allowing one set of resources and game code to be compiled for different target hardware platforms. It is this portability that enabled the same managed code lists to create effective *Call of Duty* lobby mods on the PlayStation 3 and Xbox 360. The common resources – 3D models, textures, event scripting, sound, and video files – can then be co-ordinated and called by a platform -pecific executable that is compiled and exported directly from the middleware environment. Instead of coding two different games, one for the Xbox 360 and another for the PlayStation 3 using different teams, it is viable to produce one game for the "lead platform" and then to export an executable for the other platforms from within the middleware engine. While this is an oversimplification of the process, the point is that at their core, most mainstream releases on Xbox 360 and PlayStation 3 utilize the same game code and are subject to the same exploits. Similarly, different games produced with the same middleware engines also share the same general vulnerabilities.

Yet it is this adoption of a limited number of middleware platforms, combined with the public release of modding tools with many multiplatform PC games, that has inadvertently facilitated illicit console modification. As the PC modding communities explore and discuss the ways in which code can be altered and new functionality integrated, due to the common code-set presented by the middleware platform, this inadvertently indicates how a console modification can be done. The only barriers are that consoles are closed systems that prevent the introduction of new code, but as we are aware, hacked consoles remove that restriction.

Providing the modder has an appropriately hacked console, they have already overcome the security measures that would prevent an ISO mod to be conducted. All they need to alter is the code and then the modification is complete. This is facilitated either through the use of an alternate file manager such as XeXmenu or FreeStyleDash, specifically created for hacked Xbox 360, or acquiring a "ripped" game ISO. This would be the same process undertaken by an individual wishing to play pirated video games, the only difference being the modder wishes to alter the code instead of using it as is.

Much like the prestige lobby, once the user transfers the ISO file onto a hard disk drive and then onto a personal computer, they are able to explore and interrogate the structure and its contents. In the case of an Unreal Engine game, one file, COALESCED.BIN, is the main target of the illicit game modder. It is this file that controls the universal environmental settings of the game-space and which player button presses are "bound" to software routines. Effectively it is this file that controls the operational and constitutive rules of the game, and through changing this, the modder not only alters the way the simulation behaves but also the way in which the player interacts with it.

In the following example, the modder binds a reduction of the game environment's gravity to the pressing of the Xbox 360 controller's 'a' button. The script is written in such a way that the effects are removed once the button is released.

"xboxtypes_a", command = "setgravity +900", on release "setgravity –900"

By searching this file for keywords such as "worldinfo", which controls the universal settings that determine the simulation, and "playerinput", which controls the routines that are bound to button presses, the modder begins to decipher the specific values and control that define that game and available interactions. By searching for common functions within action-orientated games, and by cross-checking them against the buttons they are bound to, such as "jump", "fireweapon", and "changeweapon", the modder is able to rapidly search other files for these terms until their settings are located – and modified. Providing the modder is prepared to spend a little time tracing the links between button binds, routines, and variables, they are able to radically alter the functionality of the game.

In addition to the game-specific variable settings the modder alters there are a number of "exec-functions" that are part of the middleware development engine itself and that can be invoked by the modder. A comprehensive list of the Unreal Engine exec-functions are distributed by Unreal as guidance to its Developer Network, which is frequented by game developers and modders alike. Among the hundred or so exec-functions are "Teleport", which teleports the player to the surface they are looking at, "Slomo", which reduces game speed, and "Loaded", which gives weapons and full ammunition. It is also possible to modify games through swapping out resources, such as the replacement of object textures or video sequences with alternatives provided by the modder. This is a case of merely replacing a file while retaining the file type and file name. Again, due to standardisation of software – in this case the widespread use of the Bink Video encoding software and its free availability for non-commercial use – modders can easily encode and introduce new sources of video into modified games.

At this point it is useful to return to the examples of ISO mods and trainers detailed earlier. The *Mass Effect 3* and *Homefront* trainers are largely the product of exec-functions bound to button presses, including Teleport, Loaded, Slomo, and Ghost. The *Batman: Arkham City* mod appears to largely be based on an adjustment of the gravity settings bound to a button press (in order to make Batman levitate), and the *Duke Nukem Forever* mod is a simple case of encoding a short piece of video using the Bink codec and replacing the original file.

The issue is that by building familiarity with an engine and through repeated game modification, patterns and consistencies become evident. Multiple mods invoke the same exec-functions (often bound to the same controller buttons) and offer the user the same pleasure – flight, infinite ammo, invulnerability, slow motion. The act of modification becomes startlingly generic. As a result it becomes very difficult to read a mod as creative innovation or even a particular challenge to the game. It is replaced with a rather mundane process of repetition following the shortest process of orientation with the idiosyncrasies of a new software release. Instead of presenting original and innovative ways of playing with and consuming a game, the modification ascribes a predictable set of functions and abilities, and is almost archaeological, unearthing hidden functions still somewhere within the game code. This is certainly the case when it comes to the ancillary outcomes of ISO modding, where modders diving into and scrutinising the game code find references to future DLC releases, such as the name of future multiplayer maps, or the much maligned "on disc" DLC, where content is merely unlocked when a purchase is made. In these cases the modder is digging into the code to ascertain what the game means, how it works, and what it still might contain in the future.

Illicit console mods therefore can be considered incredibly rapid things to produce, providing one has the requisite hardware and inclination. This rapidity of production, combined with the number of people engaged with the activity, alter the significance and pleasure of the mod production. It moves from being a creative act of subversion to a race for status. In terms of the *Mass Effect 3* mod video, the exclusivity becomes more important than the actual contents. To have modded it takes priority over what the mod offers. It shares some of the same pressures exposed in glitchers' scavenger hunts. One modder I spoke with told me:

> It's definitely a race, me and a few others always try and be the first to release a mod! … I'll keep looking for when an ISO is about to be uploaded, it's normally a week before the first release, and the moment it is I've got to download it and mod it. … I spend way more time recording a video that shows off the mod than modding the game itself.

By looking at the comments on an ISO mod/trainer video it is possible to get a sense of the lifespan of a mod video. Initially, supportive and receptive comments tend to be made, such as those commenting on or congratulating the modder for their efforts and, if unavailable, requesting access to the mod. However, many of the responses that follow appear to be strongly opposed to the activity. Aggressive and oppositional language is frequently used to question and denigrate the activity. I asked the modder whether the mods were produced in opposition to the contexts of production and consumption – as a protest against the game, the developers, or the economic model – but the line of argument, with notions of weak tactics, authenticity of the resistant reader, and the power of the institutional wasn't recognised.

> Games are pretty expensive, but if I want one I'll buy it. I love video games and play them normally as well as modding them. As for developing them, that'd kind of be my ideal job. … I'd really like to work making games but there aren't any colleges that do it or studios near here and besides, everyone wants to do it.

ISO modding and trainer creation appeared to be a pleasurable way of interacting with the game at a deeper level. It also developed some level of recognition and reputation, both positively within modding circles and negatively within the public. While many of the comments on the videos were initially positive, subsequent comments were oppositional or negative, and the modders frequently had to come to terms with a certain level of infamy and hostility from other viewers. This even extended to people who were involved in the games industry.

> They know exactly who we are and I can tell you they hate what we do. I've had emails and comments from people at Epic complaining about my mods, and videos are always being taken off YouTube, but I just ignore it, it's par for the course.

The pleasures, according to one modder, were what engaging with the code allowed him to see, the way it enabled him to further imagine how the game was produced. These are the digital equivalent of maker's marks within the structure and resources used to create the game, similar to the "fake background" label on a piece of scenery in the *Duke Nukem Forever* highway-barrier glitch in Chapter Four. What's more, the modder was curious as to why things like this were left in the game, assuming they were put there for players to access via unanticipated and often counterplay means.

> It's the code, I like looking at how they've built the game ... but you also get to explore bits of levels that are hidden. Like the secrets and Easter eggs that the devs leave in the games. Why do they leave them in the games unless they want people to see it? It doesn't make sense.

What is curious is that once again, despite receiving negative comments from developers and public alike, he still strongly associated his modding as play and refused to accept direct responsibility for the implications of the mods he had produced, although he expressed frustration that others had misused his mods. This echoes some of the stances taken by glitchers regarding game-breakers.

> ... sometimes the mods I make are misused. ... one of my ISO mods was misused and they made the multiplayer of [—] unplayable. Don't get me wrong, the multiplayer was pretty crappy in the first place, and I told people to use the mod fairly but the game was ruined, you couldn't do anything without being up against people using the mods and then the only people playing online were modders. ... I felt kind of gutted that it was my mod that people used to do it. ...

Once again this raises a dynamic seen in the grief-play, glitching, and modded lobbies examples. The modder failed to see any direct link between his actions, any damage made to the game, and the economic and legal implications. While at its heart the motivation for modding was evidently not one of hostility or destruction, nor a lack of funds (the modder showed me his collection of hardware platforms and game releases) but an ambivalence or neutrality towards the economic context of gaming. If this is resistance, it is certainly diffuse and passive.

The modder held the belief he had every right to access the games, their code, and their platforms. His view appeared to sit somewhere between a hacker hands-on-imperative and a fan-culture ownership of the text. Yet when I presented these ideas to the modder, he recognised neither the distinction nor even the contested space of ownership and access.

> It's a gut feeling. It's just what I do. ... I don't share anything that might really damage a game, and if I do I warn people to use it fairly. When I download an ISO I do it just to mod, that's it. ... It's not like it's a lost sale, I wouldn't have bought the game, and if I do play a game I always buy a copy and keep it. ... I don't think that Microsoft will come after me. Loads of people do this and nobody gets anything more than a console ban.

FROM ISO MODDING TO SOFTWARE DEVELOPMENT

While all of the modification practices in this chapter are reliant on relatively hands-on intervention and alteration of code, the use of hex editors, and a suite of rudimentary productivity applications, there are also a number of bespoke modding tools or modding frameworks that have been released. These are generally PC software applications, including Modio and Horizon, which offer a single interface to allow users to easily navigate, view, and modify the content of video-game console storage, some of which enables the automated creation of modified patches, radically lowering the technical barrier to mod development. They make modding, piracy, and the general use of hacked consoles accessible to those with a lower threshold of technical understanding and can therefore be regarded as instrumental in the development of mainstream console-modding culture.

In addition to these popular software tools publicly released through sites such as Free60.org, there is a body of less well-known software that has been intentionally restricted by its creators and is only available to trusted sources and for the right fee. This kind of restricted software represents a further layer of commercial exploitation of *Call of Duty* modding and an interesting level of organization and self regulation from within the most skilled elements within the modding community.

What this creates is a small number of privileged hackers and modders who restrict knowledge and access to the processes to those who are trusted and are willing to pay the entrance fees. In the context of *Call of Duty*, lobbies were quietly reinstated by a small cadre of hackers after the previous vulnerabilities had been patched. The complex process by which they reinstated the prestige lobbies allowed them to once again earn income from their operation but also resulted in the increase in lobby access costs pointed out by Bob. This met the demands of the audience but the costs ensured sufficient exclusivity to prevent the deflation of modded lobby fees caused by overabundance while avoiding the adverse impact of security updates motivated by conspicuous modding. In fact, during their operation these third-generation prestige lobbies were never expressly confirmed or advertised, although many speculated they existed. While there were rumours that it was possible to overcome the Xbox LIVE security, and some had mentioned a process called "Project Rainbowzzz", there was little reliable evidence to prove its existence and many were skeptical, regarding it as purely conjecture.

PROJECT RAINBOWZZZ

On September 9, 2012 the Project Rainbowzzz leak ended any speculation. The leak not only confirmed it was possible to connect infected consoles to Xbox LIVE, it also revealed it had been going on for some time. What more, it also told users precisely how to do it, including links to all the necessary files and a decompiled software package titled Project Rainbowzzz. Up until that point, Project Rainbowzzz had been a highly restricted process that allowed players to connect to Xbox LIVE via remote servers and proxies, meaning that connection was made without ever having direct access to the Project Rainbowzzz files. Instead, the individual wishing to connect their JTAG or RGH to Xbox LIVE was required to connect their Xbox 360 to a server owned by the Project Rainbowzzz developers using the FreeStyleDash homebrew application. On connection, the server made the necessary modifications needed to allow connection to Xbox LIVE directly into the Xbox 360 system's memory and then forwarded the console to the service. Once these credentials had been placed on the modified machine, it would appear to be legitimate and could go onto Xbox LIVE.

The developers of Project Rainbowzzz had decided on this model to prevent the method and its files from being shared with the community, to mitigate against reverse engineering, or perhaps to just ensure its judicious use and protect revenue streams, as well as to avoid the democratic release of the technique that had been seen with infections. Importantly, Project Rainbowzzz was not restricted to enabling *Call of Duty* lobbies to operate but enabled hacked consoles to connect to Xbox LIVE for the use of any game or mod.

> I present: PROJECT RAINBOWZZZ
> Price: FREE
> --Tired of seeing this stolen, cracked and then passed around to every one and their brother to try to sell something that isn't theirs.
>
> If certain people want to hate ... well then don't hate on me. I didn't leak the files to myself. When all these randoms start to get it, then things are out of control. Plus I am not using those leaked files here

anyway, just the source code I created from reversing the xex, which was leaked anyways so wtf is the point.

(Se7ensins.com 2012)

The Project Rainbowzzz release not only allowed players to connect their JTAGs and RGHs to Xbox LIVE servers, at least until Microsoft released a security patch that altered and strengthened the Xbox LIVE validation challenges less than a week later. It also confirmed the existence of a body of hackers/modders who were technically proficient and willing to withhold developments for commercial gain and who used this as a way of generating significant income and deploying it in a highly restrictive and monopolistic manner. These hackers held none of the egalitarianism tied in with hacker ethics or the hands-on-imperative. Their work, and the way they had managed to keep the process secret for so long, earned them significant income and kudos. In later correspondence Bob, the commercial hardware hacker, treated these individuals with deference, calling them the "uber-intelligent top of the Xbox tree".

The "uber-intelligent" can be understood as those actively engaged in the production of modding frameworks and other utilitarian homebrew, especially that which clandestinely connected to legitimate sources such as Xbox LIVE or the Microsoft Developer Network. It does not necessitate that they deploy them for financial profit, just that they can understand and utilize the system on a level beyond the average player, hardware hacker, or modder. They are the equivalent to Tmbnc, who developed the JTAG hack but oriented it towards the gaming ecosystem. While my attempts to correspond with the individuals behind Project Rainbowzzz were unsuccessful, I was able to make contact with another prominent modder, iHcJames, who Bob regarded as one of top of the tree. What he explained to me represents that most antagonistic aspect of counterplay I encountered, complete with legal dealings with both Activision and Microsoft, but yet his motivations still squarely fell within seduction with video games.

IHC.DLL: A SOFTWARE RELEASE

iHcJames, a friendly and unassuming Englishman in his early twenties, had become known within modding communities for having created IHC. DLL, a piece of software that enabled modders to reintroduce *Call of Duty* infection lobbies after the security patches deployed by Activision. Whereas the original infection lobbies used the conventional process of setting up a system-link game in order to infect the physically attached retail console, the developers removed this vulnerability and IHC.DLL was expressly written to reinstate the process. In effect it was a new application executed from within the *Call of Duty* game that simply changed the settings on any attached system, reinstating the exploit and becoming the foundation for the infection variants that were subsequently developed and are still used to this day.

This kind of software represents a shift in complexity when compared with JTAG and infection lobbies. It is software written to interface with Xbox 360 hardware and games and with an awareness of the functionality and security measures on Xbox LIVE. IHC.DLL is software designed to circumvent these systems for a specific purpose, irrespective of the security measures placed on the game through title updates. In turn, IHC.DLL and other software produced by iHcJames enabled modders to engage in a wide range of counterplay forms while also bringing back some of the commercial lobbies that had existed previously.

Adopting the hacker-ethic, hands-on imperative, iHcJames broke systems and software apart, looking at the ways they attempted to communicate with each other to develop models of how they worked. For iHcJames it was protected developer software, such as Developer Network update disks and private beta code, which were instrumental in building his understanding of the Xbox 360 console ecosystems and the security processes that surrounded Xbox LIVE and the Developer Network, therefore enabling him to develop ways of interfacing with these services and ultimately gain illegitimate access. Occasionally exotic and unexpected software ISOs are shared on the modding- and hacking-related community sites and peer networks, and it was through this process and largely through luck that iHcJames acquired a Microsoft Developer Network update disk. He explains:

> I got hold of a developer network update disk that updates a developer console to a new dashboard (OS version), the ISO was leaked online. … I reverse engineered it and figured out what it connected to, [including] the different development environments such as Xbox LIVE, [and] Partner net. I then created a piece of software to run on my JTAG that connected directly to these and allowed me to look around and see what was there.

From this privileged and unauthorized position, iHcJames was able to access developer resources and connect to channels used to distribute developmental builds, private beta builds, waypoint stages, media review code packages, and unreleased DLC. He created a simple brute force application, which scoured the networks for available software download packages that were indexed and cached, enabling him to download those of particular interest at a later date. This approach, however, brought iHcJames to the attention of Microsoft, who carefully licenses and controls the access credentials and developer console hardware that can legitimately connect to the Developer Network, which iHcJames' JTAG consoles were purporting to be.

Each connection to Developers Network was logged by Microsoft and, much like a JTAG going onto Xbox LIVE, when detected as spurious, the console, or rather its unique keyvault, was invalidated. iHcJames stated he had developed a way for generating developer console keyvaults and he used this to continually keyvault his JTAG to enable it to reconnect and explore the Developer Network some more. Little did iHcJames appreciate how seriously Microsoft protected their network and the extent to which the development of IHC.DLL had been scrutinized by Activision.

> This is partly how I eventually got into trouble with Microsoft – each time I connected to the dev network it generated a new certificate and it looked like I had 50 or so developer consoles. They must have thought I had an unregistered studio at my house and understandably they wanted to take a look, but these consoles didn't exist, they were just Keyvaults I'd generated.

Soon, after repeatedly connecting to the Developer Network, iHcJames says representatives visited him from Microsoft and Activision, which marked the beginning of a protracted and on-going legal relationship between the modder/hacker and platform-holders. The representatives "came to see me asking about the developer consoles, and they ended up taking away two of my consoles and a USB drive with my developmental work. They had expected to see more on account of the Keyvaults but that was what they took".

Up to this point, iHcJames was able to use his access to the Developer Network to interrogate game and platform processes, understand what resources were utilized, what variables were called, and ultimately what information controlled the states of the software being played. Once this information was understood it was a relatively simple step to begin to develop homebrew software that used the same resources or protocols, mimicking aspects of the commercial code. This was precisely the method iHcJames used to develop IHC.DLL, which he publicly released on March 24, 2012 on Se7ensins.com and which was quickly adopted by many. Unlike Project Rainbowzzz, IHC.DLL was distributed widely and was subsequently edited and modified by other modders and hackers. All iHcJames asked for was to be credited in the code.

The release of IHC.DLL is somewhat curious, since it inevitably desta-bilised the equilibrium that had existed in which only the highly proficient, top-of-the-tree modders/hackers were able to modify lobbies and generate income. As a release it was therefore likely to have been viewed with disdain by some of the most organized and secretive of the modding/hacking community, namely the top of the tree, but regarded as a hugely positive development to those, like Zakhaev, wishing to return to the height of infection lobby-modding. Initially the public IHC.DLL release seems foolhardy. Why release such a powerful and valuable tool to everyone? However, the release makes more sense when you read the announcement post in full. Within it, iHcJames includes a full explanation of how the software works and, cru-cially, detailed instructions for how it could be patched. While it is rather technical, it illustrates iHcJames' intent.

Hai Infinity Ward How you can easily patch this, say bye to activeaction, or if you use it for some file from a zone, check the strlen, doubt it would be long enough for the activeactionception. As this requires a title update, you may be able to fix this with a hot-fix, if you can set dvars at the menu (between each game) or before it adds activeaction to the cmd buffer just clear it.

(Se7ensins.com 2012)

While it only makes slight sense, the tone is clear. It is simultaneously illustrating that iHcJames understands the software but is reaching out to the developers as equals while also generating kudos within modding circles for his audacity. iHcJames' statement appears very similar to Fail0verflow's presentation at the Chaos Communication Congress. The IHC.DLL release adopts the conventional hacker/hands-on-imperative rhetoric, presenting the information to all parties and exposing an identified flaw. It also resonates with the practices of the glitcher, such as chaoticPERFECTION's video message to Epic Games. But, like that example, it also retains an ambivalent and hostile aspect. It shows iHcJames understands the processes and has the capability to produce homebrew software. Perhaps more importantly, the IHC.DLL release can be considered part of a carefully managed promotional campaign leading to the crescendo that is the release of another application, a modding framework known as Project AC1D. In addition to the message to Infinity Ward on the IHC.DLL instructions, iHcJames stated, "I am working on Project AC1D (Yes it will be released soon, be patient – may also be adding Modern Warfare 2 support)" (Se7ensins.com 2012), a teaser statement that alludes to iHcJames' most contentious middleware project and one that ultimately placed him in direct opposition to Activision.

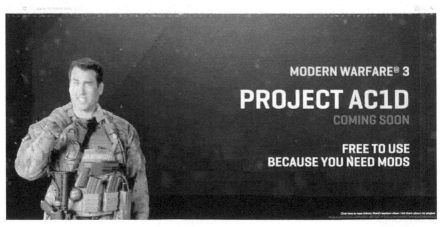

Figure 6.5 Modding, iHcJames' ill-fated Project AC1D announcement webpage.

PROJECT AC1D AND ANTAGONIZING ACTIVISION

Project AC1D is an unreleased intermediary modding framework to be run on a hacked Xbox 360 that would allow users to modify almost all aspects of the *Call of Duty: Modern Warfare 2* and *Modern Warfare 3* games. Built through the same skillset that enabled IHC.DLL, it would allow players not simply to alter the game settings, as with prestige and infection lobbies, but even the very construction and layout of game maps themselves. AC1D was therefore a fully fledged game modification and generation tool. As iHcJames explained, "I wanted to produce a Garry's Mod for Call of Duty", referring to the hugely successful user-created modification tool for Valve's source engine that was subsequently adopted by Valve and sold as a commercial release (2006). It was with the hope the same might occur with Activision that potentially motivated the development of Project AC1D, and in turn coloured the release of IHC.DLL, thus explaining the motivation for its public release and the direct message to the developers, Infinity Ward. The intention was to make them aware of his abilities, his willingness to parlay, and, like so many of the other counterplayers I spoke with, the hope he might eventually be recruited within the industry.

> I make the stuff impressive to show off what I can do in terms of programming and, of course, I love Call of Duty ... I tried to make a big image out of the modding I did in attempt to impress studios and jump into a career of game programming/security, but the only thing I have received from Activision and Microsoft are legal issues.

iHcJames had been working on Project AC1D for some time prior to the IHC.DLL release. On February 22, 2012, iHcJames published a teaser release on Se7ensins.com, inviting members to "Follow the release countdown @ http://www.iHcJames.com/AC1D/". Beneath it was a reply post that included a YouTube video link to what appeared to be a *Modern Warfare 3* modified lobby running online, something that was not possible at the time. This had been the relatively quiet announcement of Project AC1D. IHcJames' IHC.DLL release was drawing fresh attention to it now that it was largely completed. In contrast to the developer-aligned announcement of IHC.DLL, the Project AC1D holding page presented a much more modder-orientated and confrontational rhetoric. While the branding of the web page might fool the inattentive viewer into thinking they are looking at an official piece of Activision promotional literature, a small link at the bottom right of the page, which invites the viewer to "Click here to hear Infinity Ward's reaction when I tell them about Project AC1D", exposes the project's antagonism and contradicts some of the message in the IHC.DLL release: "Walking to the studio, Im gun [sic], NOOOOO GOD, NOOO, PLEASE NO, NO, NOO, NOOOOOOO – RIP Infinity Ward". Thus Project AC1D, which Activision was certainly aware of, was betrayed as malign, openly antagonistic, hostile, and incendiary, and due to his Developer Network intrusions and IHC.DLL release it was evident that iHcJames was at least competent.

iHcJames had been working on Project AC1D for the majority of March 2012, and had alluded in the IHC.DLL release that the project was nearing completion. In its current state, iHcJames asserted that it enabled:

> Extract ... access to all of the functionality of the Call of Duty script. I could do whatever I wanted to do it allowed me to patch the flags, the entities, aspects of the map, everything, it's because you're editing the memory directly instead of the files.

iHcJames uploaded successive videos charting the progress of AC1D, and when its functionality was combined with that of IHC.DLL, it would imply the modification tool would not only offer sophisticated manipulation but was likely to be able to run online. This would not simply reinstate the wide-scale modifications seen in JTAG prestige lobbies previously but increase the deviation further as a result of the level-editing capabilities. Put simply, a software release like Project AC1D, even if utterly illicit, could cause significant damage to Activision's franchise and business model. Even though the software and vulnerabilities would likely eventually be patched, having an example of *Call of Duty* with a level editor would likely raise questions over the need for annual releases and place Activision in an unnecessarily problematic situation. iHcJames detailed the extent to which the game resources were available for modification through AC1D.

> While all of the scenery of the levels were "baked" [compiled] and therefore couldn't be edited all the other entities, like barrels, and their locations could be. AC1D gradient was the name of the editor that I created, it allowed you to move and save the locations of all of those unbaked entities like barrels and cars, but not baked stuff like buildings.

It was this versatility twinned with the antagonistic stance of the holding page that presumably made Project AC1D such a comprehensive perceived threat and necessitated an urgent response from Activision.

> Having these map tools would allow a user to edit any of the maps and save them, and share them, and of course this would mean that DLC maps could easily be distributed. This is perhaps where the major issue with Activision came in. If AC1D gradient was available they [the player] could share content – and by doing so it'd undermine the money made from DLC.

iHcJames had posted a sequence of developmental videos charting the progress of his Project AC1D code. The first, uploaded on March 3, consisted of a proof of concept, but less than a month later, on March 30, iHcJames posted a number of interactive menu and weapon variable tests that demonstrated much of the functionality of Project AC1D was complete. The first showed real-time modification menus that could be accessed during play, demonstrating the menu being used and the player shifting from a conventional weapon and crosshair view to that of a camera-guided missile.

Other weapon tests accentuated the versatility and granularity of the modification options and their potential for spectacle, such as through changing the individual variables of weapons. These not only allowed well-known count variables but also timing, spread, and damage alterations to be made. In the video sequences shown, a machine gun fires hundreds of heat-seeking single-use rockets, the player spins, creating a torus from their exhaust trails before the rockets radiate out in search of their eventual targets. As there are no other players in the map, the rockets thump down into the ground, randomly creating plumes of smoke on impact. Other alterations in the video include a shotgun that has its fire rate increased so dramatically that it spews a plume of fizzing projectiles like a sparkler. Each of these examples illustrates the versatility of Project AC1D and the extent to which it represented a shift in the sophistication of illicit modding tools, bridging the variability of modding within a simple graphical user interface. With IHC.DLL and the weapon interface completed, iHcJames was then going to move on to the most ambitious and incendiary aspect of Project AC1D, the AC1D gradient-level editing component. However it was at this point his activities suddenly and dramatically ceased.

iHcJames told me that early in the morning on Saturday March 31, 2012, he was roused by someone knocking on his front door. The person purported to be an attorney representing Activision and promptly served him with a cease-and-desist letter for Project AC1D. The letter, which he later allowed me to copy, made it clear Activision was fully aware of his activities and of the ways he had communicated his progress and assisted others in their mods on modding-orientated websites. iHcJames' creation of "a modding framework for MW 3 that would permit members of the public to alter and modify elements of the game without the authorization or consent of Activision", and his activities advertising the framework and "specifically by releasing modding tools and instructing others how to use those tools", were listed as violating a number of legal restrictions, including the DMCA, and were ultimately presented as "acts of unfair competition under the laws of the United States and European Union". The cease and desist left iHcJames with no uncertainty. If Project AC1D were to cease immediately, Activision would seek no further damages, but if he did not comply, the case would be escalated and copyright violation reported and pursued.

The language used in the letter highlights the severity of the infringement and the potential legal ramifications to iHcJames, but it also betrays that Activision simply wish to prevent Project AC1D from being developed and a protracted, and potentially expensive, legal challenge is not its aim. For what is in effect a legal threat, the tone of the letter shows restraint and even an element of warmth towards iHcJames, going so far as to recognise he is a fan of the *Call of Duty* series but that his actions are both "unlawful and have the potential to cause serious harm to Activision", largely through impairing the game's multiplayer component. The friendliness iHcJames read within the wording of the letter, and the familiarity he felt with subsequent interactions with Activision representatives, later became problematic, but at the point of serving the cease and desist, it was highly effective. iHcJames ceased development of Project AC1D immediately.

In addition to stopping any further activity related to Project AC1D, iHcJames was also required to surrender its source code and notify Activision of the various locations in which it was stored. This would prevent further development, enable the framework to be removed from circulation, and, one would assume, enable Activision to reverse-engineer its code to identify what vulnerabilities it exploited. Activision's intervention had prevented the release of a modding framework that iHcJames suggested would likely have been completed by the end of the weekend. Activision was able to protect its franchise and intervene in a way that, despite the dramatic immediacy of an attorney visiting the modder at his home, showed considerable restraint and sound judgement. In the end, apart from a flurry of forum posts across modding sites discussing and judging iHcJames' response to the visit and his choice to cease development, Project AC1D disappeared quietly and no major modding framework undermined *Modern Warfare 3*'s multiplayer experience.

However, instead of feeling fortunate to have narrowly avoided prosecution for a swathe of violations, in subsequent interviews iHcJames spoke of a growing frustration and disappointment with the outcome.

> I was obviously pretty annoyed at Activision because I put a lot of hard work into this project ... and because the stuff that I do isn't particularly intended to damage or undermine their games. I tried to get this across to them but they wouldn't really listen about that.

He stated his intention with Project AC1D was to encode "a feature where if you try and connect a retail it'll kick it, exiting the game" in order to prevent the subversion of conventional multiplayer matches, but this was not made clear from the videos and posts made during its development and was certainly contrary to the tone of his countdown website page. And much like the misplaced belief that Epic Games would see glitchers as peers, iHcJames' approach failed to adequately appreciate he had already violated terms of service, user agreements, and international copyright law by this point, and his protestations were irrelevant, misguided, and naïve. Manipulating game code without consent and authorization is violation, so to be defending it by reducing its functionality is moot.

Unfortunately it wasn't entirely clear from my discussions with iHcJames whether Activision had ever made this position clear beyond the original cease and desist, since he was convinced the interactions had been relatively positive. iHcJames received a number of conference calls from individuals purporting to work at Activision: "they asked me for a lot of information and advice, and implied that this might lead to jobs in the future". Whether this was misapprehension on his part or an intentional strategy to extract information, iHcJames latched onto this aspect. Despite the initial discussions, the insinuations of potential employment came to nothing and, reassured that Project AC1D had been mothballed and the vulnerabilities identified, Activision stopped contacting iHcJames. While some would likely feel thankful they avoided legal penalty, iHcJames found the situation frustrating in the extreme.

> You've part-produced it because you think it's cool, you've announced it because you want the reputation and status, but you're in the situation that you can't finish it because people will leech the recognition or you'll get legal hassle. Also I heard nothing back from them [Activision] and that really annoyed me.

What became curious as I spoke with iHcJames, in addition to the conflicting attitudes regarding the role of author and reader, was the extent to which he demonstrated a conflicted antagonism towards Activision and Microsoft. I believe he was genuinely captivated and seduced by the video games and platforms he explored and altered, and explained he held a strong desire to work in game development in some capacity. He saw the release of illicit modifications as a way of entering into, and later re-establishing, dialogue with various parties within game development and simultaneously increasing his reputation within the modding communities – much like the symbolic dialogue implicit in glitching. This meant the ceasing of Project AC1D was highly problematic for iHcJames, as it placed him in limbo with developers and modders alike. After a while he began to start new modding and hacking projects in order to do something I call "release to re-engage" and that he described as: "When I release stuff it is due to the fact that I want to get my name back out and up on their radar".

iHcJames' release to re-engage process can be seen in a number of relatively high-profile examples: a leaked DLC for *Modern Warfare 3* called Terminal and something that appeared to look curiously like Project AC1D called uTor Engine. Both of these releases generated significant attention from the modding community and the games press, and was certainly likely to have got iHcJames back on Activision and Microsoft's radar. In the Terminal example, iHcJames once again used his Microsoft Developer Network brute-force application to access an unreleased DLC package for *Modern Warfare 3* that contained a remake of map from *Modern Warfare 2*, based at an airport and known as Terminal.

Although there had been speculation over the map's existence due to file-names found within a PC patch for *Modern Warfare 3* (much like the ISO modding archaeologists), iHcJames' unauthorized acquisition and subsequent video documentation titled "MW3 Terminal – It's Coming Back!" was the first authoritative evidence of its existence. The leak raised concerns over the integrity of Activision and Microsoft's security systems and created specula-tion over iHcJames' status within the modding community and on a number of gaming fansites. Was he a rogue Activision developer? How did he con-sistently expose and access information? In the wake of the Terminal video release, Activision formally announced the Terminal map was in production and it would be a free gift to the *Call of Duty* community, released just three weeks after iHcJames' leak, on July 17, 2012. As Activision and Micro-soft were already aware of iHcJames' identity they intervened once again, reopening communication with the hacker and escalating their warnings fur-ther. While there was certainly a negativity to their interaction on account of the very real legal threat, iHcJames saw it as re-engagement and another opportunity to interact with the people who produced the games in which he was so interested. He had suddenly become important to them again.

Two months later iHcJames yet again utilised the same brute-force method to obtain a beta version of the *Call of Duty: Black Ops 2* (2012) multiplayer application and once again released a video. This was more than a month before the game's commercial release date and before the multi-player game mode had been featured in the game press. The video served as a showcase, demonstrating the weapons and design features that would have normally been the preserve of a carefully negotiated press release or magazine exclusive. iHcJames' release undermined this capability, and the video generated significant global attention and subscribers to his YouTube channel as it was picked up by the games press. However, as with the IHC. DLL release, iHcJames used the *Black Ops 2* video to additionally introduce his new coding project called uTor Engine.

The video also retained the antagonism inherent in the Project AC1D web-site. The video starts with a uTor Engine logo and details of iHcJames' web-site. This swiftly fades into a clip from a promotional interview with one of the developers of the game, talking about the additional security tools built into *Black Ops 2*. However, behind the developer iHcJames superimposed what appears to be the as-then unreleased *Black Ops 2* multiplayer mode.

> We've been working on our anti-cheat systems, our proprietary anti-cheat systems, we really want to protect the integrity of the experience that people have online so we're not only reliant on systems that are already in the world but are … developing and coming up with our own.

As soon as the developer stops talking about the security systems, the video cuts to the countdown of a *Black Ops 2* multiplayer match. As soon as play commences, the player appears to initiate modding tools, flying around the map. At this point the game had not been officially released, had not had its multiplayer component shown to the world, and had apparently already been hacked. I interviewed iHcJames shortly after the release of the uTor Engine. At that point he told me Activision and Microsoft had not yet re-engaged. However I expected they would have done so with vigour. I spoke with iHcJames later in the year, asking whether he had made any more progress on the project, but he said he was now interested in other things. Up until the time of writing, uTor Engine has not been released to the public and I assume it remains largely mothballed.

HACKER COMMUNITIES?

The kind of hacking/modding seen with Project Rainbowzzz, IHC.DLL, and Project AC1D/uTor illustrates a different type of counterplay enabled by technical proficiency, an attitude of entitlement of access, and a disregard for copyright protection, resonating with the hackers' hands-on imperative. These appeared to be some of the defining characteristics of the top of the Xbox tree that still resonated to some degree with the other counterplay forms I encountered. I wondered if the fluid community structures that enabled the communal development of glitching were also seen in this kind of counterplay. When I asked iHcJames, Bob, and other people within the modding community about this, they were circumspect.

There was a general consensus that while once there had been a culture of collaboration and sharing within more proficient members of the community, the development and exploitation of commercial applications of modding, the kind of revenue that could be developed, and the legal risks attributed to this had made modders and hackers isolated and unwilling to share. Many of those who developed the modding methods and software processes changed their attitude to their activity after seeing their work exploited by "leeches" for profit, choosing to withhold projects or to leave the scene entirely.

> Back in 2010 people used to release stuff to help each other out. … People used to share the methods they'd found, like: ooh look I've spawned a car that you can destroy – but then people used to put all these things into one file and charge for lobbies. And people stopped helping each other, because it was all about making money. People stopped sharing.

The profiteering was problematic for modders. It constituted a theft of reputation, and as a result of its overabundance, ultimately made hacking more difficult, increasing the likelihood of aggressive intervention on the part of developers, which necessitated new techniques to be developed. Sharing had led to the tragedy of the commons, and as a result, hackers and modders became reticent, tending to work independently or in close-knit groups that stressed secrecy, reliability, and reputation. This was illustrated in iHcJames' attitude to other modders.

> I know quite a lot of people but I don't identify with a group or clan – I do almost all of my stuff on my own. … I know a lot of underground modders, but I stay away from that. Their idea of modding is just to make loads of money and do lobbies, but I'm not interested in that.

He implied the majority of commercial services related to *Call of Duty*, such as prestige lobbies, were now under the control of a small group of underground modders that effectively franchised the modifications to operators on a percentage fee basis. Instead of running the lobbies and generating income directly in multiple small transactions, they simply sold access to the tools necessary for a lump sum – around ten percent of all income generated. Meanwhile the underground modders retain control of the system, and if an operator fails to pay their money or falls out of favour, their access can be removed remotely without leaving any residual files in their ownership. The underground modders in effect were deploying portals to allow others to counterplay.

> All that happens is that you connect to their server, it loads an XEX into memory and you boot from that – that's after they verify your credentials, CPU key etc. of course. It lets the hoster say "look what I've made" and advertise the lobbies directly, and both the underground modders and hosters are happy.

Even within the constraints of this system, significant income could be generated. In effect, what this did was concentrate the income into a small number of modders instead of being shared by any modder with some understanding, a JTAG, and some keyvaults. Bob corroborated iHcJames in terms of what he knew about the business structure.

> The very intelligent people … sell slots on their "online method" and set the prices for the hosters to charge. Now a large percentage was going to the people who developed the online method, and the hosters were seeing about 20–30% in the end, which was easily thousands over the time they hosted. I know someone who hosted lobbies for the first month for those people, and he made like $14,000. From one months work, 3–4 hours a day, 5 nights a week.

iHcJames attributed the release of Project Rainbowzzz, which was one of the tools used by an underground modding group, to in-fighting within one hacking/modding team, revolving around one member's expulsion, accused of misconduct. He saw it as a mark of the fracturing and secrecy of the hacking and modding community that Project Rainbowzzz could be hidden and subsequently released, and it was symptomatic of the fractured and secretive community structures. As retribution, the ejected modder obtained the software directly from the team's servers, decompiled it, and posted the files onto a number of modding forums. Despite quick patching on Microsoft's part, the released code was sufficient to allow others insight into the processes involved and to subsequently modify this to circumvent the security interventions that preceded it. The release of Project Rainbowzzz temporarily subverted this business model until the new security patch prevented the majority from connecting to Xbox LIVE. iHcJames was adamant that the modding teams were swiftly able to reassert their business.

> There's a newer version [of Rainbowzzz] available that overcomes all of the challenges [Microsoft introduced], but that's secure and they've tightened up their security enormously.

While it appeared the widespread sharing was becoming less common within the modding-scene teams, there were still occasions when partial information or hints were given but not fully explained, the donor always asserting their authority or mastery. This was the case with iHcJames' own method for connecting a JTAG or RGH online. "I found it independently but was given pointers by other people". He said this was one of the advantages of reputation. Files and information are often passed on to him anonymously, perhaps by those who appreciate his work or members of underground modding teams, and those able to demonstrate their aptitude were often spontaneously given access to materials others were not.

> The people that really know what they're doing are an insular community. If you know what you're doing you just end up in that group who knows what they're doing. And they sometimes share stuff with each other.

It is not the case of an explicit group but a sense of equivalence and recognition based on reputation. One assumes that in large part, through the maintenance of the boundaries between leechers, the public, and the top of the tree, those in the privileged category are able to limit the distribution of all the tools they develop. The fractured community may share information but it retains the capacity to keep a great deal private. The hands-on imperative has distorted into individual silos of knowledge. In terms of scale, iHcJames thought there were perhaps a thousand people who "mod seriously"; "the amount of people that code good stuff is no larger than 100–200 globally, with a lot of them in the US", and, by contrast, "if you want to get down to the nitty-gritty assembly stuff there's no more than 20–30 people".

This paints a picture of a counterplay ecosystem where a small group of people, enough to certainly fit into a normal-sized lecture theatre – the hardware hackers who develop the processes that open the system, such as

Tmbnc; those developing the modding methods; the top of the tree, such as iHcJames; those producing good stuff – are supporting the counterplay activities of many thousands more. People playing mods, people paying to get unlocks and prestige, people wanting to beat other glitchers to discover exploits, and grief-players. At least on the Xbox 360 console we can trace an ecosystem of counterplay. But what of it? How does this help us to better understand counterplay as a practice, apparently engaged with by many but defined in violation of etiquette, rule, and law?

In terms of both hacking and modding, both phenomena can be clearly attributed to the rhetoric of pathogen. They explicitly contravene the limitations of use and, through duplication or distribution, have the capacity to undermine. They are reliant on technologies that constitute violations of copyright law and their application has further escalatory potential. Both hacking and modding impact on the experience of the games but also their commercial functions, enabling piracy and alteration that undermine the need to purchase new releases.

In relation to modding, resistance is inverted. Much like glitching or grief-play, the modded game is dependent on the status quo. It is defined in contrast to the normal operation of the game and its structures, and attempts to offer an alternate mode of play, not a permanent replacement. Those using mods – although less so those conducting them – appeared to be generally aligned with the pre-lusory goals and attitude of the game. Many were highly dedicated players who saw the use of a modded environment as an interesting temporary extension of play or a shortcut to the required functionality and trappings that would support appropriate play. By contrast, those producing mods appear to have different focuses, including the generation of income, the spreading of entertaining play modes, and the creation of identity and reputation as seen with the branding of mods and the demand to quickly mod and release, such as when glitching.

Software development such as that conducted by iHcJames takes on a hybrid position. It utilises and repurposes the existing text and requires its continuation, but introduces new functionality that has the capacity to alter it for extended periods or even in perpetuity. This can be seen with the unpatched status of IHC.DLL or, rather, its continual redevelopment by the wider modding community, despite the instruction of how to prevent it. Curiously, however, while some hardware hackers still aligned with the counter-cultural nature of hacker ethics, I found little evidence of the same with modders or software producers. They did not view their actions as in opposition to the games but instead saw them as semi-legitimate uses, or failed to see the issue in what they were doing. They regarded their activities as creative amplifications, not negations.

Within the development of new illicit software the discourse of mastery seemed important, notably mastery of the system and an understanding of the technological processes involved. This is partly dependent on a level of technical expertise but also a willingness to actually interact with video games in a transgressive manner. But even for those who displayed both ability and intent, there were other serendipitous events that facilitated counterplay, such as the random e-mail that offered a clue to a software workaround, a disgruntled software leak such as Project Rainbowzzz, or the gift of a Developers Network update disc. Without these events and interactions, without the diffuse communities that still exist (but in much less visible forms), illicit modding and the mastery it represents would not take place. For example, iHcJames uses techniques and abilities to assert mastery: mastery of the system and mastery of access, which in turn gives preferential information.

Unlike glitchers, who openly shared their findings and obtained much vicarious pleasure from seeing rank-and-file players glitching and altering play, within modding this mastery was not always egalitarian and shared, and instead, information and techniques were withheld to be used by a dominant few. This presents an interesting parasitical dynamic iin which the developers are placed at a disadvantage and the modder (or modding group) attempts to clandestinely take mastery of the space, using it for their own ends, including revenue generation, as seen with Project Rainbowzzz. Developments of this nature are only understood by a minority until they are publically released, such as the Project Rainbowzzz leak. It is impossible to check iHcJames' assurance that other unleaked processes and systems exist, although having seen the documentation that surrounded his own unreleased and uncompleted Project AC1D and uTor Engine software, it is likely others with similar intent and skills will have produced things.

Yet paradoxically, we should remember that for all of iHcJames' assumption of mastery within the game-space, of doing, taking, and interacting and its unsettling and pathogenic resonance, his primary goal was to be recognised and to enter into dialogue with members of the games industry. With him, at least, it appeared counterplay – even of such an extreme, oppositional, and escalatory nature to the extent that it resulted in direct legal sanctions – did not originate from malice but out of a desire to become closer to the games and Dyer-Witheford and de Peuter's empire that opened the discussion.

Outside this, there are certainly authentic and inauthentic ways of illicit modding and software coding: plagiarising code vs. giving props, the speed of release, the spectacularity of the modification. This in turn creates the benchmarks for three separate but overlapping communities. First, hardware hackers, who generally locate themselves around XboxHacker.org and Free60.org and are often critical of the practices of both game modders and, to a lesser extent, coders, who demonstrate understanding of the system that the modders need not. Part of the hardware-hacker community has realised the commercial potential for their work, such as through the creation of hacking teams and the industrial production of hacking components e.g. Team Xecutor's CoolRunner boards. Individuals associated with the commercial teams are secretive and distant, the assumption being that they are pseudonyms of individuals active within the more authentic hacking circles.

Coders appear to be a diffuse community linked through an understanding of the various skills of their globally distributed peers such as iHcJames. This community appears to be becoming more reticent, due to the increasing commercial significance of their work, and becoming enmeshed in protective and secretive illicit enterprises. These individuals share much of the alignment and approach that hackers demonstrate but focus on the code and systems instead of the hardware. As a result, their actions place them in direct line of sight of the panoptic security systems. Unlike hardware hackers, their activities connect and interrupt

Finally there are software modders who reside on websites such as Se7ensins.com and who utilise the techniques developed by the hardware hackers and coders. Their process of distinction is focused on other modders, and they are frequently critical of the production and content of other mods. Once again there are attempts to commercialise these through the creation of paid-for-access mods and on a scale that bridges the coder and modder communities in the case of those facilitating more recent mods and connections on the *Call of Duty* franchise.

These then create a set of identities based on competence, understanding, and their alignment with commercialism. Those who display competence are given the most status, as seen with the notion of the top of the tree, the ill-defined and secretive individuals who display expertise and exploit it accordingly, for profit or reputation. At a lower level, individuals are keen to highlight their identity as a modder or hacker. Mods have frequent branding and recognition of contribution and are careful to assert authority and identity. Even the function of the lobbies, prestige lobbies in particular, focuses on the communication of hierarchy and identity to differentiate a player from another – the accumulation of markers of skill, prestige, icons etc. they do not deserve. Paradoxically, the widespread use of these mods had the inverse impact. Anybody who cared enough about prestige markers now had them, there became uniformity of expertise, and now players carefully scrutinise the player profiles for a hint of illegitimacy or, in most cases, simply assume everything to be bogus.

Illicit modding and the hardware hacking it is dependent on resonate with the discourses of the carnivalesque. They each represent an invitation to misrule and a challenge of authority, supported through promise of different pleasures and power relations. The open system of the JTAG or RGH is capable of executing unsigned code and therefore it is prone to periodic manifestations of chaos and hostility. Despite this capability, however, the security countermeasures deployed by Microsoft have reduced this universality, although releases such as IHC.DLL go some way to re-establishing it. This has had the impact of shifting the use of mods, hacks, and software into less visible and less connected spheres. As a result, the mod/hack loses its communality and becomes fragmented and individualised. Outside occasional flourishes of misrule, it becomes used for piracy, revenue generation, and modding practices within the minority. It therefore lacks the universality of the carnival that glitching still retains.

GAMEOGRAPHY

Batman Arkham City. 2011. Rocksteady Studios. Warner Brothers Interactive Entertainment.
Bioshock. 2007. 2K Games. Irrational Games.
Call of Duty: Black Ops. 2010. Activision. Treyarch.
Call of Duty: Black Ops 2. 2012. Activision. Treyarch.
Call of Duty: Modern Warfare. 2007. Activision. Infinity Ward.
Call of Duty: Modern Warfare 2. 2009. Activision. Infinity Ward.
Call of Duty: Modern Warfare 3. 2011. Activision. Infinity Ward / Sledgehammer Games.
Call of Duty: World at War. 2008. Activision. Treyarch.
Duke Nukem Forever. 2011. 2K Games. Gearbox Software.
Garry's Mod. 2004. Valve Corporation. Facepunch Studios.
Gears of War. 2006. Microsoft Studios. Epic Games.
Homefront. 2011. THQ. Kaos Studios.
Mass Effect. 2007. Electronic Arts. Bioware.
Mass Effect 3. 2012. Electronic Arts. Bioware.
Medal of Honor. 2010. Electronic Arts. DICE Los Angeles.

REFERENCES

10thprestige. 2010. http://10thprestige.com/. Accessed January 15, 2011.
Consalvo, M. 2007. *Cheating: Gaining Advantage in Videogames.* Cambridge, MA: MIT Press.
Postigo, H. 2007. "Of Mods and Modders: Chasing Down the Value of Fan-Based Digital Game Modifications." *Games and Culture,* 2 (4), 300–313.
Postigo, H. 2008. "Video Game Appropriation through Modifications: Attitudes Concerning Intellectual Property among Modders and Fans." *Convergence: The International Journal of Research into New Media Technologies,* vol 14, issue 1, 59–74. http://con.sagepub.com/content/14/1/59.short.
Postigo, H. 2010. :Modding to the big leagues: Exploring the space between modders and the game industry." *First Monday,* 15 (5). http://firstmonday.org/htbin/cgiwrap/bin/ojs/index.php/fm/article/viewArticle/2972. Accessed March 6, 2011.
Se7ensins. 2010–2014. http://www.se7ensins.com/. Accessed January 15, 2011.
Sotamaa, O. 2004. "Playing it my way? Mapping the modder agency." Internet Research Conference 5.0, Sussex, U.K. September 19–22, 2004.
Sotamaa, O. 2007a. "On modder labour, commodification of play, and mod competitions." *First Monday ,* 12 (9). http://firstmonday.org/ojs/index.php/fm/rt/printer-Friendly/2006/1881. Accessed March 9, 2011.
Sotamaa, O. 2007b. "Perceptions of Player in Game Design Literature." Situated Play, Proceedings of DiGRA 2007 Conference. September 24–28, 2007.
Sotamaa, O. 2010. "When the game is not enough: Motivations and practices among computer game modding culture." *Games and Culture,* 5:3, 239–255.
The Tech Game. 2009–2014. http://www.thetechgame.com/. Accessed January 15, 2011.
US Department of Justice. 2014. "Four Members of International Computer Hacking Ring Indicted for Stealing Gaming Technology, Apache Helicopter Training Software." http://www.justice.gov/opa/pr/four-members-international-computer-hacking-ring-indicted-stealing-gaming-technology-apache. Accessed October 8, 2014.
Xbox360xperts. 2010–2014. http://xbox360xperts.com/dashboard/. Accessed January 15, 2011.

7 Understanding Counterplay in Video Games

In this book we have traced a wide range of apparently counterplay practices, ways of playing games that work against a broad matrix of expectations, rules, and laws and that ultimately counter the "configurations, processes, rhythms, spaces, and structures" of video games (Apperley 2010, 103). We have touched on the ambiguity of incendiary user-generated content and seen a range of outputs that appear to have been created as a casual expression of vulgarity (Sporn), an intentionally offensive and provocative statement (the 9/11 LittleBigPlanet level), highly inflammatory and problematic content (the Neo-Nazi car), and then the confusing, celebratory, but inadvertently transgressive combinations of intellectual property (LBPdius). This has shown us that counterplay manifests itself diffusely, highlights its subjective nature, and transgresses the hail-and-response model, as well as the problems associated with attributing meaning to an act without access to the protagonist. We have seen the identification of counterplay depends primarily on an observer, a victim, and the public, rather than the protagonist, and there is wide disagreement over what constitutes counterplay among players.

We found that as a result of this, many saw a low-level background noise of vindictive counterplay within video games but that in large part, this was ignored. It was either that it was considered a constituent part of the laddish culture of contemporary video games or that the pragmatic demand to not being seen to respond, and thus not escalate the act nor become a target, has masked the extent to which counterplay is problematic to players. Grief-players used the lack of outcry as testament that their actions weren't problematic, while simultaneously deriving pleasure from those who did vocally defy them. To further complicate this, it appears victims and those silent witnesses who observed counterplay acts not only added tacit support to counterplay but were often willing (under certain circumstances) to re-perform the acts on others, though not necessarily targeting those who initially caused the issue. This presents a tit-for-tat culture in which it appears players occasionally express frustration – with the game, with having experienced counterplay – towards others through counterplay and this takes the form of "displaced abjection" (Stallybrass and White 1986, 19), attacking whomever strays into view at the wrong time. We see player feuds that telescope over years and spread throughout diffuse friendship groups and allegiances, but that appear more of a contextual justification for a flurry of counterplay rather than a meaningful retaliation. Alongside all this there is the pervasive sense that players are constantly scrutinizing the play of others for legitimacy, applying the normalizing gaze, and being similarly judged by others.

There seems to be a compelling desire to appear to be an appropriate player – the measure of this differs according to the context and individual – but it seems that for the majority of counterplayers, this was connected to a yearning to become closer to the game – to be seen as an expert, as a great player, or simply avoid being seen as an inauthentic player. This dynamic drives some to play harder and longer but for others, it results in buying a modded controller to win more multiplayer games, get a hacked console to find glitches faster, or seek out illicit services in order to get prestige. Lastly, for some the identity transcends simply being a good player and moves into something deeper: a desire to become closer to the developers and other entities that produce these games in the hope of employment or simply interaction. We see this in iHcjames, in mapMonkeys, and in many other counterplayers with whom I played and spoke.

We have seen an ascetic approach to games, where the methodical, archaeological scrutiny, and deep reading of simulation and code expose a profound and unique understanding and enable the creation of identity. We find glitchers, hardware hackers, and modders who dive into hardware, software, and networks, interrogating them in order to bring nuggets of information to the masses or only to their peers. In doing so, these individuals obtain status and identity but also serve a role within wider social groups. Their discoveries, interpretations, and developments are readily consumed and used by the public, whether it is a glitch to be exploited, information about an impending DLC release, or a new way of introducing mods, spreading subversion and playful chaos.

This presents a highly contradictory and problematic picture. Counterplayers are seduced by the games to the extent they wish to get closer to them, to help produce them, and to be seen as authorities on some level. That despite the very real negative impacts of counterplay: upsetting players, undermining the commercial operation of games, and breaking the law. It seems that for many, this is motivated not out of a yearning for resistance, destruction, and change but out of a wish to be consumed by the games, to use them as spaces for almost the worship of play in all of its chaotic forms, freed from the regulation of games. But it appears that within this search for getting closer and understanding the games, or in the cases where the explicit aim is to commercially exploit those desires, the authority of rule and order appears to diminish. In the heat, energy, and excitement of play the restriction of law appears to become secondary and lost in the power of the prank or the potential offered by counterplay. From my research it appeared that many counterplayers were simply so caught up in the pleasures of play, or the escalatory and risky-laden pleasures of dark play (Schechner 1988), that they either failed to realize the extent to which they were violating rules, convincing themselves of the legitimacy of their actions, or simply focused on the illicit thrill as justification for it all.

While this characterizes many of the engagements I had while writing this book, it does not cover the entire spectrum. There are certainly aspects of counterplay – such as the creation of hardware hacks for profit, the exclusive illicit mods such as Project Rainbowzzz, and piracy in particular – that are difficult to reconcile as anything but illegal entrepreneurialism. Within such a context those conducting commercial mods and prestige services are simply meeting a demand that is not offered by the game developers, and suggests there is significant demand for radical creative tools within games, allowing far greater customisation and alteration than is currently available. Once again, this highlights the compelling nature of being seen to play authentically. Neither of these demands should necessarily be read as opposition or misalignment with the game but a product of its compelling seductiveness. Those driving the development and deployment of hacks and modifications are players who wish to experience more or be seen to be more closely aligned.

In the case of *Call of Duty* modded lobbies, the urge to reduce time and enable players to access to unlocks and awards they have not earned is a logical by-product of a game designed to reward play over a 60+ hour timeline but also within a highly visible and connected context. This suggests the expectations placed on players, the implied player, whether an illusory theoretical apparition or something legitimately defined during game development, is perhaps too reductive in approach and restrictive in its expectations. Perhaps this better betrays the success of contemporary video games, in that they have become global and ubiquitous, played by a broad cross-section of people. Now we all play, there are so many kinds of players and ways of playing that it is inevitable market demands, pockets of transgression, and an unpredictable and abrasive culture form.

The backdrop of all this is that the discourses of legitimacy are still deployed by observers and protagonists, understood by observers as some of the reasons why counterplayers do what they do, and similarly as genuine motivations that counterplayers offer. However, this is not entirely the case. Whereas we might think we see resistance, this was the discourse most absent from counterplayer testimonies, and this is curious. Despite the apparently resistant counterplay acts, few counterplayers really wished to change things, nor did they contest the authority of rule. It was more the case that in their efforts to play, their perspectives shifted and the rules became irrelevant or at best, only peripheral. It appeared that while at first, the illicit thrill of transgression did have resonance, this was a pleasure that soon became mundane, while playing with the video games did not. Counterplay simply became an alternate way of playing, an additional part of the repertoire of play.

While I am uncertain whether this really enables us to understand counterplay, I would like to think it offers another voice or perspective, one that does not instantly adopt the discourse of pathogen, nor absolve the counterplayers for their transgressions, but attempts to describe how and what counterplayers do. In that sense it allows us to understand what counterplay means to those who conduct it. Counterplayers are problematic. They offend individuals, they subvert carefully designed mechanisms, they spread chaos and misrule, and they can be parasitical, but everyone I spoke with expressed a love for games, for play, and a sincere respect for game developers. It was just many other players they seemed less enamoured with, either feeling inadequacy or disgust in the face of others' play and ultimately exposing the fact that our attempts to rationalize, understand, and label counterplay are much the same mechanisms that drive and motivate it.

The risk here is that my general observations will become too abstract, so in an effort to draw this to a close, I will present key dynamics that appear to underpin the counterplay practices I encountered to help you to better make your own judgements about understanding counterplay.

- **Seduction not resistance:** counterplayers do not appear particularly critical of the games they are seen to oppose, alter, or subvert. They expressed little desire to resist, nor any particularly strong sense of tyranny and repression. Instead those hacking, pirating, modding, glitching, and grief-playing expressed a seduction with the video-game form and, occasionally, a near deification of those who create them. Perhaps what is most important here, however, is the subtext. The seduced care deeply about the games they are seen to damage and as a result, punitive sanctions are unlikely to be fruitful. As I discovered, these counterplayers merely dust themselves off and start again, using a new console, a new identity, a new project;
- **Desire for recognition:** players are constantly subject to and engage in a process of scrutiny and judgement of play. This can be seen as an unintended repercussion of the shift of play into the realm of the networked video game. Within this context, combined with the ubiquity of video-game play as an activity, players constantly see distasteful play, expert play, and interpret hierarchies of play legitimacy according to whatever criteria they deem most valuable. What this creates is a flexible model of group identities, allegiances, notions of worth, and legitimacy: players to be emulated, players to be placated, players to be trolled. We see this in something like Booster Busters, where the playerbase decrees that counterplayers are illegitimate and are free to be abused, harassed, and reported. Likewise we see the same dynamic inverted with the grief-player who harasses because of the illegitimacy of conventional play. We can also trace this through glitching and modding, where the pressures to be seen to be a legitimate or authentic player are met through illicit means, or where legitimacy is read in a different manner and becomes about showing expertise and sharing strategies. Curiously, the desire for recognition even extends to the many desperate attempts to engage with developers and game publishers. I believe the constant observation and

scrutiny attributable to contemporary video games is a critical influence on counterplay;

- **Laddish culture and the carnival:** players find themselves in an abrasive play culture that frequently resonates with ritual laughter, offense, the singling out of individuals for persecution, and a hostile competitiveness. This is not to say all contexts and play acts are suffused with this, but this laddish culture has become part of the lexicon of play, something that is tolerated and engaged in to an extent. For me, this resonates deeply with the notion of the carnivalesque. Within this concept, we are able to move from beyond a reductive reading as the action of a crass minority into a way of playing that the majority engage in or contribute to as an occasional aspect of play. Perhaps it is most useful to consider the interdictions and structure presented by seduction (that motivates players to more deeply interact with a game) and the constant scrutiny (that makes players both aware of hierarchy, of better players, and of subordinate, illegitimate players), and then consider that within this context, a descent into misrule is both meaningful and pleasurable;

- **The primacy of play and irrelevance of rule:** ultimately the combination of seduction, scrutiny, and laddish culture creates fertile ground for chaotic, powerful play experiences but when we are deep within play, rules, laws, expectations, and even any sense of repercussion become diminished. When these are placed in the social context of multiplayer games, social networks, gaming forums, and word of mouth, the activities take on an escalatory mode and the pleasures, the establishment of hierarchy and human connections, become more meaningful than distant arbitrary law or rule. This resonates deeply with Schechner's dark play, and is the simple observation that when we are playing, external frames begin to dissipate and fade. We see this in Zakhaev's yearning for mods and his derank lobbies, iHcJames' illicit software development, and Ocelot's grief play.

GAMEOGRAPHY

Forza 2. 2007. Microsoft Studios. Turn 10 Studios.
LittleBigPlanet. 2008. Sony Computer Entertainment. Media Molecule.
LittleBigPlanet 2. 2011. Sony Computer Entertainment. Media Molecule.
Spore. 2008. Electronic Arts. Maxis.

REFERENCES

Apperley, T. 2010. "Gaming Rhythms: Play and Counterplay from the Situated to the Global," *Amsterdam Institute of Network Cultures* [online]. http://www.network-cultures.org/_uploads/TOD%236%20total%20def.pdf. Accessed June 22, 2012.

Bakhtin, M. 1984. *Rabelais and His World*. Bloomington: Indiana University Press.

Booster Busters. 2014. https://www.youtube.com/user/XBoosterBustersX. Accessed November 18, 2014.

Bourdieu, P. 1990. *The Logic of Practice*. Cambridge, UK: Polity Press.

Dyer-Witheford, N. and de Peuter, G. 2005. "A Playful Multitude? Mobilising and Counter-Mobilising Immaterial Game Labour." *The Fibreculture Journal* [online]. http://journal.fibreculture.org/issue5/depeuter_dyerwitheford.html. Accessed September 6, 2014

Dyer-Witheford, N. and de Peuter, G. 2009. *Games of Empire: Global Capitalism and Video Games*. Minnesota: University of Minnesota Press.

Evil Controllers. 2014a. *Evil Controllers*. http://www.evilcontrollers.com/.

Schechner, R. 1988. *Playing*. Chick, G. and Sutton-Smith, B., eds. *Play & Culture*, 3–19.

Schechner, R. 2013. *Performance Studies: An Introduction*. New York: Routledge.

Stallybrass, P. and White, A. 1986. *The Politics and Poetics of Transgression*. London: Routledge.

Bibliography

Index

Milton Keynes UK
Ingram Content Group UK Ltd.
UKHW030903141024
449569UK00032B/1851